PERSONNEL MANAGEMENT
THEORY AND PRACTICE

PERSONNEL MANAGEMENT
THEORY AND PRACTICE

VOLUME I

ARUN KUMAR
RACHANA SHARMA

ATLANTIC PUBLISHERS AND DISTRIBUTORS

Published by
ATLANTIC PUBLISHERS AND DISTRIBUTORS
B-2, Vishal Enclave, Opp. Rajouri Garden, New Delhi-27
Phones : 5413460, 5429987
E-mail : info@atlanticbooks.com
Web site : www.atlanticbooks.com

Sales Office
4215/1, Ansari Road, Darya Ganj, New Delhi-02
Phones : 3273880, 3285873, 3280451
Fax : 91-11-3285873

Typeset at
APD Computer Graphics, Delhi
Printed in India at
Mehra Offset Press, Delhi

PREFACE

In the modern industry, humanistic considerations have pervaded all the aspects of management theory and practice. Personnel, therefore, have acquired the central place and personnel management has become the task of not only a democratic government and a welfare state but also of an enlightened employer, businessman and manager. Employee management and development, from labourer to manager, have become an important subject of research. It may be said without exaggeration that personnel management is the most important area in the field of management. Therefore, no apology is needed for writing a book on this subject.

This book deals with syllabi prescribed by Indian universities and Institutes of management on B.B.A. and M.B.A. levels in personnel management and administration. While matter has been drawn from authentic and standard works of Indian and Western scholors, it has been narrated in a simple and lucid style, free from technical jargon. Data have been given to support statements. Tables, Figures and Charts have been used to illustrate complex subjects. Questions at the end of each chapter have been drawn from the examination papers to help the students to prepare for examinations.

In writing this book, while the senior author has widely utilised his experience in multinational corporations, the junior authoress has utilised her vast knowledge of psychology to make this book an ideal guide, both in theory and practice. It is a text-book for the students and reference book for the teachers.

Suggestions, if any, for the improvement of the book in the next edition will be highly appreciated.

ARUN KUMAR
RACHANA SHARMA

CONTENTS

Volume I

1

Introduction to Personnel Management

In the present day industrial and business management, different terms, such as 'Personnel or Staff Management,' 'Personnel Administration', 'Labour Relations', 'Labour Management', 'Man-Power Management', 'Employee Relations', 'Industrial Relations', etc., have been used interchangeably. The phrase 'staff executive' in-charge of 'personnel management', 'personnel administration', has been variously designated, reflecting changes in status and functions. Richard Calhoon points out : "From the earliest term 'employment manager' evolved the more general term of 'Personnel Manager' in the 20s and 30s. During the late 30s and 40s, the terms 'Industrial Relations', and 'Labour Relations' became more popular concurring with the rise of collective bargaining and the expansion of other functions (the executive being known as 'Industrial Relations Officer or 'labour Relations' 'Director' or 'Manager' or 'Labour Welfare Officer' or simply 'Labour Officer'). Then, in the late 40s and 50s, a limited number of organisations and industries espoused the designation 'Human Relations' (the executive being known as 'Director' or 'Manager') as more in keeping with the over-all organisational behavioural responsibilities. As of 60s, however, the key word is 'personnel' to describe the general functions in the vast majority of cases."[1]

This chronological growth in terminology indicates that as a branch of knowledge Personnel Management is still in a formative stage. Prof. Yoder Manpower management used the term "Industrial Relations", which is the most inclusive of these terms and which describes the more all-inclusive functions of "Manpower Management" which relates to procedures through which human resources are organised and directed towards the attainment of organisational, social and individual goals. Yoder further subdivides it into "Personnel Management/Personal Administration" and "Labour Relations." He

1. Calhoon, Richard, *Managing Personnel,* 1964, p. 18.

uses the first two terms interchangably to refer to the management of manpower. They represent the employers' relationships with individual employees (in different activities); and "Labour Relations" represent the relationship between the management and organised unions, and indicating the negotiation and administration of collective agreements or labour contracts. I have preferred the use of "Personnel Management" "the Management of Human Resources,"[2] because it is highly inclusive and imbraces all the above concepts. Even otherwise, at present, the terms "Personnel Management" and "Industrial Realtions" for purpsoe of accuracy are widely used and the executives are designated as Personnel Officer, Personnel Director, Personnel Man, Personnel Executive, Staff and Personnel Manager, Employment Manager, Labour Welfare Officer, Labour Liaison Officer, or Labour Officer or Chief Industrial Relations Officer. In India he is called 'Labour Officer', 'Labour Welfare Officer', 'Personnel Officer', 'Personnel Manager,' 'Employee Relations Officer', 'Industrial Relations Officer etc.

Definition of Personnel Management

1. *Yoder, D., and Others* : "It is that phase of management which deals with the effective control and use of manpower as distinguished from other sources of power."[3]

2. *Yoder, D.* : "The management of human resources is viewed as a system in which participants seeks to attain both individual and group goals."[4]

"Its objective is to understand what has happened and is happening and to be prepared for that will happen in the area of working relationships between the managers and the managed."[5]

3. *Jucius, M.J.* : Personnel administration is : "The field of management which has to do with planning, organising, directing and controlling various operative functions of procuring, developing, maintaining and utilising a labour force, such that the : (*a*) objectives, for which the company is established are attained economically and effectively; (*b*) objectives of all levels of personnel are served to the

---

2. Yoder, D., *Personnel Management and Industrial Relations,* 1972, p. 11.
3. Yoder, D., Heneman, H.G., Turbnull, J.G. and Stone, C.H., *Handbook of Personnel Management and Industrial Relations.* McGraw-Hill Book Company, New York, 1958, p. 6.
4. Yoder, D., *Personnel Management and Industrial Relations,* Prentice-Hall of India, New Delhi, 1972, p. viii.
5. Yoder, D., *Ibid.,* pp. 4-5.

highest possible degree and (*c*) objectives of the community are duly considered and served."[6]

4. *Thomas G. Spates* : "Personnel administration is a code of the ways of organising and treating individuals at work so that they will each get the greatest possible realisation of their intrinsic abilities, thus attaining maximum efficiency for themselves and their group, and thereby giving to the enterprise of which they are a part its determining competitive advantage and its optimum results."[7]

5. *Edward Flippo* : "Personnel Management is the planning, organising, directing and controlling of the procurement, development, compensation, integration, maintenance and separation of human resources to the end that individual, organisational and societal objectives are accomplished."[8]

6. *W. French* : "Personnel Management is the recuritment, selection, development, utilization of and accommodation in human resources by organisations. The human resources of an organisation consist of all individuals regardless of their role, who are engaged in any of the organisations activities."[9]

This definition states that personnel management is planning, co-ordinating, and controlling of a network of sub-processes and facilitating systems pertaining to the recuritment, selection, utilisation, development of and accommodation of human resources. The sub-processes comprise the most vital aspects of personnel management, leadership, justice determination, task specialisation. staffing, performance appraisal, training and development, compensation, collective bargaining and organisation development. According to French : "Personnel management is a major component of the broader managerial function and has roots and branches extending throughout and beyond each organisation. It is a major sub-systems of all organisations."[10]

7. *Scott and Others* : "It is that branch of management which is responsible, on a staff basis for concentrating on those aspects of operations which are primarily concerned with the relationship of

---

6. Jucius, M.J., *Personnel Management,* Richard D. Irwin, Homewood, Illinois, 1973, p. 25.
7. Spates, Thomas, G., *An Objective Scrutiny of Personnel Administration,* American Management Association, New York, Personnel Series No. 75, 1944, p. 9.
8. Flippo, Edwin, B., *Personnel Management,* McGraw-Gill — Kogakusha, Ltd., 1980, *International Student Edition,* p. 5.
9. French, Wendell, *The Personnel Management Process : Human Resources Administration,* Houghton Mifflin Company, New York, third edition, 1974, p. 3.
10. *Ibid.,* p. 3.

management to employees and employees to employees and with the development of the individual and group. The objective is to attain maximum individual development, desirable working relationship between employers and employees and employees and employees, and effective moulding of human resources as contrasted with physical resources."[11]

This definition puts emphasis on the staff group personnel activities and on assisting the operational personnel in performing the personnel duties (*i.e.* maintenance of personnel records; selection, transfer and promotion of employees; and the responsibility for seeing that the company's policies relating to personnel practices and procedures are carried out).

8. *Dunn and Stephens* : "The personnel management is the process of attracting, holding and motivating people involving all managers-line and staff."[12]

An analysis of this definition will show that personnel management is principally concerned with three activities, *viz., attracting people,* by offering suitable monetary and non-monetry rewards; *retaining them* in the organisation by improving work environment, etc. and *motivating them* by following progressive practices and human policies conducive to bring about personal satisfaction to the employees.

9. *The Institute of Personnel Management, London* : "Personnel Management is that part of the management function which is primarily concerned with the human relationships within an organisation. Its objective is the maintenance of those relationships on a basis which, by consideration of the well-being of the individual, enables all those enaged in the undertaking to make their maximum personal contribution to the effective working of that undertaking"[13] (1945).

"Personnel Management is that part of management concerned with people at work and with their relationship within an enterprise. Its aim is to bring together and develop into an effective organisation the men and women who make up an enterprise and having regard for the well-being of the individual and of working groups, to enable them to make their best contribution to its success" (1965).

The essence of the definitions is that Personnel Management is

---

11. Scott, Wilter Dill., Clothier, Robert C., and Spriegel, William R., *Personnel Management : Principles, Practices and Point of View.* Tata McGraw-Hill Publishing Company Ltd., New Delhi, Sixth Edition, 1977, p. 11.
12. Dunn, J.D., and Stephens, E.C., *Management of People,* McGraw-Hill Book Company, New York, 1972, p. 10.
13. Institute of Personnel Management, *Functions of Personnel Department,* London, 1949.

concerned with *man at work*; and with *their group relationship*, with a view to acheive the objectives of the organisation through their maximum personal contribution towards the work-goal achievement. The new definition places emphasises on the 'group aspect'. In this definition three objectives are explicit : (*a*) to maintain good relationships within an organisation, (*b*) to enable each person to make his maximum personal contribution to the organisation as a member of the working group and (*c*) to acheive these things through respect for human personality and the well-being of the individual.

10. *The Indian Institute of Personnel Management* (now National Institute of Personnel Management) : "Personnel Management, Labour Management or Staff Management means quite simply the task of dealing with human relationships within an organisation. Academically the three aspects of Personnel Management are (*i*) *the welfare aspect* concerned with working conditions and amenties such as canteens, creches, housing personal problems of workers, schools, and recreation; (*ii*) *the labour or personnel aspect* concerned with recruitment, placement of employees, remuneration, promotion, incentives, productivity, etc., (*iii*) *the industrial relations aspects* concerned with trade union negotiation, settlement of industrial disputes, joint consultation and collective bargaining. All these aspects are concerned with human element in industry as distinct from the mechanical."[14]

11. *Lawrence Appley* : "It is a function of guiding human resources into a dynamic organisation that attains its objectives with a high degree of morale and to the satisfaction of those concerned. It is concerned with getting results through people." According to him, "all management is 'personnel management' as it deals with human beings, its development can best be discussed in terms of human development, philosophical, psychological, spiritual and physical."

12. *Pigors and Others* : "It is method of developing potentialities of employees so that they get maximum satisfaction out of their work and give their best efforts to the organisation."[15]

13. *C.H. Northcott* : "Personnel Management is an extension of general management, that of prompting and stimulating every employee to make his fullest contribution to the purpose of a business."[16]

---

14. Institute of Personnel Management, *Personnel Management in India,* Calcutta, 1973, pp. 29-30.

15. Pigors, Paul and Myres, Charles A, *Personnel Administration : A Point of View and Method.* McGraw Hill Book Co., Kagakusha Ltd., Tokyo, 1961, second edition 1961, p. 11.

16. Northcott, C.H., *Personnel Management : Principles and Practices*, Sir Issac Pitman and Sons, London, 1958, p. 12.

14. *Dirks, Howard M.* : "It is a function concerned with developing and utilising the manpower resources of the business to the optimum extent in achieving the objectives of that business."[17]

15. *Sikula, A.F.* : "Personal Administration is concerned basically with manpower on 'people', organisational resource of output."[18]

16. *Richard Calhoon* : Personnel Management involves the task of handling the human problems of an organisation, and is devoted to acquiring, developing, utilising and maintaining an efficient work force."[19]

CHARACTERISTICS OF PERSONNEL MANAGEMENT

1. Specialised branch of general management. Personnel Management is a specialised branch of General Management. Therefore all the principles of general management apply to this branch of management.

2. Definite principles and policies. Over and above the general principles of management, there are definite principles and policies of personnel management which help overall development of human force.

3. Management of human resources. Personnel Management is the management of human resources in the industry. Best possible results are secured by managing this source of power in an effective manner.

4. Defines inter-personnel relationships. Personnel Management defines the relationship between (a) employer and employee and (b) employee and employee. The word employee includes not only the workers at the lowest level but the employees at all levels and types of management such as craftsmen, foremen, operators (low level), department managers (middle level) and general manager or chief executive (top level) are also included in it.

5. Considers development as individual and as member of a group. Personnel Management considers the development of individuals at work, as an individual and as a member of the group. Therefore, in formulating personnel policies and solving the human problems of an organisation intelligently their individual character and the entity as a member of the group are considered so that the intrinsic abilities of

---

17. Dirks, Howard M., "Personnel Administration", in Maynard, H.B. (ed.) *Handbook of Business Administration,* New York, 1967, Section 11, p. 11.

18. Sikula, Andrew F., *Personnel Administration and Human Resource Management,* John Wiley and Sons, Inc., New York, 1976, p. 5.

19. Richard Calhoon, *Managing Personnel,* New York, 1964, p. 4.

the workers may be developed to the best use of the organisation and the goal of the organisation is attained to the maximum possible extent.

6. Considers labourer as a human being. The whole philosophy of personnel management is based on the assumption that labourer is a human being. Humanly treatment should be given to him so that he can recognise his intrinsic abilities and these may be developed and motivated towards the best interest of the organisation.

Thus, Personnel Management is an approach, a point of view, a technique of thinking and philosophy of management concerned with the overall development of men at work.

FUNCTIONS OF PERSONNEL MANAGEMENT

The function of personnel management may be divided into two parts — Managerial functions and Operative functions. These are as follows :

FUNCTIONS OF PERSONNEL MANAGEMENT

Managerial Functions	Operative Functions
1. Planning	1. Procurement of Personnel
2. Organising	2. Development of Personnel
3. Directing	3. Compensation to Personnel
4. Controlling	4. Employees' Benefits Schemes
	5. Maintaining Good Industrial Relations
	6. Record Keeping
	7. Personnel Planning and Evaluation
	8. Personnel Research and Audit.

1. Managerial Functions

(i) Planning. It is the main function of management. It is concerned with manpower planning; studying labour turnover rate, forecasting the future requirements of personnel and planning for selection and training procedures, etc.

(ii) Organisation. It involves the establishment of inter-relationships within organisation. By identifying the various sub-groups headed by individuals in managerial jobs as well as operative jobs, it provides a structure for the company.

(iii) Direction. It includes issuing instruction to the workers, developing communication network, interpreting various industrial laws and integrating workers.

(iv) Control. It provides basic data for establishing standards, makes job analysis and performance appraisal, etc. All these techniques assist in effective control of the qualities, time and efforts of workers.

2. Operative Functions About Personnel

(i) Procurement. It is concerned with the obtaining to the proper kind and number of personnel necessary to accomplish organisation goals. It deals specifically with such subjects as the determination of manpower requirements, their recruitment, selecting, placement and orientation, etc.

(ii) Development. Development has to do with the increase through training, skill that is necessary for proper job performance. In this process various techniques of training are used to develop the employees. Framing a sound promotion policy, determination of the basis of promotion and making performance appraisal are the elements of personnel development function.

(iii) Compensation. Compensation means determination of adequate and equitable remuneration of personnel for their contribution to organisation objectives. To determine the monetary compensation for various jobs is one of the most difficult and important function of the personnel management. A number of decisions are taken into the function, *viz.*, job-evaluation, remuneration policy, incentive and premium plans, bonus policy and co-partnership, etc. It also assists the organisation for adopting the suitable wages and salaries, policy and payment of wages and salaries in right time.

(iv) Good industrial relations. It covers a wide field. It is intended to reduce strifes, promote industrial peace, provide fair deal to workers and establish industrial democracy. If the personnel manager is unable to make harmonious relations between management and labour industrial unrest will take place and millions of man-days will be lost. If labour-management relations are not good the moral and physical condition of the employee will suffer, and it will be a loss to an organisation *vis-a-vis* a nation. Hence, the personnel manager must create harmonious relations with the help of sufficient communication ystem and co-partnership.

(v) Record keeping. In Record-keeping the personnel manager collects and maintains information concerned with the staff of the organisation. It is essential for every organisation because it assists the management in decision-making such as in promotions.

(vi) Planning and evaluation. Under this system different type of activities are evaluated such as evaluation of performance, personnel policy on an organisation and its practices, personnel audit, morale, survey and performance appraisal, etc.

(vii) Research and audit. It is concerned with the research in newer motivational techniques and auditing, its effect on the workers of the organisation etc.

IMPORTANCE OF PERSONNEL MANAGEMENT

1. Harmony in management-employees relationship. The personnel function is concerned with the relationship of management and the employees. The management has to get the work done through the employees who implement the plans. Despite tremendous technical development the man still remains the main factor of production. He plans, thinks, produces and sells the products. Thus, production, marketing, finance, accounting, products research and development, all the functions are performed by human beings. As Peter Drucker says, "The proper or improper use of different factors of production depends upon the wishes of the human resource. Hence, besides other resources, human resources need more development." If employees are satisfied and motivated they will contribute their best towards the attainment of organisational goals. Without this no object of organisation can be realised. Apply has aptly said, "Management is the development of the people and not the direction of things." Management and personnel administration cannot be separated, though in a relatively large organisation, personnel management activities are characteristically carried out by a separate department having a title such as Personnel Department or Personnel Management, Industrial Relations Department and so on. The specific designation may vary from company to company. Personnel department is primarily interested in the selection, training, development and motivation of employees. The activities involved in personnel management affect the entire organisation. As every manager has to deal with his subordinates, he must know the techniques to deal with them successfully.

2. Wide Scope. Thus, the scope of personnel function is very wide. It is concerned with the maintenance of the organisation. It aims to achieve both efficiency and fairplay. It seeks to bring together and develop into an effective organisation the men and women who make up an enterprise enabling each to make his own best contribution to its success. It seeks to provide fair terms and conditions to those who are employed. To conclude with an apt observation of M.W. Cumming : "The personnel function is basically concerned with the relationship of management with the employees and employees in all matters other than actual work itself."

3. Duty of Manager. In a large enterprise, the various functions in the personnel division are grouped into departments. The major divisions usually contained in the personnel department are employment, record keeping, job evaluation, performance appraisal, safety and health, education and collective bargaining, etc. Though these are operative responsibilities of personnel department but the personnel function is the duty of each manager. It is so because each manager has to deal with the people and his main responsibility is to get the work done through and with the people. His main duty is to deal with his subordinates and co-workers fairly and nicely. The importance of proper personnel management has been summed up by Mayer in these words, "Those industries who care not for the needs and feelings of human resources, they are only a heap of machinery. They could not be called industrial organisation at all."

4. Development of people. L.A. Apply says that "Management is the development of people and not the direction of things, Management and Personnel Administration are one and the same. They should never be separated." Personnel function is to achieve both efficiency and justice. It seeks to bring together and develop into an effective organisation the men and women who make up an enterprise enabling each to make his own best contribution to its success both as an individual and as a member of a working group. It seeks to provide fair terms and conditions of employment and satisfying those employed in an organisation. It is not concerned with the effective utilisation of manpower only but equally with the organisational maintenance also.

The importance of personnel management may be summed up in the words of Glean Gardiner as follows : "By centralizing the personnel function in a personnel department, too many people have assumed that you can centralise human relations, it was perhaps the error in thinking of the production, people and general manager who felt that it would be very helpful if we could just put all our personnel headaches into one that left somebody else worry about them for all of us. The personnel function is by no means a one man function or a one man department." Thus, each manager is essentially a personnel manager.

SUBJECT MATTER OF PERSONNEL MANAGEMENT

The subject matter of Personnel Management is human being *i.e.*, employees of the organisation. It is that part of management process which is concerned with the effective utilisation of the labour resources of an organisation. Human labour has always been a significant factor of production. The proper or improper use of the different physical factors of production depends upon the wishes of the human resource of the organisation.

SCOPE OF PERSONNEL MANAGEMENT

Earlier, the business organisations were mainly one man show.

The proprietor, manager and even worker was the one and the same person. With the development of modern industries and management techniques, the organisation structure became complex. The increase in the size of the industrial units, their development and importance has led to indirect management, *i.e.*, indirect relationship among workers and management. Besides, a significant change in the viewpoints and attitudes of the workers as well as management has come about. Therefore, the scope of personnel function has become wide. The major divisions usually contained in the personnel department of a modern industrial organisation are employed record keeping, job-evaluation, performance appraisal, health and safety, education and training, wage surveys, wage determination and administration, redressal of grievances and in some organisations, collective bargaining also. Following are two descriptions of scope of personnel management :

1. Indian Institute of Personnel Management

(i) Labour requirement, selection, test and their best utilisation.

(ii) Conditions of working, remuneration system, management of working condition and labour services and convenience.

(iii) Amicable settlement of the industrial disputes and maintenance of good industrial relations.

2. Strauss and Salyes

(i) Recruitment of labour, selection and placement,

(ii) Analysis, description and evaluation of the work,

(iii) Compensation and schemes of appraisal work,

(iv) Keeping records of the personnel,

(v) Welfare programmes,

(vi) Special services like safety, inspection and control,

(vii) Training and educational programmes,

(viii) Labour relations,

(ix) Public relations and

(x) Personnel Appraisal and development.

Thus, the scope of personnel management is very wide. It is not limited to industrial and business field only. Its importance is extended to every type of organisation whether commercial, religious, social or political wherein people work in groups. The basic concept of management is the art of getting the work done through and with the people. Hence, the use of personnel management extends to all kinds of enterprise, big or small, efficient or inefficient, commercial or non-commercial, private or public enterprises.

NATURE OF PERSONNEL MANAGEMENT

According to Scott, Clothier and Spriegel, "Viewed from the standpoint of the enterprise as a whole the personnel division is a staff unit." Personnel department enjoys both the ranks-line department as well as of a staff department. Personnel function is both a staff activity as well as a line function.

1. Line function. Personnel function is said to be a line function because all the functions co-operative in the process of earning profits for the organisation. All activities are carried out by persons and personnel management department, controls the functions of these persons. It plans, organises and channelises their efforts of the common goal of the organisation. The personnel manager motivates them, creates an atmosphere of sound human relations, industrial peace and so on. Thus, personnel department can rightly be said to be a line department. As an activity or function the personnel function is a line responsibility because each manager whether a production manager or a marketing manager has to deal with persons. Hence, he must have sufficient knowledge how to deal with them.

2. Staff function. Personnel function is also a staff function. In business organisations, the main function of a personnel manager is generally to advise the Board of Directors or General Manager in personnel matters. He helps in formation of sound personnel policies and maintaining good industrial relations between the management and the workers. He assists and serves the workers and other departments too. He provides efficient workers to different departments through proper recruitment and training, etc. He keeps necessary personnel records, makes job evaluation, makes performance appraisal and chalks out the programme of executive development, workers' training, etc. He acts as mediator between the management and workers' union in case of industrial dispute.

OBJECTIVES OF PERSONNEL MANAGEMENT

(A) *General Objectives* : General objectives express the basic philosophy of top management towards the labour force engaged on the work and its deep underlying conviction as to the importance of the people in the organisation. Therefore personnel management must formulate and adopt a basic creed and make it known to its employees and the public. The statement of basic objectives should include the following as the most important objectives :

1. Maximum Individual Development. The employer should develop the personality of each individual. If an act of the employer adversely affects the personality of the individual, he should avoid it.

He should establish and support such human values that may have social recognition and importance. Employees should always be regarded as co-owners or partners of the organisation and given a due importance in the organisation. As each individual differs in nature therefore the management should recognise his individual ability and make use of such ability in an effective manner.

2. Defining relationship of employer and employees. Personnel management seeks to have a desirable working relationship between the employer and employees so that they may co-operate with the management. This is possible only when there is complete mental revolution. The top management should realise that labourer is a human being and humanly treatment should be given to him. The workers should co-operate with the management in accomplishing the goals of the management.

3. Efficient moulding of human resources. A man is the only active agent of production who engages the other factors of production to work the management should emphasise the effective utilisation of human resources as contrasted to physical resources so that maximum production at minimum cost is possible. Without effective moulding of human resources, other factors of production will be ineffective.

(B) *Specific Objectives* : These refer to the various activities of the personnel department such as the following :

1. Selection. Personnel management selects type and number of persons required to the organisation concerned.

2. Orientation. Personnel Management ensures proper orientation and introduction of new employees of the organisation to their jobs.

3. Training. Personnel management seeks organisation of suitable training facilities for better job performance and to prepare a man to accept the challenge of higher job.

4. Better working conditions. Personnel management aims at provision of better working conditions and other facilities such as medical facilities, facilities of provident fund, gratuity, leave with pay etc. so as to help to hold the competent and qualified personnel in the service of the organisation.

5. Incentives. The objective of personnel management is the provision of sound or fair and effective wages and salary administration and other incentives which will result in the highest possible productivity of workers.

6. Retirement. An objective of the personnel management is that a full and fair consideration should be given to an employee when his services are terminated or he leaves the organisation. He should hold a good impression of the management at the time of retirement.

7. Trade Unions. Trade unions today play an important role in the industrial life. Personnel management seeks to maintain good relations with representatives of trade unions on mutual confidence and respect.

8. Personnel Research. Personnel research keeps the management equipped with recent development and trends essential to take sound decisions without any further delay as regards personnel matters.

To conclude, the objective of personnel management is to satisfy the men at work. The management should be aware of the problems faced by the workers and try to solve them effectively with the least controversy.

TRAITS OF PERSONNEL MANAGER

According to survey made in U.S.A. in the year 1958, in 60 per-cent companies personnel manager was called Personnel Director, in 10 per cent as Personnel Officer; in 10 per cent companies as Personnel Manager; in 10 per cent companies Public Relations Officer and Personnel Manager and in 10 per cent companies he was termed as Employees Officer. In India, Personnel Manager is treated as a member of the top management team of the organisation. He is an executive requiring essentially the same executive qualities as other executives. He needs technical competence in the areas of his division's specialities. He needs not be a specialist in all the areas of the personnel division, yet he should have a high degree of skill and competence in at least one of the areas.

1. Philosophy of social justice. Personnel management should have a keen sense of social justice and be fully appreciative of the rights and interests of the men and women as well as of the economic necessities of management. His philosophy of social justice should include two fundamental concepts :

(i) Industry is a partnership between management, men and owners whose objective is profits through service.

(ii) Industry can profit greatly by developing and co-ordinating the capacities, the interest and the opportunities of each worker and of each member of management.

2. Interest and common-sense. Personnel Manager should take interest in people and possess a wealth of common-sense which will protect him from sentimentality on one side and from coldness on the other.

3. Sound advice. He must be qualified to advise management on matters of personnel and capable of talking without fear of favour with any executive in the organisation.

4. Qualities of head and heart. He should possess legal, social, human and managerial qualities of head and heart as well.

5. Responsibilities

1. *Geoge Henon* :

(i) Responsibilities towards Personnel System.

(ii) Responsibilities towards the Top Management.

(iii) Wage and Salary Administration.

(iv) Protection of Physical Resources.

(v) Assistance in Cost in Expenditure| Control.

(vi) Maintenance of Records.

(vii) Maintenance of Industrial Peace.

2. *Scott, Clothier and Spriegal* : "The chief personnel officer should be a specialist in organisation theory and as such be an effective adviser to top management in organisational matters, as well as being able to organise his own division (department) in such a manner as to minimise frictions, promote goodwill and release the latent energies of his own people and associates to be expanded on their primary assignments."

3. *M.W. Cumming* : "Top personnel manager aims to achieve both efficiency and justice, neither of which can be pursued successfully without the other. It seeks to bring together and develop into an effective organisation of the men and women who make up an enterprise enabling each to make his own best contribution to its success both as an individual and as a member of a working group. It seeks to provide fair terms and conditions of employment and satisfying work for those employed."

POLICIES OF PERSONNEL MANAGEMENT

According to George D. Hasley, following principles of sound personnel management are useful in building good worker morale :

1. Care and skill should be exercised in the selection of employees.

2. Introduction to the job should be friendly skilful and adequate.

3. Each employee should be made to feel that his efforts are really appreciated.

4. Careful and thoughtful consideration should be given to the probable effect each rule, each notice, and each practice will have on the feelings of all concerned.

5. Employees should have a part in planning those things which affect their working conditions (whenever it is practical to do so).

6. There should be a sense of security and reasonable freedom from worry.

7. There should be constant and intelligent effort on the part of management to be absolutely fair in every policy and every practice.

8. Each employee should have a feeling of pride in the worthwhileness of his work and his company.

9. The organisational set up be such that there is no confusion in any one's mind as to his duties or responsibilities.

10. Conditions should be such that working proves to be satisfying social experience as well as means of making a livelihood.

SEQUENTIAL METHODS OF CLASSIFYING PERSONNEL FUNCTIONS

Procurement	Retention	Development	Relations	Administration
1. Recruitment	1. Promotion	1. Training	1. Govt. Rules & Regulations	1. Application & co-ordination of Personnel policies and programmes.
2. Selection	2. Transfer	2. Appraisal	2. Policies	2. Personnel Records and Reports.
3. Introduction	3. Wages & Salary Administration.	3. Rating	3. Union relations	3. Personnel Research and Statistics.
4. Placement	4. Management of Fringe benefits: (a) Financial (b) Education (c) Housing (d) Health (e) Recreation (f) Other Welfare Activities.	4. Development Programmes.	4. Community Relations	4. Evaluation of Personnel Administration.
		5. Relations with Govt. industrial machinery.	5. Personnel Audit.	
			6. Collective Bargaining.	
			7. Grievance Procedure.	

NEED FOR A SEPARATE DEPARTMENT OF PERSONNEL MANAGEMENT

1. Job Analysis. The personnel administration must have information about the job specifications describing details of the duties involved for long job. The information will help to fill vacancies. It will also enable assignment of substitutes from among employees of the same or other organisation units, in case of temporary absences due to sickness, vacations, or other reasons. The personnel administrator must be currently informed about all conditions and charges in manpower. He should use books and tables to record all requirement and changes pertinent to his field of responsibility. Many personnel administrators use visual charts containing slots for every employee that is needed, and names and other data for jobs currently filled. These visual instruments permit quick orientation just like a balance sheet in an account book. Hence, it is essential to have a separate department of Personnel Management.

2. Reduction in the cost of production. There are a number of techniques to bring about reduction in the cost of production. A proper control over the wastages and leakage caused by labour is the most important. Hence, it is desirable to have an independent department of personnel administration.

3. Contented Manpower. A satisfied labour force is a *sine qua non* of personnel administration. It requires the provision of welfare amenities, implementation of social security measures and such other activities that may bring labour and capital closer to each other. The successful working of such activities necessitates the existence of a separate department of personnel administration looking after the problems of labour, trying to meet its demands, chalking out schemes of social security, providing welfare amenities, etc.

4. Trained and efficient labour force. This is the age of scientific technology and automation. If any country aspires to keep abreast with the march of time and come out with flying colours the modern cut-throat competition, it is all the more necessary to provide the most up-to-date training to those who have to handle the machines. Efficiency can also be achieved by means of proper training. Training within industry is a popular feature in most of the American concerns. Thus, there should be an independent department of personnel administration having a training sub-division for a careful appraisal of the above problem.

5. Scientific Recruitment. Recruitment is the most important function of the employment department, a part and parcel of the department of personnel administration and management. The recruitment process is largely responsible for the disposition and allocation of manpower. Unskilled or thoughtless recruitment may occasion the misuse, misapplication and underutilization of labour. It may direct manpower into positions in which participants will not utilize their

FUNCTIONS OF PERSONNEL ADMINISTRATION DEPARTMENT

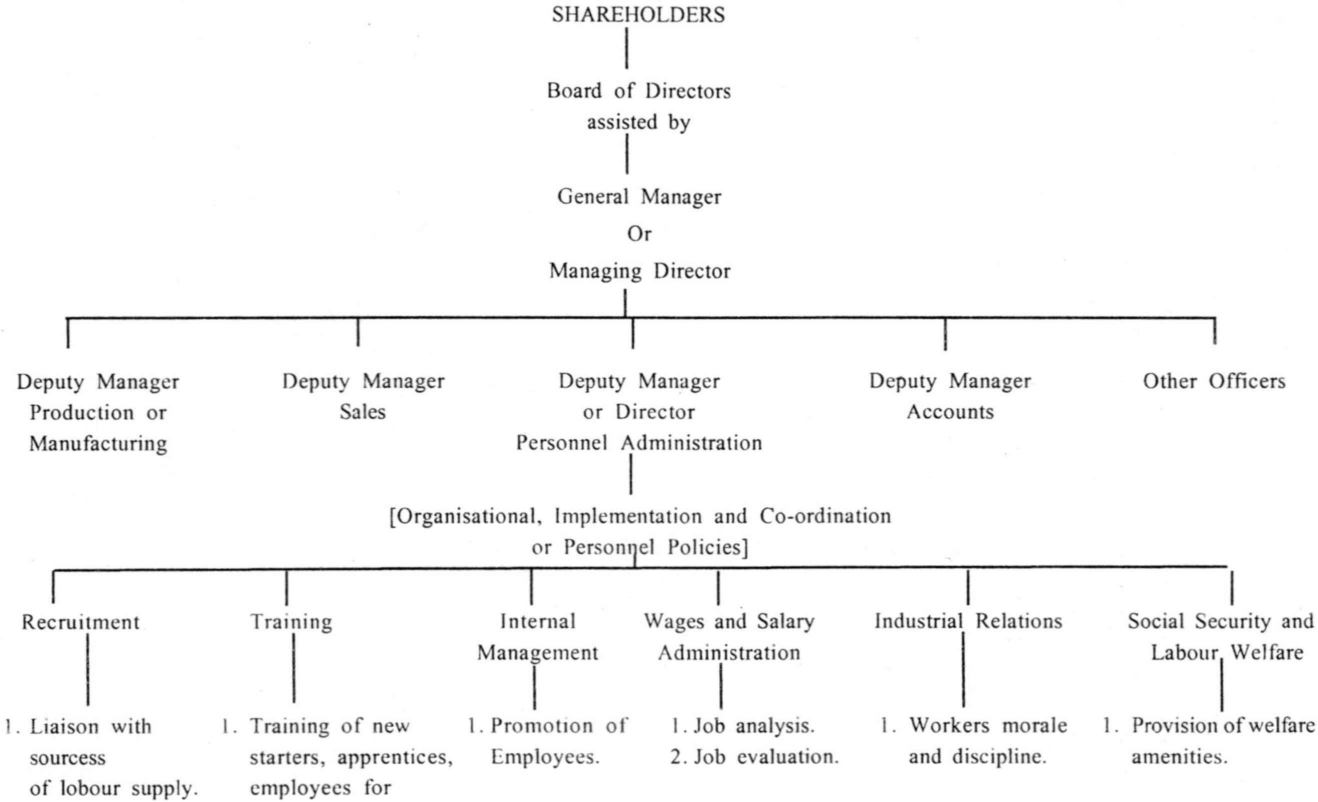

2. Interview applicants.	transfer and promotion, instructors, supervisors etc.	2. Transfer of Employees.	3. Wages surveys. 4. Employee rating.	2. Labour legislation interpretation.	2. Implementation of social security legislation.
3. Tests and Physical Examination 4. Maintenance of Personnel statistics. 5. Granting of employees.	2. Encouraging additional education through night schools; attendance at technical and evening classes, lectures, films, dramatic musical and other societies. 3. Supervision and control of notice-boards. 4. Suggestion-scheme. 5. Work-tours. 6. Library. 7. Works-magazines.	3. Demotion. 4. Termination of services.	5. Wage incentives. 6. Profit sharing. 7. Workers' participation in management.	3. Attending labour grievances. 4. Labour-management co-operation 5. Arbitration.	3. Other social security measures, like provident fund, old-age pension, employees' insurance, etc.

highest talents, where they will not secure the training or experience essential to their maximum contribution or where they may face long periods of idleness or numerous changes from one inappropriate job to another equally inappropriate. Scientific selection seeks to separate the most likely and promising from among those made available by recruitment. This necessity of scientific recruitment of manpower further emphasizes the need of having a separate department of personnel administration and management.

6. Scientific promotion, demotion and transfer. Promotion of deserving employees from the lower to the higher cadre, demotion of the guilty and inefficient and suspension of the indisciplined workers requires scientific treatment. Promotion, demotion, interdepartmental transfers, suspension, etc., should be based on certain scientific principles. A strict observance of these rules requires the establishment of an independent department of personnel administration and management.

7. Cordial Employer-Employee Relations. Cordial relations between the superior and the subordinates is the key to the maintenance of industrial peace. Industrial production is bound to suffer without peaceful atmosphere. This can be achieved only when industrial relations is scientifically and properly tackled. There must be a department of industrial relations as a wing of the major department — the department of personnel administration and management — whose primary function should be to link the top management with the working people. If both, labour and capital, surrender a little and proceed hand-in-hand with a feeling of goodwill and co-operation there is no power on the earth that may hinder production.

The department of personnel administration and management should be under the charge of a capable and experienced senior officer of the concern. He may be designated as the Deputy Manager or Director of the Department of personnel administration and management. There may be several Deputy Directors under him for his assistance, who may be entrusted with different activities and functions which may be undertaken by the department of personnel administration and management.

FUNCTIONS OF A PERSONNEL MANAGER

In promoting the optimum utilization of the abundant human resources by providing expert professional and competent advice to management resources by providing expert professional and competent advice to management in the areas of selection of employees, training and development, job evaluation, wage and salary administration, men-boss relations, human relations, etc. Personnel Manager have a great responsibility. In the words of Shri V.V. Giri, "They (Personnel

Managers) should assist employers not only in formulating proper, humane and progressive personnel policies and procedures, but also in implementing them effectively in an industrial organisation. Personnel managers should command respect of both sides of the industry-labour and management and they must follow an independent attitude and must have in view the promotion of the organisation's health as well as the health and prosperity of the individual employee." Following are the functions of a Personnel Manager :

1. To select personnel. Personnel Director (or Manager) in industries carries on sound policy of recruitment. Proper selection of personnel is the first task which confronts him. To the old methods of recruitment such as interviews and recommendations, modern method adds psychological testing used in addition to normal trade tests or recruitment tests and interviews.

2. To carry on scientific placement of recruits. After proper selection of personnel, the personnel manager should do the judicious and scientific placement of the recruits. This requires the skill of matching the man, the job and the supervisor so that the department where he is put, can work with optimum efficiency.

3. Induction and training of new recruits. This is another fundamental assignment of the personnel manager. Induction and training should start immediately on personnel's appointment as they are important for orientating an employee and training him up for his job. These help the department to avoid some accidents which could happen if the employee is completely unacquainted with the working conditions. A brief idea of the organisation and a detailed training of the department where he is scheduled to work will help the employee as well as the department.

4. To establish good industrial relations. An important function of the personnel manager is to establish industrial relations. Industrial peace is of vital importance for the peace and prosperity of an organisation. The bigger the organisation the greater is the task of the personnel manager.

QUESTIONS FOR EXERCISE

1. Explain the salient characteristics of Personnel Management.
2. Define Personnel Management and explain its importance.
3. "The activities involved in personnel management pervade the entire organisation." Comment on this statement and discuss the importance of Personnel Management.

4. "Personnel Management involves two categories of functions — managerial and operative." Describe these functions in detail.
5. "Management is Personnel Administration." Comment.
6. "Personnel Management is a basic management function that pertains to all levels and types of management." Discuss.
7. "Personnel Management is a way of approach, a point of view, a technique of thinking and a philosophy of management." Elucidate the statement by describing the main characteristics and importance of personnel management.
8. "Personnel Management is clearly a management function and not a 'third force' as practised in some industries." In this context discuss the various functions of a Personnel Department.
9. "Personnel Management is a basic management function pertaining to all levels and types of management." Discuss.
10. "The activities involved in personnel management pervade the entire organisation. They are not performed solely by those in the personnel department." Explain this statement and bring out the importance of personnel function in a business enterprise.
11. "Management and Personnel Management are one and the same." Explain this statement.
12. "Personnel administration is a line responsibility, but it is also a staff function," Examine this statement carefully.
13. "The objective of Personnel Management, Personnel Administration or Industrial Relations in an organisation is to attain maximum individual development, desirable working relationship between employers and employees and effective moulding of human resources as contrasted with physical resources." Discuss the objectives of Personnel Management.
14. "Managers are not born but made". Discuss.
15. What are the traits required in a personnel manager? Explain the responsibilities of a Personnel Manager in a large-sized business organisation.
16. What are the policies and principles of Personnel Management?
17. What is the need of a separate personnel department in business enterprises?

2

Development of Personnel Management

DEVELOPMENT OF PERSONNEL MANAGEMENT IN INDIA

The development of personnel management in India can be studied under two heads : (A) Development before Independence and (B) Development in post-Independence era.

A. Development Before Independence

1. Appointment of labour welfare officers. Before Independence nothing commendable was done either on the part of employers or on the part of Government for the development of industrial relations. The development of personnel management in India was as late as in 1920 when labour welfare activities were initiated by some Indian business enterprises like Tata Group, British India Corporation, Calico Mills, Empress Mill, etc., who appointed labour welfare officers to look after the interest of the working people and of the enterprise in relation to the human problems.

2. Industrial unrest. The year 1920 was the year of industrial unrest. Employers and the Government took various steps to resolve better industrial relation including the recognition of trade unions. But satisfactory progress in industrial relations could not be seen on the whole.

3. Governmental efforts. Before and during World War II, the Government (Central and States) were the leading agencies in India to develop and improve the labour relation in Indian industries. In 1934 with the efforts of Bombay Government, the appointment of the labour welfare officers was made compulsory in industries employing 500 or more workers throughout the State of Bombay to resolve the labour disputes with labour commissioner as the chief conciliation officer. Industries in other states also appointed the labour officers.

4. Royal Commission on Labour. In 1939, Royal Commission on Labour recommended the appointment of labour officers so that the labour problems might be reconciled amicably. The Union Government convened a tripartite labour conference to discuss the extent of labour laws in Indian industries, to evolve a system of grievance handling and to establish conciliation system in industrial matters.

B. Development in Post-Independence Period

1. Labour legislations. Government of India did commendable work in this direction. On the recommendations of the Central Labour Investigation Committee 1946, several labour legislations were enacted such as, Labour Disputes Act, 1947, Industrial Employment Act, 1946, Factories Act, 1948 etc. The Factories Act, 1948 provided the appointment of a labour welfare officer in every industry employing 500 or more workers for the purpose of helping the management in providing welfare measures to the workers as enunciated in the Act. Now the urgency of appointing personnel or labour officer is being felt even in such industries where there is no legal compulsion to appoint welfare officer as there is a need of such agency to guide the management in tackling the ticklish labour problems by providing the specialised services. The services of these labour welfare officers are not up to the mark even now because of their taking a biased view. While dealing with the workers, they consider themselves as an agent of management.

2. Training. The Government arranged for the training of workers and management personnel in India and started several training centres and institutes for imparting training in industrial relations. In 1949, for the first time in independent India 'Xavier Institute of Labour Relations' was established. Several other institutions were started later on such as Indian Institute of Personnel Administration, Calcutta, Indian Labour Management Institute, Bombay, Institute of Industrial Relations, Bangalore, Federation of All India Labour Welfare Officers, and Indian Productivity Councils, Shri Ram Centre for Industrial Relations and Human Resources at Delhi.

3. Reforms during emergency. In the middle of 1975, the government proclaimed the state of emergency in India and took several administrative steps to eradicate the system of bonded labour, to give momentum to the scheme of workers' participation in management in Indian industries and to extend the scheme of apprenticeship.

4. Post-emergency labour legislation. In 1978, a comprehensive Industrial Relation Bill was introduced in Parliament in order to improve the labour relations in industries through collective bargaining by consolidating Trade Union Act, 1926; Industrial Employment (Standing Order) Act, 1946 and the Industrial Disputes Act, 1947. But due to dissolution of Lok Sabha in 1979 the bill could not be passed. In 1981 the President promulgated an ordinance giving powers to the Government to ban strikes in essential services for six months. The essential services include Railways, Post and Telegraph, Telephone, Docks, Airports, Banks, Petroleum, Water and Sewer Disposal, Defence and Hospitals. The Government was empowered to declare any service as an essential service. In 1982, Government amended several labour laws, including Industrial Disputes Act, Industrial Employment (Standing Order) Act, 1946. The Government also amended the Employees State Insurance Act in 1984.

EVOLUTION OF PERSONNEL MANAGEMENT

1. Early Philosophy (Before 1900). The history of modern personnel management began with the name of Robert Owen. Owen is called the founder of Personnel Management. In 1813, he wrote a book, *A New View of Society*. In it he propounded the need of better industrial relations and improvements in the service conditions. His attitude towards workers was very cordial, liberal and patternalistic. He got good houses constructed for his workers by the side of his factory. He eliminated child labour and provided healthy conditions. Mr. J.S. Mill, Andrew Yule and Charles Bewarage contemporaries of Robert Owen, developed personnel management as a science and supported the idea of wage incentives, profit sharing and labour welfare, etc.

2. Efficiency and Productivity Movement (1900-1920). During the last year or 19th century arrived the age of efficiency and productivity movement. The two decades of 1900-1920 were the years of scientific management movement. Taylor's Scientific Management thought was accepted during this period. Taylor opposed the idea of trade unionism and workers' organisation. The main contribution of these two decades has been the increase in the size of units, introduction of scientific thinking into actions, job analysis, standards costing, scientific selection and training of workers and the idea of mental revolution.

3. Period of Welfare-ism and Industrial Psychology (1920-1930). Up to 1925, the personnel management had taken a definite form. Staff line organisation became the basis of personnel management. The opposition of scientific management movement by workers introduced the need of industrial psychology. Industrial psychologist developed many new techniques like psychological testing, interviewing, workers training and non-financial incentives. They helped to give a professional form to personnel management. The personnel management began to be realised as a profession and a specialist's function.

4. Period of Human Relations (1930-1950). Prof. Elton Mayo and his companions conducted Hawthorn experiments as the beginning of human resources having greater influence on production than that of other psychical resources. Worker must be treated as a human being. His social, psychological and moral instincts should be fully recognised by the management. Due to these experiments the commodity concept of labour changed to social concept. The decade of 1940-1950 was very important for the development of personnel management. During the decade, many new techniques were developed for the selection, training and induction of workers. The personnel philosophy became people-oriented. Trade unions flourished and provision of fringe benefits for the workers became common.

5. Modern Times (After 1950). The history of personnel management since 1950 upto current times is the age of modern developments. It is the period of the citizenship concept of labour where the workers have full right to be consulted in determining the rules and regulations under which they work. The concept of industrial democracy has imposed many new responsibilities upon the personnel managers of industrial houses. In modern times, the personnel management is widely accepted as an independent discipline. One finds two important developments during this period : After 1960, the personnel management began to be realised as a behavioural science which centred completely on human elements with the study of organisational behaviour as its main crux. After 1970s the belief of 'open social and industrial system' became very popular for business organisations. In modern times, personnel management is fully recognised as a profession dealing with the management of human resources. Some authors call it manpower management. These developments widened the scope of personnel management.

APPROACHES TO PERSONNEL MANAGEMENT

1. Commodity approach. This was the first or traditional approach towards workers which took birth from the factory system of production. It is also known as a Factor of Production Approach or Mechanical Concept of Labour. The observation that wages are high when labour is scarce in relation to demand and wages are low when labour is in excess of demand gave rise to the idea that affected by the law of supply and demand, labour is like a commodity and it may be bought like other commodities. The approach was supported by the proponents of scientific management movement. It developed the idea of economic concept of man. Money was accepted as the only and most effective motivator for more work. The absence of government intervention and lack of labour laws created the situations of labour exploitation. The factory owners took them as a cog in the machinery of production. It led to the machinery labourer concept of labour. The employer regarded his employees as operating organisms or machines, capable of a certain amount of output. Thus, philosophy led to an impersonal attitude towards workers. Hence, the worker's mind was diverted to protection rather than to production. With the growing knowledge that neither the commodity nor the machinery conception of labour was complete, the resulting inefficiency led to the beginning of the welfare protective movement.

Evaluation. The commodity approach of labour prevailed upto the end of 19th century. It made the condition of workers worst. They were loaded with more work, low wages, unhealthy working conditions and other types of exploitation. It led to class-struggle. Eventually, the trade unions came into existence to protect the rights of the workers.

2. The protective approach. After First World War, employers began to realise that the welfare of their employees had a direct effect upon their productivity. Hence, were introduced safety measures, lunch rooms, rest rooms, bulletin boards visiting nurses and a horde of ameliorating movements. The provision of housing, labour welfare measures, recreational and medicinal facilities were considered to be the duty of the employer. The employer without a welfare movement was considered backward. Robert Owen, the famous British industrialist, was an ardent proponent of this viewpoint. He used to say that an employer should treat his employees like his wards. But labour organisations attacked these welfare efforts of the employers. The visiting nurse was looked upon as spy, bulletin boards were interpreted as devices of propaganda, the costs of safety devices were sometimes objected to on the grounds of lowering wages. According to Scott, Clotheir and Spriegel : in many instances labourers took the attitude : "Put the money in our pay envelops, and we will take care of ourselves."

Evaluation. However, this attitude of workers towards labour welfare measures could not last for a long time. Today labourers claim these provisions as a matter of right. Various labour legislations have made them obligatory on the part of the employees.

3. The humanitarian approach or social approach. The period of human relations approach stressed the human use of human assets. The experiments of Prof. Elton and their associates asserted that the factory is a social system and its employees are human beings having their mind, heart and human values. Management should behave with them with dignity respect so that they would like to put their hearts with the work. The human approach maintained that the workers had certain 'inalienable' rights as human beings. These rights were as important as the right of other persons, and it was industry's duty to recognise them. All men are equal in the sense that they have many of the same impulses and reactions. The industry has a moral obligations not only to permit its workers to enjoy their rights, but to encourage and help them to make as much of themselves as possible. Psychologists stressed labour-management relations. They pointed out that men differ from one another in mental abilities, emotional stabilities, traditions and sentiments more than physically differences. These differences should be recognised. The worker cannot be separated from his job. A reciprocal relationship exists between the job and the market. The worker influences the nature and volume of performance, his job in turn influences the attitudes of the worker.

Evaluation. These developments led to an emergence of social approach to labour. The workers movement became more organised. It demanded more and more share in the prosperity and development of the business. This led to the development of the citizenship concept of labour. This mooted the idea of industrial democracy. As in a democracy a citizen has certain fundamental rights and a voice in determining and exercising these rights so do workers as industrial citizens have a right to be consulted in determining the rules and regulations under which they work. The legal recognition of this concept of labour is relatively recent in origin. More and more participation of workers in management is in offing. Industrial democracy is self-government by the workers, determining the mutual relationships of employer and employee, terms of employment, conditions of labour, rules and regulations affecting employees and the relationship of employees to each other. It accepts that 'the employee is both a social and economic entity, possessing different characteristics in various work situations.'

LOWER STATUS OF PERSONNEL MANAGEMENT IN INDIA

1. Insufficient Appreciation. In India personnel managers have been viewed as contributing little to the essential functioning of an organisation due to the fact that they were entrusted with such tasks as did not offer challenges. They generally prepared routine plans, programmes and procedures, handled employment details, did wage and salary surveys, and handled employee welfare programmes. Other executives were involved in many challenging tasks such as financing and looking after complex production problems. This lack of involvement on the part of personnel managers often led to frustration among them. The personnel function itself was placed at a lower level in the organisational structure. Untrained persons, who were not needed anywhere else, were employed in this department with the resulting low status and prestige of the personnel manager and his department.

2. Low position in the organisation. The personnel function was given a low status in the organisational structure. Line manager were reluctant in seeking help from the personnel department, mainly because personnel executives were contacted for the solution of a single problem. There was hardly any personnel planning, personnel programme and personnel policy in the organisation.

3. Lack of expertise. Frequently, a mediocre line manager was asked to perform personnel functions. Sometimes this was done : "to kick him upstairs" or "to reward him for his good performance elsewhere." As a result, he did not command the respect of his subordinates. As incompetent managers could not anticipate the problems of an organisation; they underestimated their possible effects. Some did not have even sufficient knowledge of, or interest in broader organisational personnel matters.

4. Poor self-image. As personnel managers found that they held low level positions, or were not fairly treated by other executives, they did not take any lively interest in their work, and often performed a static role.

Present Rising Status

These weaknesses influenced the status of personnel managers. But today the top executives have begun to realise that in order to meet the changing needs, there should be "human resources experts" well versed in the diverse aspects of personnel management. These experts must be knowledgeable, competent and committed personnel specialists capable of making meaningful contributions to their organisations and utilizing human resources very effectively.

Today, the Personnel Department is enjoying good status in the overall organisational structure. High sounding designations such as Personnel Director, Senior Personnel Manager, Manager, Human Resources are being used for them. The personnel manager, very often serves as a key member of the top management team. In a large company, vice-presidential position is usually assigned to the top personnel man. He has ultimate responsibility for all personnel and industrial relations policies. He assists in decision-making, organisational planning, executive development and community relations policy.

GENESIS OF PERSONNEL MANAGEMENT IN INDIA

The Royal Commission on Labour (1931) recommended the appointment of labour officer in order to "protect the workers from the evils of jobbery and indebtedness, to act as a spokesman of labour and to promote an amicable settlement between the workers and the management." The Commission made following observations :

1. Exclusion of labour. The jobber should be excluded from the engagement and dismissal of labour and that, instead, a Labour Officer should be appointed for this purpose.

2. Traits of Labour Officer. The traits required of a Labour Officer should be integrity, personality, energy and the gift of understanding individuals. He should have a linguistic facility. If he is of the right type workers will rapidly learn to place confidence in him and regard him as a friend.

3. Powers. All labour should be engaged by him and none should be dismissed without consulting him.

4. Duties. The Labour Officer should fulfil many duties and should particularly initiate and administer welfare measures.

REASONS FOR RECENT HIGHER STATUS

1. Technical factors. (i) *Industrial Revolution* : Industrial Revolution brought in revolutionary changes in the method and techniques of industrial production. The industries were shifted from the former workshop to new mills and factories. Steam and power supplemented or substituted the efforts and energy of people. Production processes were simplified by the use of new machineries and techniques. On the other hand emerged other problems relating to men, materials and machines. The existing principles of management were suitably changed or amended or new principles were developed in order to reconcile the situation.

(ii) *Experiments in social sciences* : New experiments and research in social sciences contributed to the growth of personnel management. For example, Hawthorn experiment in the field of psychology affected the attitudes of the employers to a great extent. Researches in behavioural science also subscribed to the development of personnel management. New techniques and methods were developed which are not being used in selecting the right person on the right job and developing them scientifically by introducing new methods of training.

(iii) *Use of science in industries* : With the advent of science new and newer products, methods, techniques and processes were developed in the fields of production, communication and marketing, affecting the industrial development and the personnel relations. New offices were created to cope with the problems of industrial development, such as engineers, production manager etc.

2. Awakening among workers. After World War I, workers started to unite. A new industrial labour movement soon became an important element in this structure. In the early stages of industrialisation the unions emerged as means of protecting the careers, levels of wages, stability of employment and status in the new industrial society of work. Some other factors also subscribed to their cause at later stages. These were : (i) Economic hardship to workers due to inflation after World War I; (ii) Political movements and success of Russian Revolution in 1917; (iii) Emergence of International Labour Organisation in 1919. The union movement succeeded in improving the labour relations in industries. The concept of industrial democracy is the outcome of the labour movement.

3. Change in Government Attitude. The change in Government attitude towards labour, management and business was mainly due to the following reasons :

(i) *Laissez faire* : Widespread acceptance of *laissez faire* viewpoint was popularised by Rousseau, Bentham and Hobbes and was further advanced by Malthus, Adam Smith and others so-called classical school of economists. It proposed a minimum of public intervention in economic activities. As the political interests of the countries could not safeguarded by this policy in World War I hence the protection policy was introduced by nearly all the countries in the world. As businessmen could get an opportunity to earn huge profits at the cost of employees the Government come to the rescue of the employees in getting them rid of exploitation by the employers.

(ii) *Change in the Concept of labour* : The change in the concept of labour from the commodity concept to other human concept was given a wide recognition. Labourer is now regarded as a human being and master of all the industrial activities. The idea of workers' participation in management has been recognised by almost all the Governments of the world.

(iii) *Labour Legislation* : Establishment of welfare states in most of the countries led to the enactment of various labour laws for the welfare of the industrial force. International Labour Organisations and other national labour agencies recommended several countries to introduce numerous labour statutes to reconcile the viewpoint of the labour and management.

Thus, the Government attitude was one of the factors in the development of personnel management or industrial relations.

4. Cultural and Social Changes. (i) *Education* : Education brought the change in the attitude of labour towards their word. They realised that work is worship and they would be more benefited if they worked hard. They could understand what was favourable and what was against their interest. Hence, they could no longer be exploited.

(ii) *Population problem* : Population problem also had its impact upon the problem of personnel management. The problem of active utilisation of men arose in the countries having a vast population like China and India. Problems of unemployment and wage fixation had direct link with the population. The other population problem is the migratory character of the labour causing absenteeism and labour turnover. These problems could be overcome by motivating the people in the right direction.

(iii) *Change in social values of the labour* : Social values of workers affect the efficiency of worker on the job. If a worker is given due regard in the society or by his fellow workers, he will be the most contented man in the society and his efficiency will be increased thereby. Large-scale production and advanced means of transportation and communication increased the social value of labour. Personnel problems increased and new personnel principles developed.

5. Change in the size of the business. Industrial Revolution and technical changes in methods and machines led to large-scale production. The use of technically-developed machines, simplification of methods and large-scale production led to development division of labour and specialisation functions requiring a large number of technical and non-technical workers. The need of personnel management was felt in order to get the work done by these people efficiently.

6. Change in the attitude of management. Some of the factors which compelled the management to make a change in its attitude towards labour were the development of scientific management, Industrial Revolution, awakening of workers, favourable attitude of Government towards labour and change in the social value of workers.

7. Change in the form of business organisation. In earlier years business was carried on under sole proprietorship. With the advent of joint stock companies as a form of business organisation, the size of the business increased exorbitantly. New management techniques developed to cope with the problems of personnel in large industrial houses.

8. Problem of co-ordination and control. Large-scale production created the problem of control over the thousands of persons working in unit. The need of co-ordination between personnel objectives, developed methods and techniques and overall objectives of the organisation was realised. New structural relationships were developed. The problems of control and coordination required an intensified study if made in the nature of working personnel.

FUTURE OF PERSONNEL MANAGEMENT IN INDIA

In future there are possibilities for the development of personnel management in India. Industrial development in India is progressing very fast. In order to sclve many problems of industrial development, it has become necessary to develop the science of personnel management. This shall be possible only when there is a revolution in the minds of Indian industrialists and they feel that workers are human beings and humanly treatment must be given to them. They should not undermine the importance of labour as compared to other factors of production. Labourers should be induced to work hard so that other factors of production may be exploited in a better way to achieve the primary goal of maximum output at minimum cost. As partners in the industry, workers can contribute much to the national prosperity. Thus, the future of personnel management in India depends upon the change in the attitude of the industrialists towards labour. The Government has announced certain steps for the development of healthy industrial relations such as effective implementation of workers' participation in management scheme and enforcement of labour laws.

CODE OF ETHICS OF MEMBERS OF NATIONAL INSTITUTE OF PERSONNEL MANAGEMENT

Recognising and accepting the responsibilities of the profession of personnel management, I as a member of the National Institute of Personnel Management, shall :

— Uphold the honour and dignity of the profession and the Institute;

— Observe and maintain integrity as the keynote of professional conduct and shall perform my professional duties with fairness, impartiality, fidelity, and dedication to the cause of the profession;

— Recognise and accept the dignity and worth of an individual as a human being, irrespective of race, religion, language, caste or creed, and strive for the development of his personality;

— Co-operate in maximising the effectiveness of the profession by exchanging freely information and experience with others and by contribution to the development of the profession to the best of my ability;

— Maintain at all times as open mind with regard to problems that I have to deal with in the course of my work and approach the problems of others with understanding;

— Not allow any interest other than professional to interfere with any official work;

— Strive unceasingly for self-development by acquiring ever increasing knowledge, skill and experience related to the profession;
— Endeavour to extend public knowledge on professional matters and try to eliminate misconceptions and misunderstandings about the profession;
— Express publicly an opinion on professional matters only when it is founded on adequate knowledge and honest conviction;
— Not damage, directly or indirectly, the professional reputation or practice of other members;
— Exercise due restraint in criticising the work of other members;
— Endeavour to give credit for professional work to those to whom it is due;
— Endeavour to provide opportunities for the development and advancement of professional men who work with me;
— Uphold the principle of appropriate remuneration for those engaged in professional work;
— Not associate in work with another member who does not conform to ethical standards and not hesitate to bring to the notice of the Institute any unethical practice adopted by any member of the Institute;
— Be faithful to my employer or client, and present clearly to him the consequences to be expected if my professional advice is not accepted;
— Advise engagement of specialists when I am convinced that such services are in the best interests of my employer or client and shall co-operate with them in their work;
— Follow professional principles and practices tactfully and courageously, keeping in mind the principles of equity in the fair distribution of work and rewards;
— Promote the concepts, methods, skills and techniques in the fields that contribute to productivity, growth, profitability and employee satisfaction;
— Not disclose any information of a confidential nature that I may acquire in the course of professional work without obtaining the consent of those concerned and
— Not accept or offer any improper gratification in any form or manner whatsoever in connection with, or in the course of, my professional work.

QUESTIONS FOR EXERCISE

1. Trace development of personnel management in India.
2. Describe the evolution of Personnel Management in modern times.
3. Explain important approaches to Personnel Management.
4. Account for the lower status of Personnel Management in Indian business houses. Trace reasons for their recent higher status.
5. Highlight the future of Personnel Management in India.

3

Personnel Management Function in India

Importance of Labour Officer

The importance of labour officers in Indian industry was realised as early as 1929. Set up in 1931 The Royal Commission on Labour recommended the appointment of a labour officer in order to "protect the workers from the evils of jobbery and indebtedness, to act as a spokesman of labour and to promote an amicable settlement between the workers and management." The Commission observed that :[1]

(i) The jobber should be excluded from the engagement and dismissal of labour and that, instead, a Labour Officer he appointed for this purpose;

(ii) The qualities required of a Labour Officer should be integrity, personality, energy, and the gift of understanding individuals and he should have a linguistic facility. If he is of the right type, the workers will rapidly learn to place confidence in him and regard him as friend;

(iii) All labour should be engaged by him, and none should be dismissed without consulting him and

(iv) The Labour Officer should fulfil many duties, and should particularly initiate and administer welfare measures.

Appointment of Labour Officers

In 1931, the Bombay Millowners' Association appointed Labour Officers, who were required to attempt to settle grievances and disputes. Under the directions of the Jute Mills Association similar officer were appointed in the jute industry in Bengal. These officers were entrusted with the responsibility of setting up food shops, promoting sports and welfare activities. In the textile industry personnel officers came up from the department concerned with recruitment and the settlement of grievances rather than from one administering welfare activities. Their functions as Industrial Relations Officers to handle grievances and prevent disputes were stressed from the beginning.

---

1. *Report of the Royal Commission on Labour*, Simla, 1931 pp. 24-25.

During the Second World War

During the Second World War, these officers were generally entrusted with the handling of welfare and labour administration. Their duties were subsequently enlarged and influenced by the social reform movement in the country, public concern for improving labour administration and the growth of the modern management movement. Their functions included activities relating to welfare, personnel and industrial relations.[2]

Legislation in Free India

After the attainment of freedom, the Government, enacted Factories Act of 1948 (Section 49) which made it obligatory for the factories employing 50 or more workers to appoint Welfare Officers. Under the Mines Act of 1952, this limit was for 500 workers. Under the Plantation Labour Act, 1951, the limit was for 300 or more workers. These Act also prescribed the manner of their recruitment, their salaries and conditions of service; and an elaborate list of duties to be performed by them, including those concerned with welfare, day-to-day personnel administration and industrial realtions.

Nominal Role of Welfare Officer

The "personnel man", who was initially known as "Welfare Officer", has moved on to be known as "Labour Welfare Officer", "Personnel Officer", "Industrial Relations Officer" and is now identified as "Human Resource Manager". In the beginning, he was neither given any particular attention or place in the organisation system, nor did professionals find themselves involved in the process. Subsequently, it was entrusted with the *policing function* within the organsiation, *i.e.,* to report on and assist the organisation in dealing with industrial discipline and getting rid of trouble-makers. At this stage, it was mostly engaged in "fire fighting tasks" *i.e.,* going to the forefront at the moments of crisis, without having crried out any preventive or organising action. At this stage the use of Welfare Officers for aiding and abetting the exploitation of the working class by certain organisations brought them on the periphery of notoriety. However, by and large, their appointment in industries remained only symbolic, satisfying the statutory requirements, without any specific, constructive role to play.

QUALIFICATIONS OF LABOUR WELFARE OFFICER

The qualification for Welfare Officer (i) a university degree; (ii) degree or diploma in Social Sciences of Soccial Work or Social

2. Mamoria, C.B., *Industrial Labour and Industrial Relations in India,* Vol II. Kitab Mahal, Alld. 1976, p. 159.

Welfare from any recognised institution and (iii) adequate knowledge of the language spoken by the majority of the workers in the area where the factories, mines and plantations are situated.

According to the National Commission on Labour, "laws were made to ensure that the managements appointed a person exclusively to look after the welfare of their workers and help them in discharging their statutory obligations in respect of welfare measures. Welfare Officers should form part of the administration in order to discharge their responsibilities effectively. Therefore, the eligibility of a Welfare Officer must be ensured before his appointment. The Welfare Officer should not be called upon to handle labour disputes on behalf of the management."[3]

After going through the views expressed by the State Governments, public sector undertakings, private employer's organisations, workers' organisations and eminent persons in the field of relations and on the role and status of welfare officer, The Committee on Labour Welfare recommended that : "The management should designate one of the existing officers of their Personnel Department as Welfare Officer to fulfil the purpose of the law. The management should ensure that only such officers of the Personnel Department are designated to look after the welfare activities as are properly qualified to hold these posts and have aptitute for welfare work.''[4]

FUNCTIONS OF LABOUR WELFARE OFFICERS

1. Supervision of

(i) Safety, health and welfare programmes; housing, recreation, and sanitation services;

(ii) looking after the working of the joint committee;

(iii) grant of leave with wages and

(iv) redressal of worker's grievances.

2. Counselling workers on

(i) Personal and family problems;

(ii) adjusting to work environment and

(iii) understanding rights and priviliges.

3. Advising the Management on Matters of

(i) Formulating welfare policies;

(ii) apprenticeship training programmes;

(iii) meeting statutory obligations to workers;

3. *Report of the National Commission on Labour*, Delhi, 1967, p. 120.

4. *Report of the Committee on Labour Welfare*, 1969.

(iv) developing fringe benefits and

(v) worekrs' education and use of communication media.

4. Establishing liaison with workers to

(i) Understand the various limitations under which they work;

(ii) appreciate the need of harmonious industrial relations in the plant;

(iii) interpret company policies to workes and

(iv) persuade workers to come to a settlement in the event of a dispute.

5. Establishing liaison with the management to

(i) Appreciate the workers' viewpoint on various matters;

(ii) intervene on behalf of the workers in matters under the consideration of the management;

(iii) help different department heads to meet their obligations;

(iv) maintain harmonious industrial realtions in the plant and

(v) suggest measures for the promotion of the general wellbeing of workers.

6. Working with the management and workers to

(i) Maintain harmonious industrial relations in the plant;

(ii) arrange a prompt redressal of grievances and speedy settlement and

(iii) improve the productivity and productive efficiency of the enterprise.

7. Working with the public to

(i) Secure a proper enforcement of the various provisions of the Acts as applicable to the plant by establishing contact with factory inspeccts, medical officers and other inspectors;

(ii) to help workers to make use of community services.

Thus the duties and functions entrusted to a Welfare Officer range from assisting the management in policy formulation and implementation to supervising welfare programme, establishing contacts with workers and the public, solving workers' problems and grievances. In the following chart 3.1 are shown the functions of a Labour Welfare Officer.

Duties of Welfare Officer

According to the National Commission on Labour, "the care of workers in all matters affecting their well-being, both at the place of work and outside, puts a special responsibility on the Welfare Officer. He should be a 'maintenence engineer on human side'. In many cases, he also handles grievances and complaints of workers relating to terms and conditions of service and domestic and other matters which lie in the domain of Personnel Management. There is, thus, virtually no demarcation between personnel management functions and welfare functions." The Commission recommended that "in order to reduce the hierarchical hiatus in the status of these two officers, there should be an interchange to encourage professional functional mobility and to eliminate the functional monopoly as well the hierarchical status problems."

CHART 3.1

Labour Welfare Officer

Labour Welfare Functions	Labour Administration Functions	Labour Relations Functions
Advice & Assistance in implementing legislative and non-legislative provisions relating to 1. Health and Safety 2. Working conditions 3. Sanitation and Cleanliness 4. Recreation 5. Welfare amenities 6. Workers' Education 7. Services like coops. grainshops, housing coops. 8. Formation of Welare Committees 9. Housing 10. Implementation of Welfare Acts.	1. Organisational discipline 2. Safety & medical administration 3. Wage & Salary administration 4. Administration of Legislation covering Industrial Relations	1. Adminsitration of Standing Orders 2. Settlement of Grievances 3. Settlement of Disputes through statutory producers. 4. Trade Unions and Union Management Relations. 5. Steps to increase Productive efficiency

The Central Model Rules, 1957, (revised) define the duties of Welfare Officers so widely (Rule 7) as to comprise :

(1) helping maintain harmonious relation between factory management and workers.

(2) redressal of workers' grievances.

(3) providing feed-back to management regarding labour's point of view "to shape and formulate labour policies and to interpret these policies to the workers."
(4) to watch industrial relations and settle disputes by "persuasive efforts."
(5) to advise maangement on the implementation of health and safety programmes.
(6) to promote productive efficiency.
(7) amelioration of the working conditions and helping workers to adjust and adapt themselves to the working environment.
(8) personnel counselling — advising workers on individual personal problems, etc.

CHART 3.2

Responsibilities and Authority of Labour Welfare Officer in India[5]

Nature of Authority	*Area of Responsibility*
(1) Advisory	
To advise To suggest To encourage To promote To secure	In the formulation of company labour policies, (a) should promote training and apprenticeship programmes; (b) induction programmes and improved working conditions; (c) welfare programmes, housing, recreational and educational facilities for workers and their families; (d) joint consultation and methods of communicating with the workers.
(2) Service	
To help To explain	(i) To workers; (a) In personal and family problems; (b) In adjusting to work environment; (c) In understanding their rights and priciples; (d) In making applications for leave etc. (ii) To Management; By helping workers to undestand the various limitations under which they have to work.
(3) Supervisory	
To inspect To supervise	(a) Welfare and benefit programmes; (b) Health and safety programmes;

5. Jain, S.C., *Personnel Management in India, Its Evolution and present status,* 1968, pp. 33-34.

To regulate	(c) Paid vacations;
	(d) Joint committees.
(4) Functional	
To ensure	(a) Implementation of labour laws;
To deal with	(b) Wages and employment.
(5) Policies	
To bring to notice of	(a) The factory management the grievances of the workers, individual as well as collective;
To Watch	(b) To watch industrial relations with a view to using his influence in the event of a dispute between the factory management and workers;
To restrain	(c) To exercise a restraining influence over workers going on an illegal strike and over the management declaring illegal lockouts, and to help prevent anti-social activities.
(6) Mediation	(a) To establish contacts and hold consultations with a view to maintaining harmonious relations between the factory management and workers;
	(b) To secure an expeditious redressal of the workers' grievances and to act as a negotiating officer with trade unions;
	(c) To help bring about a settlement of an industrial dispute by persuasive efforts and
	(d) To maintain a natural attitude during a legal strike or lockout and to help in bringing about a peaceful settlement.

Impediments to the Progress of Personnel Management in India

1. Legal Status of Personnel Officer. The legal status of a Personnel Officer requires him to work in the field of welfare and day-to-day personnel administration and industrial relations. But since the personnel function is a line responsibility and a staff function, it cannot be properly performed by a personnel officer.

2. Attitude of Employees. The attitude of the employees towards personnel officers has not been favourable. Management in India is still traditional and does not take the personnel officer into its confidence. "The line executives are often regarded as those who get the material, cut it up, put it together and ship it out, while staff executives are those who attempt to prevent the line boys from doing their jobs." Such ideas about the role of the personnel managers generate frustration among them. In the words of Peter Drucekr, "the personnel manager tends to conceive his job partly as a file clerk's job, partly as a house-keeping job, partly as a social worker's job and partly as a fire-fighter to head off union trouble or settle it."

3. Preoccupation with Litigation. Personnel officers are even now required to spend a major portion of their time in attending to disputes and the grievances of workers. The plethora of labour laws has encouraged trade unions to keep some matters always under litigation for the advancement of their selfish interests. This factor keeps a personnel officer preoccupied in litigation and away from his more important duties. As a result, he has neither the time nor the inclination for long-range planning.

4. Professional Impediments. Lack of professional training facilities, a sense of insecurity and lack of job satisfaction among a large number of personnel executives drive them away from the profession.

5. Ordinary Calibre. The profession has not so far attracted the most meritorious among young persons. Mostly those of ordinary calibre has found place in this profession. One of the reasons being that this profession is still considered by many to be somewhat like a *pinjrapole*, an abode of useless cows.

6. Age Old Curriculum. The educational institutions for personnel men have still the age-old curriculum which falls far short of equipping the incumbents the desired type of fast changing knowledge and skill — which could enable them to deal with human problems effectively at the first instance.

7. Lack of Initiative. The urge for updating the personnel people themselves is also mostly absent, which keeps them from being developed. The lack of initiative renders them obsolete and incompetent for the challenging jobs.

8. Personal Aspirations. Their pre-occupation with their own personal aspirations nake them overlook and, at times, ignore the expectations of all others, including the organisations.

9. Wrong Tendencies. By and large such professionals have not been tested in any trying situation when actually put in it, they have generally emerged as failures. Then tendencies like making false promises for cheap popularity and taking credit for the performance of others make it difficult for them to be acceptable to others.

10. Lack of Professional Courage. Lack of couarge to take responsibility for decisions based on their advice have been their greatest handicaps. The professional courage to disagree is a rare virtue. Absence of such professional courage of conviction and lack of confidence in their own competence often compel them to take the line of least resistance.

11. Alienation. Often the personnel man-whether due to professional zeal or personal ambition try to impose their will on other professions. This has been responsible for their alienation. They should shed this trait and make an effort to integrate the expectations of all other professional in industry without creating the feeling of an imposition.

12. Lack of Total Acceptance. Personnel management has not yet been accorded the totality of acceptance by all concerned. The result of faulty decision on the management of human resources is not, by and alrge, felt immediately and the responsibility for it can safety be shifted to someone else. Unlike professions such as engineering and medicine, where the result of any faulty action or decision becomes almost immediately obvious, the loss felt and the person responsible identified. As the acceptance of "man-management" as a profession has to come from employers is trade unions as well as the government. The profession an easy prey to politicalisation by government machinery, trade unions and even by those within the organisation.

Professionalisation of Personnel Management

S.M. Pandey, an expert in Personnel Management, has offered following useful suggestions for professionalisation of personnel management :[6]

(1) The employers and the organisation having professional men should give the same status as extended to other professions, and give the personnel man's advice the same weightage as given to others. The areas in man-management should be left to be handled by personnel managers and they must be allowed to contribute their utmost in the formulation of sound personnel policies... It is high time that management of human beings is not made to like anybody's business. The idea, that by virture of being a man, everybody is capable of handling other human beings, must go. The practice of encroachment by all and sundry in the area of man-management must stop.

(2) The trade unions must recognise this profession as a speciality in the area of man-management and deal with accordingly... *Firmness with fairness must replace the practice of appeasement of the trade unions without creating any misunderstanding.*

(3) The Government must also professionalize personnel management in the public sector, which is supposed to be the model for others to follow... The Government should reduce its involvement in the day-to-day relationship of workers and managers, and should encourage bipartism to paly its role in its fulness. *It should remain*

6. Pandey, S.N., Presidential Address, "Management Human Resource : The Task Ahead", reproduced in *Personnel Today,* Vol. 1, No. 1, April-June, 1980, National Institute of Personnel Management, Calcutta, pp. 6-7.

the watch dog to restrain, direct and guide the parties as an when required.

(4) On the side of the management themselves, it is expected that *personnel management should read the writings on the wall.* It must be able to identify the goals of the organisation with those of theirs, by appreciating the needs and aspirations of all others.

Future Role of Personnel Manager in India

About the future role of personnel manager in India, S.N. Pandey observes :[7]

"Just as the business of finance men is to manage the finances of the organisation to get the optimum return on investment, just as it is the business of production men to utilise the various resources at their disposal in such manner that optimum output is obtained, so is the business of 'personnel men' to manage human resource ensuring harmony, motivation, satisfaction and commitment."

"The line managers and other functionaries should continue to directly deal with the 'men' under them and, therefore, this relationship must continue. The personnel men's role should be to aid and assist the line managers and others in such a way that the human resource is put to its optimum use. Areas of expertise like wage negotiations, implementation of compensation plans, collective bargaining, recruitment, training in organisational development, management development, manpower planning, manpower audit, employees' service, community development and social welfare and the like are the areas which need professional strategy and skills of personnel men. *In these areas they must be given a decisive role to play.* By virtue of education and training as well as the time at their disposal, personnel men will be most suited persons to handle these matters."

"The concept of 'line' and 'staff' functions must undergo a change and the word 'adviser' (staff) and 'line' need be redefined. Because in a highly competitive and interdependent process of production, where group dynamics plays significant role, drawing an 'iron-curtain' between these two functions cannot work. It is the teamwork that matters and will matter most in dealing with people. An organisation is an organic system, and management a composite team. The various disciplines in management must be cohesive and given equal importance. From this angle, *personnel function should be given appropriate place at all levels of management.*"

"Status is earned and not asked for. Each personnel man will have to undergo a serious introspection about his role and himself.

7. *Ibid.*

The power always lie in one's effectiveness and usefulness. It also lies in its capacity to influence other organisational disciplines as well as workers. In a nutshell, personnel man's power and status will depend to a large extent on how pragmatic is his approach.''

"In a fast changing society as our own, self-development in professional field is a continuing feature which must be kept up at all levels best obsolescene would eat our vitalities."

Mr. Billimoria has very rightly said that the future role of personnel officers will depend upon :[8]

(i) The responsibilities delegated to personnel officers and their relationship with their bosses, and subordinates;

(ii) Having authority delegated to them for co-operative or service functions;

(iii) Their being able to function unfettered in giving objective advice;

(iv) Their guarding themselves constantly against obsolescence;

(v) Their placing adequate emphasis on personnel research, without which they will turn into corporate refugees;

(vi) Their preparing an adequate training base for the new members of the profession;

(vii) Their ability to slash through procedural brambles in order to achieve results and

(viii) Their being prepared to accept the full responsibility of their position as senior executives of an enterprise.

---

8. Billimoria, R.P., "The Future Role of Personnel Officers", in *Readings in Personnel Management*, The Indian Institute of Personnel Management, Orient Longmans New Delhi, 1970, pp. 58-59.

4

Personnel Policies, Procedures and Programmes

Labour policy in India derives its philosophy and content from the Directive Principles of the Constitution and has been evolving in response to specific needs of the situation to suit requirements of planned economic development and social justice. It has been envisaged that growth of the economy would not only increase production but also absorb the backlog of unemployed and under-employed and a substantial proportion of the additional labour force. Seventh Plan laid emphasis on harnessing the country's abundant human resources and improving their capabilities for development. Personnel policies are part of labour policy.

PERSONNEL POLICIES

Definition

1. *Edwin B. Flippo* : "A policy is a man-made rule or predetermined course of action that is established to guide the performance of work towards the organisation. It is a type of standing plan that serves to guide subordinates in the execution of their task."[1]

2. *James B. Bambrick* : "Policies are statements of the organisation's overall purposes and its objectives in the various areas with which its operations are concerned — personnel, finance, production, marketing and so on."[2]

3. *Dale Yoder* : "A policy is a predetermined and accepted course of thought and action that is defined and established as a guide towards accepted goals and objectives."[3]

---

1. Flippo, Edwin B., *Personnel Management,* McGraw-Hill Kogakusha Co. Ltd., Tokyo, 1976, p. 84.
2. Bambrick, James B., "Developing Workable Personnel Policies" in *The Personnel Man and His Job*, D.B. Taraporevala & Sons, Bombay, 1967, p. 88.
3. Yoder, Dale, *Personnel Management and Industrial Relations*, Printice-Hall of India, Pvt. Ltd., New Delhi, 1972, pp. 26-27.

4. *Industrial Relations Glossary* : Labour policy is "the principle of objective established by a company for the guidance of the management in its relations with employees."

5. *Richard P. Calhoon* : "Personnel policies constitute guide to action. They furnish the general standards or bases on which decisions are reached. Their genesis lies in an organisation's values, philosophy, concepts and principles."[4]

Characteristics of Personnel Policies

1. Personnel policy is a statement of objectives for the guidance of management in its relations with employees.

2. Personnel policy is a predetermined course of action.

3. Personnel policy is the recognized intention of the top management and guide to the subordinates in the execution of their task.

4. Personnel policy provides general standards or bases on which decisions are taken.

Policies, Procedures and Practices

Explaining the difference between policies and procedures says Ernest C. Miller, "Policies are general instructions-procedures and specific applications." Policies respond to 'what' and 'why' whereas practices explain the way of executing the policies. They transform the policy into action. 'practices', on the other hand, "are what is actually done in the organisation."

NEED OF PERSONNEL POLICIES

1. To achieve the objectives of the organisation. Policies are guide to action towards the objectives of the organisation. Hence, they must be known and well understood by every one in order to concentrate efforts on the objectives.

2. To achieve uniformity in decisions. Personnel policies furnish the general standard on which decisions are taken. Various line authorities take decisions in an organisation keeping in view the personnel policies. Thus, uniformity of action is maintained in similar cases. There is the least possibility of worker's exploitation through biased decision. If the person in authority is transferred and the other person takes charge of the office the decisions to be taken by the new authority are similar to those which have already been taken in similar circumstances by the former authorities due to the predetermined policies of the organisation. This brings simplicity and uniformity in action.

---

4. Calhoon, R., *Personnel Management and Supervision*, Appleton Century Crofts, New York, 1967, p. 21.

3. To delegate authority. Personnel policies make delegation of authority possible, which means assigning the work to others and give them authority to do it. Personnel policies help executives at various levels of decision centres to act with confidence without consulting the superiors every time. Personnel policies give a manager liberty to choose the alternatives provided and to decide upon the action.

4. To achieve better control. Personnel policies specify relationship among organisation, management and workers. Therefore, each group works for the achievement of the large objectives of the organisation without any policy conflicts. Thus, personnel policies provide better control.

5. To evaluate efficiency. Personnel policies serve as standards in execution of work. Efficiency of a group may be evaluated by its performance in the light of the policy. After assessing whether organisation has achieved the desired results set in the policy, personnel policy may be amended or a new policy may be formulated in the light of the actual performance.

6. To create confidence among employees. Personnel policy provides the workers a security against exploitation and creates confidence in employees who may know where they stand in the organisation.

7. To motivate. Personnel policy introduces the employees to the objectives of the organisation. It guides the workers in achieving the objectives. They work enthusiastically and with loyalty to get those objectives.

8. To guide the management. Personnel policy provides guidance to management in relation to the personnel problems. Personnel policy decides how to get the work done by the people or how to behave with them.

FORMULATION OF PERSONNEL POLICIES

1. Due to day-to-day problems. Formulation of personnel policies and their development is the sole responsibility of top management. Their main purpose is to assist the top executives in reaching the decision in a given situation. If the policy fails to suggest a solution to the problem in a new situation it may be amended suitably or a new policy may be formulated to cope with the arising situation. Thus, the development of personnel policies depends upon the day-to-day problems arising in an organisation.

2. Role of Personnel Manager. In a position of staff officer the personnel manager assists the line authorities in formulating and developing the personnel policies. While developing the personnel policy we must have in mind the needs, goals and objectives of the organisation. The personnel policies should be flexible enough to offer sufficient scope for the department administrator to meet different situations.

3. Factors in policy formulation. A company having operations in various parts of the country or having global operations must adjust its policies in such a fashion as to enable the regional manager to develop specific principles to meet the requirements of their areas. Personnel policies should not contravene the basic policies of the organisation. Each group must be represented in the formulation and development of the personnel policy, otherwise it will be very difficult to bring the policy into action.

The laws of the country, social values and customs and employees aspirations should be taken into account in designing the personnel policies. These should be integrated in such a manner that these could not purport the economic and social objectives of the organisation.

4. Communication Policy. Personnel policy is a total commitment of the organisation for carrying out the work in a specified way. It should be communicated to all concerned. Any amendment and change in it should be brought to the knowledge of all employees and executives so that they may have full knowledge of the intentions of the organisation. If such policies adversely affect their interests they should be given full liberty to raise objectives. Cooperation from all sections may be sought in reviewing and finalising the policy.

OBJECTIVES OF PERSONNEL POLICIES

1. To achieve maximum individual development. The main objective of personnel policy is the maximum individual development. It should be designed in such a way that a healthy competition and effective co-operation among workers may be promoted and better results may be achieved.

2. To achieve maximum use of human resources. Personnel policy aims at the best and the maximum use of available human resources. Individual development of workers is not much advantageous to the organisation unless they are used in the best manner possible. There should be a direct relationship between man and the job. Right man should be placed on the right job. The job should be assigned to the man most interested in that work and has sound knowledge of working. He should be so developed that he may be able to accept the challenge of any eventuality of job. Maximum individual development and the maximum use of human resources should be a continuous process.

3. To develop good industrial relations. Personnel policy aims at good employer-employee relations. The promotion of good industrial relations requires co-operation between the management and workers. Nothing is possible unless there are good industrial relations. Taylor emphasised the principle of Mental Revolution which aims at the conciliation of the antagonistic views.

4. To achieve individual satisfaction. Personnel policies aim at individual satisfaction. The management should consider social values, customs and employees aspirations in formulating and developing personnel policies. Individual satisfaction is linked to the monetary and non-monetary incentives provided by the organisation to its workers. This ensures good wage and salary administration. The general attitude of the management towards labour should be reflected by personnel policies. Due recognition given to the work will promote cooperation and loyalty.

5. To protect worker's interest. Personnel policies should protect the interest of workers and recognise the trade union activities.

6. To provide opportunities. Personnel policies provide the opportunities for promotion to workers within the organisation.

7. To motivate people. Personnel policies seek to motivate the people at work and increase their morale.

8. To provide job-security. Personnel policies seek to provide security to job.

9. To promote loyalty. Personnel policies promote and develop among the workers a sense of loyalty to the organisation so that a sense of common interest may develop.

10. To develop sense of responsibility. Finally, personnel policies develop a sense of responsibility in executives.

CONTENTS OF A PERSONNEL POLICY

1. Name of the company. This includes a complete historical review of the development of the company and full details regarding persons in management.

2. Mode of selection. This includes sources of recruitment and methods, procedure and techniques for selection.

3. Working conditions. Working conditions such as working hours, leave rules, top most authority-levels, channels for promotions and rules regarding suspensions and retirement etc. should be clearly mentioned in personnel policy.

4. Training programmes. Full details regarding training programmes, planning and objectives of training programmes for existing and new employees are included in personnel policy.

5. Procedure for handling grievances. Procedure for handling grievances should be mentioned in detail, *i.e.*, to whom should they contact in case of any grievance and when, where and how?

6. Rules and regulations. Rules and regulations governing accidents, unfair termination, maintenance of discipline and standing orders should be clearly defined in the personnel policy.

7. Description of offices. Full information regarding numbers and positions of various offices in the organisation, their grades, wages, allowances and perquisities attached to their bonus and incentive wage plans, methods of payments and priorities should be given in the personnel policy.

8. Provision for labour welfare. Provision for labour welfare and service activities such as education, entertainment, canteen facilities, financial assistance, profit sharing, benefits of provident fund, compensation for accidents etc. should be made, is a personnel policy.

9. Industrial relations. Full details regarding maintenance of industrial relations, *i.e.*, notice period for strikes and lock-out rules for declaring strike illegal, monetary and other losses of strikes and lock-outs to workers etc.

10. Representation in collective bargaining. Personnel policy should include full particulars regarding representation in collective bargaining.

11. Line of Communication. Line of communication and authority relationship should be ascertained in personnel policy.

12. Methods of consultation. The personnel policy should clearly mention the methods and procedures of joint consultation.

13. Fulfilment of needs. The items to be incorporated in the personnel policy may be more or less according to the needs of the organisation.

PRINCIPLES OF PERSONNEL POLICY

1. Common interest. The principle of common interest must be given due recognition in designing personnel policies. Economic success of the enterprises, the interest of the employer and the employees. It benefits all the concerned parties — employees, employer and the Government. Employees must have a chance for a better standard of living, better security and opportunity for living a fuller and better life. In return the employer must be able to get the maximum possible return. A successful business enterprise contributes substantially to the national exchequer and creates propriety all around.

2. Development. The organisation must provide ample opportunities for the growth of employee's personality. People want to improve their status, to earn more, to shoulder higher responsibility. Personnel Policies should lay down rules for the opportunities for development to those who are willing to contribute something to the prosperity of the organisation and to sacrifice their time and efforts for undergoing training to improve themselves on the job.

3. Recognition of work and Accomplishment. There must be direct relationship between work and accomplishment. A job should provide for sufficient wages and benefits that will enable an employee to buy his bare necessities. The personnel policies should take into consideration the employee's expectations such as reasonable security on the job against accidents, sickness and old age.

4. Recognition of Trade Unions. As the trade unions play an important role in the development of industrial relations, therefore, the management must recognise them. The personnel policies, should incorporate the clause for amicable settlement of the dispute with the trade unions through negotiations and collective bargaining.

5. Participation in management. Employees' representatives should be given participation in decision-making bodies of the organisation so that they may realise their responsibilities towards the management and workers. The success of any programme or policy depends considerably upon its willing acceptance by the employees. If the decisions regarding personnel affairs are taken in the presence of workers' representatives, there shall be better employees' satisfaction and morale. It will also minimize resistance to change.

6. Face the change. Employees always resist change which may be pleasant or unpleasant one. An assignment to an Indian technician abroad on company's expense may be a welcome change. But unwelcome change may relate to loss of income, loss of status, reassignment or retraining activities and broken friendship. Therefore, the employees should be prepared by the management well in advance to face the change as and when warranted. This may be done through bulletin boards, company magazines and newspapers, committee meetings, union-management meeting, broadcasting system and so forth. In this regard management viewpoint should be reflected in personnel policies.

To conclude, personnel policies be designed to promote common interest, create safe and healthy working conditions, give proper recognition for work and accomplishment, recognise impact of change on people, encourage employees' participation and recognise the functions and responsibilities of the trade unions.

AN IDEAL PERSONNEL POLICY

1. Protecting interests. An ideal personnel policy must protect the interests of all parties associated with the enterprise, *i.e.,* workers, entrepreneurs, consumers, government and community. All concerned parties must get their due share in the total production of the enterprise.

2. Precise and certain. Ideal personnel policy should be precise and clear to the point and complete in every respect. It should not lead to varying and conflicting interpretations otherwise unneccessary disputes would arise in the organisation.

3. Flexible. An ideal personnel policy should be flexible enough to adjust and adapt any change in economic, social, legal and technological factors from time to time without disturbing the present norms and ideals.

4. Stable. An ideal personnel policy should be reasonably stable and permanent. Frequent changes should not be allowed as it would lead to confusion. It should be a long-term policy.

5. Framed within overall policies. An ideal personnel policy should be framed within the overall policies of the enterprise with the objective to achieve the organisational targets through better personnel planning and organisation.

6. Integrative. The ideal personnel policy must integrate characteristics of all people. It must fully take into account the differing capacities, capabilities, interests, aspirations, beliefs and temperamental make-up of the people for whom it is meant.

7. Uniform. An ideal personnel policy should be applicable to all members and all units of the enterprise although variations are possible keeping in view the nature of work and regional variations.

8. Acceptable. An ideal personnel policy must possess acceptability among the people for whom it has been formulated. This will reduce the number of disputes and will help maintain the discipline in the organisation.

9. Properly communicated. An ideal policy should be properly communicated to all those for whom it is intended so that all employees could know their rights, liabilities, duties and obligations in advance and could behave likewise.

10. Responsive to prevailing trends. An ideal personnel policy should be capable of being adjusted to the prevailing norms and trends of the business society. It should not be against the prevailing trends. For example, if the current thinking is in favour of workers' participation in management the personnel policy should not be against it.

Suggestions by Calhoon

Calhoon suggests that such a policy, being a guide for management decisions, should include these features :[5]

1. It should affirm the long-range purposes of personnel relations. At best, such pruposes are derived from well thought-out principles of philosophy, sociology, and ethics. Thus, they reflect mature social principles or ideals in human relations.

2. It commits management representatives at all levels to a reaffirmation and reinforcement of this purpose in their daily decisions and behaviour.

3. It indicates the scope for discretion when a long-term purpose is interpreted in a variety of specific situations and over a period of time.

Origin and Sources of Personnel Policies

1. The past practice of an organisation;
2. The prevailing practices among sister concerns in the neighbourhood and throughout the country in the same industry;
3. The attitudes, ideals, and philosophy of the Board of Directors, top management and middle and lower management;
4. The knowledge and experience gained from handling day-to-day personnel problems;
5. Employees suggestions and complaints;
6. Collective bargaining programmes;
7. State and national legislation;
8. Changes in the country's economy;
9. International forces, such as may operate in times of wars;
10. The culture of the plant and its technology, its business environment, its social and political enviornment;
11. The extent of unionism;
12. The attitudes and social vlaues of labour;
13. The ethical points of view or the social responsibility of the organisation toward the public and
14. The goals of the organisation.

TYPES OF PERSONNEL POLICIES

Jucius identifies two types of polices *viz.,* functional or organisational groupings of policies and the centralised policies.

---

5. Calhoon, R., *Managing the Personnel*, Appleton Century Crofts, New York, 1964, p. 36.

1. The functional grouping of policies. These are those policies which are grouped for different categories of personnel, *e.g.*, for the management dealing with personnel planning, organising and controlling or for management concerned with functions of procuring developing and utilising manpower.

2. The centralised policies. These are framed for companies with several locations. They are formulated at the head office and apply through out the organisation.[6]

3. Major policies. These pertain to the over-all objectives, procedures and control which affect an organisation as a whole. Such policies are formulated by the Board of Directors, and a framework is established within which major executives fit the remaining policies necessary to carry out the major objectives of an organisation.

4. Minor policies. These cover relationships in a segment of an organisation, with considerable emphasis on details and procedures. Such policies are the outgrowth of major policies and preserve their unity of purpose.

Coverage of the Policies

According to Calhoon, the subject matter of personnel policies is as varied as the practices of the Personnel Department; and any itemization would serve merely as a laundry list.[7] The norms of personnel policy vary from industry to industry, and with its management structure, the economic and social conditions prevailing in it at a particular time, the attitudes and ideals of the top management. They also vary with changes in public opinion, area and regional traditions, customs and practices, the country's industrial system, the labour and industrial policies of the State and the Central Governments, the influence of trade unions, national agreements between representatives of employees, managers, employees and the government. The policies and influences of business associations, employers' federations, technological development, competition and social approval, the prevailing attitude of the organised labour, government regulations, the extent of unionisation in a particular industry. The decisions of tripartite conferences, Industrial or National Tribunals or Labour Courts — these, too, determine the norms of personnel policies. In other words, they cover such a wide variety of items and are so broadbased that every possible item which affects the interests of one in an organistion is included in them. However, it is virtually impossible for any organisation to have policies which cover every type of contingency because new

---

6. Jucius, M., *Personnel Management*, pp. 73-74.
7. Calhoon, R., *op.cit.*, p. 36.

issues or questions usually crop up from time to time for which no policies exist or for which an organisation is still in the process of writing a policy. In such cases, therefore, it has to work without policies until such time as it frames them.

View of NICB

The National Industrial Conference Board of the USA is of the view that the following matters should be included in a personnel policy :[8]

1. History of the company's growth.
2. Employment practices and conditions of employment — minimum hiring qualifications, preferred services for recruiting personnel, physical examination, psychological and occupational interest and aptitude test; methods of wage payment and pay period, hours of work, overtime work, shift work and shift relations; the basis of promotion and promotion channels, lay-offs, and re-hiring, discharge, voluntary separations; seniority rights, guaranteed employment after attaining a certain length of service and when an employee is considered as a regualr employee.
3. Grievance redressal procedrue.
4. Safety rules and regulations, and responsibilities of employees while at work.
5. General practices — employee identification, punching time cards and reporting in and out of the plant or department; checking of tools, purchases from the company usually at a discount; procedure for getting pay; absence, leave of absence, change of address and solicitation on company premises.
6. Mutuality of interests and need for co-operation between management and men.
7. Employee financial aids — savings, loans, credit co-opeatives, mutual benefit associations, group insurance, profit sharing, bonus plans, incentive plans, partial or full payment of tuition fees for attendance at professional institutes.
8. Educational opportunities — apprentice training, factory schools, vestibule schools and on-the-job training; training for promotion, provision of training facilities.
9. Employees' news sheet and house journals.

---

8. National Industrial Conference Board, "Personnel Policies in Factories and Offices," in *Studies in Personnel Policies,* Nos. 145 and 154.

10. Communication media and suggestion system.
11. Heath and hospitalisation — medical, health and safety services and programmes.
12. Vacation with pay.
13. Sickness, death and maternity benefits or allowances.
14. Freedom for the employees to discuss any item of interest with the management.
15. Company stores.
16. Social security and other kinds of compensation and unemployment and accident compensation, provident fund, pension, gratuity, compensation for employees injured while on duty, invalidity.
17. Collective bargaining and recognising the employee's rights to join any union of his choice, recognition of a particular bargaining agency, procedure to be followed in settling grievances or the interpretation of a bargaining contract, and the right of an individual to be heard.
18. Procedures for disseminating information on company policies.
19. Maintenance of discipline and adherence to rules; penalties available.
20. Garnishments.
21. Public relations.
22. Labour-management relations and union-management co-operation.
23. Prohibited activities such as smoking, gambling, imbibing liquor and soliciting on company premises and during working hours.

Coverage of personnel policies in India

1. Policy on Recruitment or hiring of Employees. Following subjects are taken into account, in finding and selecting right calibre and number of people required to perform the operations of the organisation : (i) whether recruitment needed; (ii) how much manpower required and at what levels; (iii) selection procedures; (iv) age limits for employment; (v) martial status, minority groups, SC/ST, women; (vi) *pre-employment* medical check-up; (vii) establishing order of preferences, between relations of employees, employment exchange candidates, and outsiders in matter of selection and (viii) induction and placement etc.

2. Policy of Manpower Planning and Development. It coveres : (i) work study, job evaluation, (ii) selection and recruitment techniques,

(iii) identifying training needs and preparing training progarammes, (iv) promotional avenues and orienting the selection and training activities to such avenues and (v) opportunities for self-development and advancement in organisation, etc.

3. Policy on Terms and Conditions of Employment. It covers terms such as hours of work, overtime, shift working, lay-off, termination of services, and welfare, wage policy, payment methods, pay period, job evaluation, etc.

4. Policy on Industrial Relations. It considers : (i) whether to recognise trade unions, and conditions of recognition, (ii) collective bargaining, (iii) grievance handling procedure, (iv) workers' participation in management, etc.

5. Policy on Communication with employees. It covers : (i) suggestion system; (ii) formal/informal meetings between top management and junior management.

According to Ram S. Tarneja, personnel policy consists essentially of the following parts :[9]

1. The objective stated in broad general terms, indicating the top managements' deep and underlying intents and convictions as to the importance of the people in the organisation.
2. Procedures for the attainment of the objectives. Procedures lay down the steps that must be followed in order that the spirit of the policy is retained intact and is reflected in management's action.
3. Rules regulations arising from the policy and procedures are aimed at clearly defining the do's and dont's that have to be observed by the employees at all levels.

Responsibility for Policy-Making

Though the actual formulation of personnel policies is the responsibility of the personnel manager; its ultimate approval, change or modification comes from the top executives : The personnel manager's decision depends upon the financial ability of a company, the obligations imposed upon it by legislation, the agreement between employers and employees, the repercussions of such decisions of the various levels of employees as well as on neighbouring industries and on the community. The personnel manager's role is one of mediating, reconciling, persuading, convincing, expressing and communicating the policy;

---

9. Tarneja, Ram S., "Personnel Policies and Practices", in Kapoor T.N. (ed.) *Personnel Management and Industrial Relations in India*, N.M. Tripathi Pvt. Ltd., Bombay, 1968, p. 51.

developing tools and machinery, guiding, directing and evaluating the effectiveness with which those tools are used in the application of policy. The responsibility for personnel administration rests squarely upon the line management. The Personnel Department assists in communicating policies to those for whom they are meant and exercises control over it in order to ensure fairness and unifromity.

Methods of Informing Personnel Policies

1. Written standard practice, procedures issued to cover company policies, with supplements to cover changes.
2. Booklets or Bulletins, issued to new employees setting forth rights, previleges, and responsibilities.
3. Verbal instructions from immediate superiors.
4. Group meetings of new employees convened regularly.
5. Union contract.
6. Company paper or house organ, giving details about company policies.
7. Conference conducted as a part of executive training programme.

MECHANISM OF POLICY FORMULATION

According to Pigors, the steps necessary in designing a policy are :[10]

(i) Initiating a policy.
(ii) Uncovering of facts by the personnel department.
(iii) Recommending a policy to the top management and eliciting the views of all concerned.
(iv) Putting down a policy in writing.
(v) Explaining and discussing the proposed policy with members of the organisation.
(vi) Adopting and launching it.
(vii) Communicating it to employees at all levels.
(viii) Administering it.
(ix) Initiating follow-up action on it.
(x) Evaluating it.
(xi) Restating or reformulating the policy.

---

10. Pigors, Paul and Pigors, F., "Who should make Personnel Policies?" in Agarwal, R.D. (ed.) *Dynamics of Personnel Management in India,* Tata McGraw-Hill Publishing Co., New Delhi, 1973, p. 86.

It should be clearly understood that "the authority for implementing personnel policy must come from the top management. The responsibility implementation rests with the line management at the level of the department head and that of administration of day-to-day matters with the lower level of management. The responsibility for assessment, review, and follow-up action should lie with the personnel department."

According to R.P. Billimoria, the success of personnel policies is determined by the following :[11]

(1) The success of the top management in determining labour policies wisely.

(2) The success of the personnel manager in interpreting these personnel policies properly, in achieving their proper execution through the line executives, and in making the Personnel Department render as nearly prefect service as possible to the line executives.

(3) The success of the line executives themselves, particularly the first line supervisors, in fulfilling their obligations to management and to the workers by interpreting policies wisely and interestedly and in promoting the effectiveness of their workers by dynamic leadership.

PROCEDURES AND PROGRAMMES

Specific procedures and programmes are needed. For the accomplishment of the objectives of personnel policies. Procedures indicate "how" a policy is to be carried out. It spells out in detail the methods, processes, movements and specific rules and regulations, and indicates the steps, time, place and personnel responsible for implementing it. It tells us where an action is to take place and at what stage.[12] It goes further than policies in helping to clarify what is to be done in particular circumstances. It is usually set up by high-level managers and observed by first line supervisors. It's mroe specific in outlining the course of action and the sequence of activities necessary for the implementation of policies. It enables an organisation to maintain control since they assign specific obligations to the staff for the performance of the various tasks. It is periodically reviewed and reissued, pointing out the amendments and the areas of slackness.

According to Brown Milton, procedures tell us "how" the work is to be done, the programme tells "what". It consists of the entire broad course of action governing employees at all levels. It can be

11. Billimoria, R.P. "Personnel Policies in Tata Steel", in Kapoor T.N., *op. cit.*, pp. 98-99.

12. Scott, Clothier and Sprigel, *op.cit.*, p. 59.

thought of as a "stable plan of action that continues over an extensive period of time."[13] It is the end product of philosophy, values, concepts, principles, policies and procedures.[14] Programmes represent simple or complex activities, presumably developed to carry out the policy. They are a step ahead of policy in that they simplify the process of decision-making and reduce it to a routine. Programmes may require appropriate action or practice at all levels throughout an organisation. Practice (*i.e.*, what is actually done in an organisation) and procedures are the specific actions that may be combined in a programme. According to Mee and Williams, "All expenditure of money, time and effort on a personnel relations programme should be justifiable in terms of the immediate, intermediate or ultimate objectives of an organisation that it is to support."

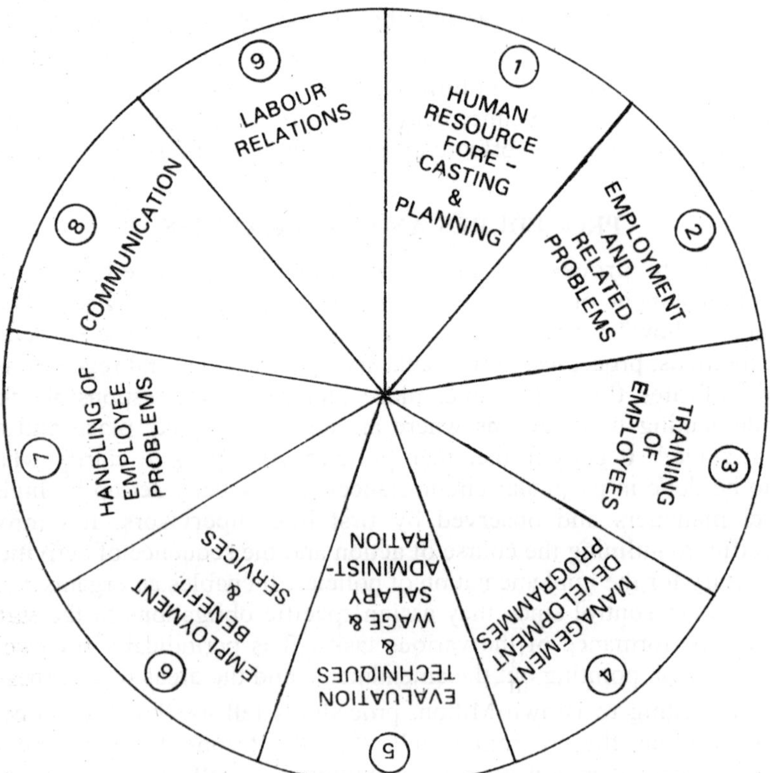

Fig. 4.1 : Human Resource Action Programme.

13. Brown, Milton, *Effective Work Management*, 1980, p. 75.

14. *Ibid.*, p. 79.

Some specific procedures and programmes

1. Human resource forcasting and planning.
2. Employment and related facts.
3. Training and development of employees.
4. Management Development programmes.
5. Evaluation techniques, wage and salary administraiton programmes.
6. Employee benefits and services.
7. Handling of employee problems.
8. Communication.
9. Labour Relations.

QUESTIONS FOR EXERCISE

1. Discuss Labour Policy in India.
2. "A policy is a man-made rule or predetermined course of action that is established to guide the performance of work towards the organisational objectives" — Edwin B. Flippo. Discuss and explain the meaning of Personnel Policy.
3. "A policy is predetermined course of thought and action that is defined and established as a guide towards accepted goals and objectives." Explain the above statement and discuss the principles of Personnel Policies.
4. What is Personnel Policy? Why is it required? How is it developed?
5. What are the principles of personnel policy? Describe an ideal Personnel Policy.

5

Industrial Organisation Structure

If two or more persons establish among them co-operative relations and make concerted efforts, the state of these co-operative relations and concerted effort is called organisation. The organisations can perform simple or complex tasks. All individuals within an organisation try to work for a common aim. The word organization is a derivative of the word *organ*. The word *organ* means a part or limb of an animal or man. Thus brain, heart, liver, arms, legs etc. are the various organs of man. The man or an animal as a whole is said to be a structure and organization. He is an organisation because his various limbs, parts or organs are mutually and cooperatively related. A group of individuals together working for a definite common aim is called an organization. The mutuality and togetherness found in a group of persons engaged in industrial production is called industrial organization.

Basic Elements of Organization

An organization may be industrial or formed for the attainment of some social or political aim. Every organization has some common basic elements. The basic elements constitute structure of an organization. Generally three elements are considered basic for any organization. Firstly, an organization must have numerous components. As a living organism consists of numerous organs and millions of cells, in the same manner an industrial organization has many wings or components and hundreds of units. These components perform their respective roles. The second element basic to an organization is the adjustment between various components. In respect of adjustment also, living organism provides best illustration. As an organism lives and functions only as long as its various organs function harmoniously, similarly, an industrial organization retains its character only as long as its various components work in a complementary manner. It is true of course, that there cannot be such ideal adjustment among the industrial components as in the case of human organism. Nonetheless without a minimum amount of adjustment there can be no industrial organization. It is not possible for workers to do any work if raw material is not supplied or the supervisory staff is missing to supervise the work. The third basic element of an organization is that it should be suited to purposive activity. This means that all elements of an industrial organization should be such as will contribute to the aim specified for it. For the attainment of different aims different types of organizations are required.

KINDS OF ORGANIZATIONS

Organizations are of two kinds : spontaneous or informal organization and formal organization. The spontaneous organizations are natural and these are not formed for any particular purpose. The organizations in the human, animal and vegetable kingdom are the examples of spontaneous or informal organizations. A sudden voluntary get together of human beings is another example of informal organization.

A formal organization is a result of deliberate efforts and is brought together for some specific purpose. Compared to informal organization, a formal organization is more systematic and works under specific rules. It is only within the framework of law and rules which brought it together that an organization remains an organization. In the event of violation of rules it is liable to break down.

The industrial organizations are always the outcome of deliberate efforts and are established with a specific aim. In an industrial organization we find both kinds of organization, that is, an industrial organization contains within it both formal and informal associations. In fact wherever men get together both formal and informal associations come into being. A deliberately organized structure brings together a lot of men. This togetherness, in turn, give rise to certain informal organizations. Besides, in as much as each industrial organization is organized to achieve certain specific aims, it has a formal character. With expansion and diversification of an industrial organization several sub-organizations under it come into being. For example, in every huge industrial complex, several organizations of workers and managerial staff come into being. These sub-organizations can be either formal or informal. However, these sub-organizations have their role and importance within the framework of the parent organization. It is however possible that sub-organizations may be in revolt against the parent organization.

In order to understand the industrial organization, it is essential that the nature of formal and informal organizations be discussed in detail.

Formal Organization

As it is clear from the above discussion, formal organization in industry is that human group which deliberately comes together for the achievement of a specific purpose or aim. According to C.L. Barnard, following are the chief features of a formal organization.

The formal organizations are not concerned with nor do they revolve around a person or persons in particular. It is not the name or heredity of the person but his status and work that are important in a formal organization. An organization requires a man to perform according to his or her status. A formal organization has a hierarchy of status. On relinquishing of a post by one person another person assumes his office and the work of the organization goes on. The members of a formal organization bear to each other impersonal and not personal relations. Their relations depend upon the plan of the organization. For example, if in an industry an *x* makes a component of a machinery and *y* makes another component and *z* fits them together, the relation between *x*, *y*, *z* is purely formal and is limited to certain processes in an industry. However, this does not mean that there are no personal relations among *x*, *y*, *z*. Indeed, in an organization, it is but natural that various members should spontaneously develop various types of relations, social, economic, religious etc., among themselves. However, these relations are informal and are not strictly essential for the maintenance and sustenance of the industry. Within the framework of an industrial organization the relations between members are formal but outside of its framework these are informal.

Another characteristic feature of formal industrial organization is that it is formal and functional, it is nonetheless in the background of vast social organization or system. The social atmosphere affects it much. The socio-economic-ethical conditions of a society affect the industrial organization directly or indirectly.

Another characteristic of industrial organization is that it is scientific and systematic. Under the formal organization the role, status and importance of all jobs is well determined. The structure of formal organization is quite explicit and these are tractable of easy investigation.

Departments of Formal Organization

Whenever an industrial organization develops and becomes vast it becomes complex and the functions within it become quite intricate. Under these conditions the organization gets split up in various departments for its smooth functions. The departments are generally considered to be parts of the organization. Normally there are three such departments in an organization. These are :

(1) Linear Organization.

(2) Functional Organization.

(3) Staff Organization.

(1) Linear Organization. Once an industry assumes gigantic proportions it requires a hierarchical system which can effectively control and manage the whole organization. This hierarchy directs the entire organization towards its pre-determined ends. This system is known as linear organization.

(2) Functional Organization. The industrial organizations have a variety of functions. For convenience each of these functions is entrusted to one department. This system of departmentalising of functions is known as 'Functional Organizations'.

(3) Staff Organization. In modern industry technological changes and inventions are taking place daily. New devices and sophisticated methods of work are being discovered daily in the fields of technology, economics, law and social sciences. The discoveries in all these fields have their direct or indirect application to industry. As a result of these there is a conceptual and practical revolution in every aspect of business management, production, marketing etc. It is not possible for everyone to be fully posted with latest developments in various fields of socio-economic and techno-legal developments. Besides, the scientific research is snowballing and requires special cadre to imbibe and absorb its impact. As the industry requires successful application of various new techniques to maintain progress, every industry keeps a team of specialists to keep track of development in science, technology, social research and law. Thus, a successful industrial organization would have experts in engineering, sociology, science and legal studies etc. This organization of experts is known as staff organization.

VARIOUS LEVELS OF INDUSTRIAL ORGANIZATION

Besides the classification described above, there are some other kinds of classification in an industrial organization. This classification is hierarchical and is according to status and position. This is also known as vertical organization. According to this classification there are different levels of posts and positions starting from labour and going upto the highest executive.

In any industrial organization, the wrung positions are occupied by those who are the founders of that organization. The capitalists themselves appoint the Board of Directors. The Board of Directors appointed by the capitalists elects the Chairman of the company. The Chairman in turn entrusts to each director one department according to his ability and capability. There is some difference of opinion with regard to the number of top managerial posts. But generally top positions are as follows : (1) Chairman; (2) Managing Director; (3) Executive Director; (4) General Manager; (5) Works Managers and

(6) Regional Sales Managers. In India Tata Oil Mills Co. Ltd. has the above described arrangement of posts.

Next to top wrung officials are middle wrung officials. This set of officials comes between the topmost and the low wrung officers and workers. The middle wrung officials are concerned with the implementation of policies and directions laid down or given by topmost officials. This set of officials must have plenty of practical knowledge. These officials are usually the specialists in the fields. The staff organization described above is the organization of these officials.

The third wrung of the industrial managers is occupied by supervisory staff. They occupy a position just above the clerical staff. Their job is to supervise work and report to the higher officials from time to time.

Thus, in an industrial organization we find hierarchy of status. The persons occupying different places in this hierarchy have their respective privileges and obligations.

PRINCIPLES OF INDUSTRIAL ORGANIZATION

In regard to industrial organization and business management new principles are being continuously established. However, certain principles laid down by relatively old experts still have their significance. Some of these experts are : E.W. Taylor, H. Fayol, C.I. Barnard, L. Urwick and P. Sargent. The laws and principles discovered and established by them have not only historic significance but have certain validity and practicability even today. These principles are based on actual experience of industrial management. Henri Fayol has laid down fourteen principles for efficient industrial management. These are :

(1) Division of Work
(2) Authority & Responsibility
(3) Discipline
(4) Unity of Command
(5) Unity of Direction
(6) Subordination of individual interests to general interests
(7) Remuneration to Personnel
(8) Centralization
(9) Scales chain
(10) Order
(11) Equity
(12) Stability of tenure of personnel

(13) Initiative

(14) *Espirite de corps.*

The above mentioned principles are crucial to every industry. By following these principles one can conveniently obtain the desired goals.

INFORMAL ORGANIZATION

Besides formal organization certain informal organizations spontaneously spring up in every industry. These informal organizations are generally complementary in nature and play a supporting role in respect of main formal organization. The informal organizations are based upon personal as against the impersonal relations of formal organizations. Wherever some persons get together there is exchange of social and personal human relations and this forms the basis of informal organizations. Many such informal organizations are found in industries. The informal organizations are neither deliberate nor do they possess neat well-defined structure. Yet there are certain preconditions for the formation of such organizations :

(1) The first type of informal organization is the totality of members of the organization bearing with each other certain relations at personal level. In the terminology of sociology this informal group is derivative or secondary group. In the secondary group members have interpersonal relations remaining within the primary group.

(2) The second type of informal organizations are those which spring upon on account of common tastes, interests or hobbies of some person. The members of trade unions, for example come together on account of commonness of interest or purpose. Certain clubs or societies develop, for example, we find dramatic clubs in many an industry. This is a clear example for an informal organization. We also have informal societies based on religion, region and language. There are also sports clubs which again an example of informal organization.

(3) The third type of informal organizations are represented by persons doing similar jobs in an industry.

(4) The fourth type of informal organizations are of very few and limited persons. There may be half a dozen poets in an industrial organization and they may form a poetry club. Again, there may be more than two persons in an industry hailing from same family. Their association will be an example of informal organization. Besides family relations, such organization may be based on friendship or intimacy.

It is imperative that there should be informal organization within an industry. The informal organizations are generally complementary to formal organization. They are not contrary to it. If care is taken to nourish the informal organizations they prove beneficial to the industry. If there is sufficient co-ordination and co-operation between industry and informal organization within it, the chances of strikes and lock-outs are minimised. Any work connected with industry can be done easily through the heads of informal organizations. The efficient managers try to maintain support with these heads.

Now the question is why is an informal organization necessary and how it comes to be established. The answer lies in human nature. Basically man is gregarious and has an instinct for establishing informal relations with his fellow beings. It is on account of this instinct that informal organizations come into being. Secondly, industrial workers are in the habit of avoiding work. They need some or other things to fill their empty hours. The informal organizations fill this bill. The habit of gossiping, smoking etc. are symbolic of this. Another reason for coming into being of informal organizations is that every worker knows well that he can be shunted from work, therefore he feels comparatively insecure. Besides informal organizations give emotional security.

ORGANISATIONAL STRUCTURE OF THE PERSONNEL DEPARTMENT

Depending upon their size the internal organisational structure of the personnel department varies widely in different companies. In small companies, personnel functions are discharged by line executives, as shows in the following chart 5.1.

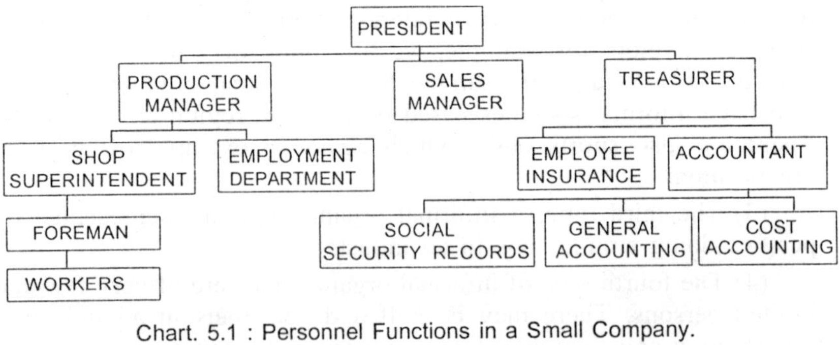

Chart. 5.1 : Personnel Functions in a Small Company.

In a large company, separate department is organised for the purpose variously knows as the *Personnel Department* or the *Industrial Relations Department*. It is headed by the *Personnel Manager* or *Personnel Director* or *Vice-President, Personnel,* or by the *Industrial Relations Director* or *Labour Relations Officer, Labour Superintendent* or *Employment Officer*. Whose position is under the President (or the

General Manager) of the organisation. Under him are Interviewing Officers, Training Officers, Secretary, Medical Doctor/Welfare Officer, head of cleaners, gatekeepers, etc. These are entrusted with the responsibility of recruitment and employment, training, industrial relations, employee services and security work.

A Personnel Department's organisational set-up is given below in Chart 5.2

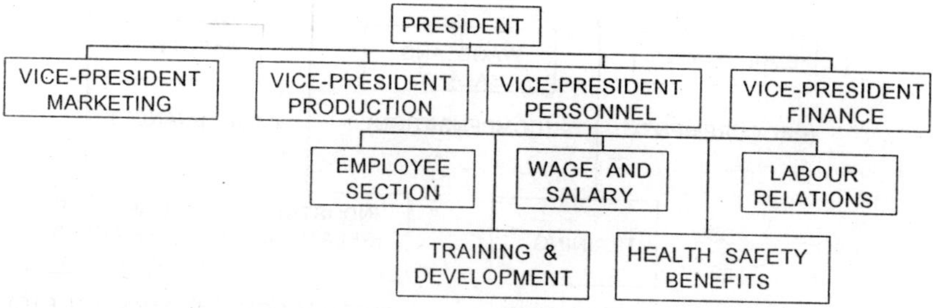

Chart 5.2 : Organisational Chart of Personnel Department.

As given in the Chart personnel manager has under him subordinates who look after the Employees section, the Training and Development section, the Wages and Salary Administration section, the Health, Safety and Benefits section and the Labour Relations section. The personnel in charge of these sections are generally known as 'employment officer', 'training director', 'wage and salary administrator', labour welfare officer', 'security officer', 'health officer', 'labour relations officer' etc.

Bases of Organisation of Personnel Department

Personnel Departments or Units may be organised on three basis :

1. Functional basis, 2. service basis, and 3. clientele basis.

1. Functional Basis. According to functional basis, Departments are grouped into different functions, such as : Procurement (employment), Development (training) Compensation (Wage and Salary administration), Integration (Labour Relations), Maintenance (Safety), and Separation (employee services, retirement). Such a division would be influenced by variables as size, abilities of personnels, and top management philosophy towards the role of the personnel. Functional basis has been given in Chart 5.3.

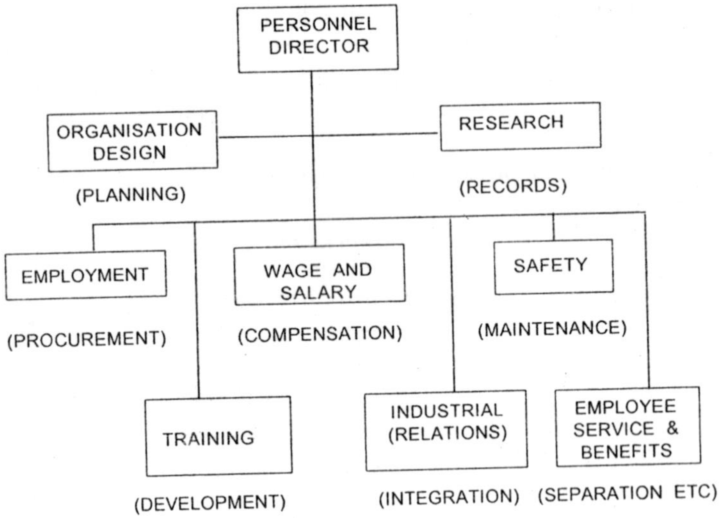

Chart 5.3 : Functional Basis of Personnel Department.

2. Service Basis. Owes its evolution to Herzbergs' theory. It takes into consideration the service rendered or the purpose achieved. It tries to prevent dissatifaction through hygienic maintenance, and promotion of satisfaction through motivators. It has been shown in Chart 5.4.

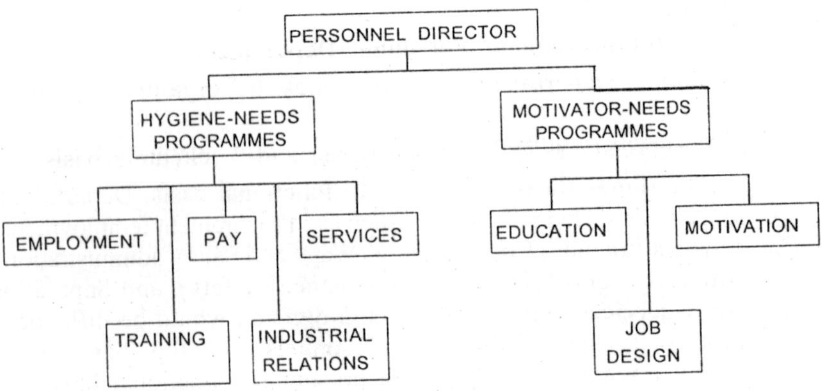

Chart 5.4 : Service Basis of Personnel Department.

3. Clientele Basis. It has been propounded by Soholik who holds that different requirements of different types of employees need specialisation. Clientele basis has been illustrated in Chart 5.5.

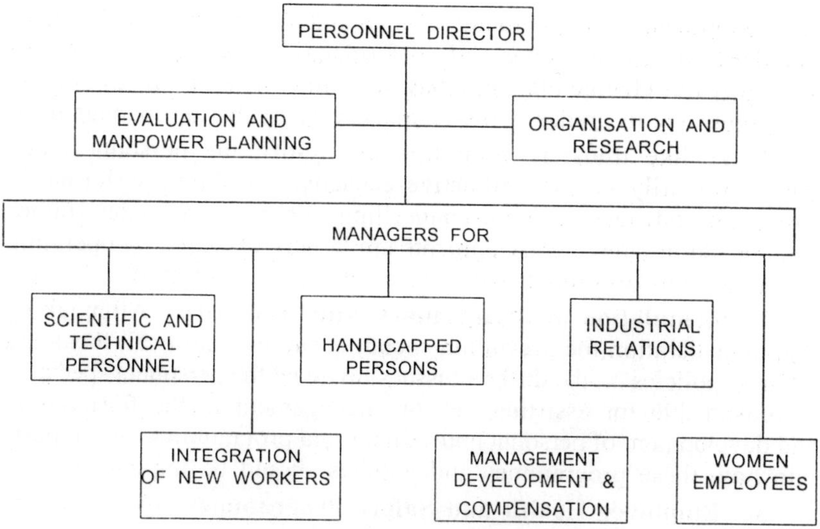

Chart 5.5 : Celientele Basis of Personnel Department.

RESPONSIBILITIES OF PERSONNEL SPECIALIST

According to Richard P. Brown, "the major responsibility of the personnel specialist or staff is that of helping all levels of management to make the company a good place to work in."[1] This means that the responsibility of personnel specialist is very wide. In developing and administering a personnel programme his role is multiple. Charles Furlog states that "the task of the personnel administrator is to see that sound personnel programmes are installed, not merely conceived."[2]

Following are the responsibilities of the personnel specialist :

1. Human Resource Planning. As he has to supply qualified employees to the various departments after making a careful screening, recruitment and selections; and maintain a cntinuous source of labour force for the organisation, he understands and knows the contents and requirements of the job. Therefore, the work of designing and installing job analysis and job evaluation plans, maintaining suitable records and undertaking wage and salary surveys in the labour market are has responsibilities of the personnel specialist. He is also responsible

1. Brown, Richard P., "What the Line Manager Expects", in the *Personnel Man and his job*, D.B. Taraporevala & Sons, Bombay, 1967, p. 37.
2. Furlog, Charles W., "The Personnel Staff : Advice or Decide," in *The Personnel Function : A Progress Report*, p. 18.

for a co-ordination of meritrating schemes and for laying down objectives standards for the assessment of performance. However, the decision to improve or change the entire pay schedule or fix the minimum and maximum pay in grades is the responsibility of the top management.

Tasks like transfer, promotion or lay-off, the personnel staff serves primarily in a co-ordinative capacity. Coaching, performance appraisal, and post-appraisal counselling, job rotation, under studies and special broadening assignments are largely executed by operating managers but co-ordinated by the central personnel staff.

2. Formulation of Porgrammes and Procedures. After taking into consideration the prevailing social, economic, political, local and national policies on the different issues involved the personnel specialist to repsonsible for assisting the top management in the formulation and development of personnel procedures and programmes. He suggests into how these programmes and policies should be implemented.

3. Employee Health and Safety Programmes. The staff acts as a live wire for the promotion of safety consciousness in the plant. Employee safety, education and health programmes (pre-employment medical examination, periodic examination of those in service, operation of dispensaries, treatment of first-aid cases and removing health hazards) are a co-opeative responsibility of both the staff and line personnel.

The personnel specialist a frame and observes the rules and regulations pertaining to disciplinary matters, together with the range of penalties for different offences, is also his responsibility.

4. Training and Development of Personnel. The personnel specialist is responsible to do the necessary research, plan and organise facilities so that the employee is sufficiently trained to perform his job satisfactorily. As the training has to do with people, the responsibility for guiding, developing and co-ordinating it as well as developing programmes and keeping these active is that of the personnel staff.

5. Wage and Salary Administration. It is the responsibility of the personnel specialist to see to that the company's wage and salary structure is sound and well administered. He provides counselling and training to the supervisory force in the administration of the company's wage policies He furnishes guidance on performance reviews and merit ratings. He spearheads the appraisal plan, which may be used by the management to provide an inventory of current and potential human resources in the organisation.

6. Labour-Management Relations. The personnel specialist is responsible to see that the employee is treated as a human being. He is required to develop a better understanding between the employees and the employers to ensure that a good labour-management relationship is established in the organisation. He is also responsible for bargaining on behalf of the management and for proceedings relating to conciliation, arbitration and adjudication of individual and group disputes.

7. Service and Benefits. The personnel specialist is responsible for administering employee benefit programmes such as insurance, accident claims, pensions, and provident fund and other fringe benefits. He operates company medical facilities, fire-fighting and plant protection units, cafeterias, etc. He encourages the formation of clubs, thrift associations and recreational activities, and arranges social hunctions. However, the actual decision to establish or expand these services is taken by the top management on the advice of the personnel staff.

8. Personnel Research. The personnel staff is responsible for conducting personnel research on improvement programmes or worthwhile innovations. It recommends or cahnges sources of employee motivation. It carries on research on effective supervisory styles, differential illness and accident possibilities in the work force; and on the relative usefulness of alternative safety devices and clothing. These researches keep the management continually informed so that better decisions and plans can be made. They also add to the management's knoweldge of improved motivation and utilization of the members of the organisation.

The personnel specialist is also responsible for maintenance of accurate and adequate records and statistics of the various personnel problems of the industrial unit. Standard tools in research, include statistics and data processing equipment.

9. Audit and Review Work. The personnel specialist is responsible for a continuing audit and reviewing of the line departments in matters of policies, procedures and programmes, particularly those which relate to accidents, grievances, absenteeism, voluntary quits and disciplinary actions.

10. Communication. It is the responsibility of the personnel specialist to aid the management in ensuring effective communication throughout the organisation through proper media. *He should be an active force behind the two-way communication programme.*

To sum up, the role and responsibility of personnel men have been very *ably stated in the following words of the American Management Association :*

"The personnel manager must function *as a technical specialist* — one who is equipped to perform skilfully the duties which the position entails; as a *student* who cosntantly strives for exact knowledge to enable him to recognise and correct the flaws and weaknesses in the programme as it evolves; and *as a leader* who has the vision and the personnel integrity to build an enduring organisation around sound principles, honest convictions and wholesome human relationship." As Beach has rightly observed : "He creates the environment in which employees can work effectively to accomplish the goal of the enterprise and, at the same time, obtain a substantial satisfaction of their need." The responsibilities of the personnel specialist have been illustrated in Fig. 5.1.

Fig. 5.1 : Responsibility of Personnel Specialist.

Decision Making Authority of Personnel Executive

In their work *Guide to Personnel Management* M.G. Miner and J.B. Miner have given following chart of decision making authority of Personnel Executive.

CHART 5.6

Decision-making Authority of Personnel Executive[3]

Responsibility shared with	*In the administration of those activities*
1. Top management	Planning general personnel policies; Manpower planning; Organisational planning; Vacations and holidays; Leave.
2. Salary Committee	Non-management pay policies; Executive compensation.

3. Miner, M.G. and Miner, J.B., *A Guide to Personnel Management,* Bureau of National Affairs, Washington, 1973, p. 14.

3. Company insurance	Group insurance; Pensions; Health and medical services.
4. Public Relations Dept.	Community relations.
5. Employee organisation	Recreation and social activities.
6. Line Supervisors	Recuriting and selection: Performance appraisal; Promotions, transfers, separations, induction, orientation, on-the-job training; Supervisory training and management development; Education and scholarships; job evaluation; Employee counselling, discipline and greivance handling; Safety and working conditions; Housing services: Trade union relations.

QUESTIONS FOR EXERCISE

1. What are the basic elements of Industrial organisation? Describe its kinds.
2. Explain levels and principles of industrial organisation.
3. Write short note on (i) Informal Organisation; (ii) Human Relations in Industry.
4. Explain the organisational structure of the personnel department.
5. Discuss and explain the rsponsibilities of a personnel specialist.

6

Personnel Record, Audit and Research

As the number of employees grows it becomes more and more difficult to remember all details and as such, they have to be recorded. Such records of all employees are kept by the personnel department, these records keeping are up-to-date, handy.

What is Personnel Record?

Personnel records are the employees' complete particulars, negative notes like notes on indiscipline, along with positive records like his achievements, promotions, training, etc., so that such details may be used for his further growth. This information is vital for effective and efficient use of human resources. Proper record-keeping is essential for the smooth working of any establishment. Some of these are statutory requirements; other records are for reference.

Uses of Personnel Records

1. Used in Promotion, demotion, transfer etc. Personnel record of employees in not kept by individual functional departments. This information is centralised in personnel department and supplied when required. It may be used at many occasions like promotion, demotion, transfer, awards, etc.

2. Preparation of Pay roll. Pay roll may be prepared from those records, easily and accurately.

3. For Government Information. Government frequently asks for different kinds of information relating to the workers, which may be supplied on the basis of such records.

4. Training needs. Training needs may be determined from these records.

5. Facilitates Evaluation. Full details of any employee at one place facilitates dispassionately evaluation of his work.

Types of Personnel Records

1. Job Descriptions. These are essential for job evaluation. Description of various jobs is kept-job wise or department wise. A copy of relative job description may go into the individual employee's personnel file.

2. Recruitment and Selection. This information is essential for those who wish to enter a job.

3. Evaluation and Training Records. This information is essential for personnel evaluation and assessment of training needs. Evaluation and training records comprise evaluation by superiors, performance appraisal, training time-tables and records as maintained by personnel department.

4. Rules of Discipline. Rule of discipline dealing with employees record of discipline, awards and punishment are essential part of record.

5. Wage and Salary Administration. Records relating to wages and salaries are also very useful for different purposes. Wage and salary administration records show the initial wages on which the employee starts and his salary escalation over the years. Sometimes, this information is supplied to Government, Trade Unions, Chamber of Commerce and Industry, etc., also.

6. Health, Welfare and Safety. These records indicate the efficiency and intelligence of the employee.

7. Industrial Disputes. Records relating to all industrial disputes may also be recorded in these records. By personnel department, all industrial disputes are recorded and any employee's special role in them is also put in his personal file. The decisions and terms of settlement are also recorded therein.

8. Leave, Transfer and Demotions. These records indicate employees interest and efficiency in his work.

Objectives of Record System

1. To supply information. The basic object of a personnel record system is to supply information when it is required. This information should give all essential details. It should not be so cluttered that lot of time is wasted to hurt the desired information about the nature of information to be stored in the personnel department to satisfy the possible requirement should be discussed with the department concerned. Record-keeping is an expensive exercise. Record management deserves the attention of the personnel manager himself.

2. To Review the system. It should be discussed and decided as to how long information of a particular type is to be retained. The system should be reviewed every now and then to check if the arrangement meets with the requirements.

3. To keep Adequate copies. It should be decided as to how many copies of a particular record are to be kept. Sometimes as a measure of precaution so many copies are made that these copies keep on cluttering files. One does not throw them away or destroy them lest they may be needed again. Therefore the manager should know when to destroy extra coipes of records.

4. To have Filing system. Proper, filing systems are essential for retrieval of the information at the time of need. Many companies such as Roneno, Remington, Godrej advise on office systems. They also give suggestions on procedure manuals which list out procedure for classification of records.

Rules of Effective Record Keeping

1. Clear objective. The objective of records should be very clear.

2. Clear use. As far as possible, it should be clear in the beginning itself as to what use the record will be put to.

3. Limits of control. Records should be within limit of control. They should contain only that much of information which could actually be made use of.

4. Quick retrieval. It should be possible to retrieve the information quickly. There is no use having information if it is not available at the right time.

5. Standardised form. The form to be completed should be clear and standardised. There should be confusion so that information is uniformly kept.

6. Up-to-date entries. Up-to-date entries, should be made in the records otherwise they can be more misleading than being of use.

7. Easy identification. It may be helpful to give every form a number for easy identification.

8. Consulting people. The people who will ultimately supply the information should be consulted while designing the forms. Their involvement and advice would be helpful in this respect.

9. Use oriented. Record keeping is a work of art. It should be use oriented and accurate.

PERSONNEL REPORT

What is Personnel Report?

The personnel department of an organisation prepares significant reports for the top management and department heads/supervisors, on the basis of personnel records it maintains. This way personnel department fulfils it obligations as a staff department. For example, a timely report to the production manager on absenteeism may draw his attention to the problem and he may take remedial action. A report to the supervisor on individual workers may help him to control them

CHART 6.1

A Specimen of Staff Record

Surname...First Name..

Father's Name...

Date of Birth....................................Place of Birth..

Age..Sex...

Height...Weight..

Nationality...............................Married/Single/Widower/Divorcee..................................

Languages known...

Present Address..

Permanent Address...

Designation..

Date of appointment...........................Date of confirmation..

Date when increment due...

Department in which posted..

Date of joining pension/provident fund...............................

Monthly contribution...

When payable (in case of death)..

Members in the family...wife/sons/daughters

Ages of children...Sons.......................Daughters.....................

Educational Qualifications...

Professional Qualifications/Training Achieved...

Promotions

To...with effect from...

Transfers

To...with effect from...

Leave Record

From...................................to...............No. of days accumulated When and how much payment is to be made

....

....

Medical/sick leave

From..................................to...(days)

....

....

Periodical medical examination when done..

Medical history of major illnesses..

Performance appraisal..

....

Warnings and censures

Date................................Remarks...

Token file No..

CHART 6.2

A. Preliminary Summary and Service

(i) Attention should be directed to :
Trends
New developments
Notable changes
Special projects
Unusual accomplishments.

(ii) It should be designed to :
Catch interest
Encourage a detailed study
Enlist co-operation
Focus attention.

B. Employment

(i) Numbers : Beginning and/or end of a period :
By departments
Whether employee is temporary or permanent
By sex
Whether hourly rated or salaried.

(ii) Labour turnover, separation and accession :
By department and/or plant
By types of separation
By quits, lay-offs, discharges
By avoidable vs. unavoidable
By reasons (marriage, home duties, frequency, pregnancy, moving, pension, death)
Comparison with local, state or national turnover.

(iii) Unfulfilled requisitions :
By department
By job.

C. Job Analysis, Recruitment and Selection

(i) Jobs analysed or reviewed :
By department
By plant.

(ii) Applications for employment :
By skill
By sex
By source.

(iii) Employee interviews.

(iv) Applicants tested.

(v) References checked.

D. Training

(i) Enrolment :
By training programmes
By new trainee programmes
Number finishing by programme.

(ii) Turnover — separations of former trainees
Cost of training.

E. Promotions, Transfers, Appraisals

(i) Promotions, by department.

(ii) Transfers, by department.

(iii) Numbers rated, by department.

F. Labour Relations

(i) New agreements — in negotiation/negotiated.

(ii) Amendments — negotiated.

(iii) Arbitrations — in process or concluded, by results.

(iv) Grievances — setteld and in process :
By subject
By the stage at which settled
By the nature of the settlement.

G. Medical, Health, Safety

(i) Deaths among employees.

(ii) Retirements.

(iii) Physical examinations.

(iv) Medical treatment.

(v) Hospital calls on employees.

(vi) Illness — number of cases by department :
By kind of illness.
By department.
By time lost.

(vii) Accidents in plant :
By department.
By cause.
By severity and frequency rates.

(viii) Workmens compensation, number of cases :
By department.
By new and recurrent cases
By amount of benefit
By cost.

H. Other Employee Services

(i) Benefit plan, membership.

(ii) Benefits offered :
By number of employees
By type death, disability, maternity
By amount paid.

(iii) Personal loans, number and amount.

(iv) Credit union :
Applications received
Applications approved or disapproved
Loans extended, number and amount.

(v) Life insurance.

(vi) Pensions — normal retirements, optional retirements, disability retirements.

(vii) House organs — circualtion costs.

(viii) Suggestions — number received and disposed of; awards for suggestions.

(ix) Cafeteria — meals served, rupee sales, csot, subsides.

(x) Recreational activities-type, participation, costs.

I. Wage and Salary Administration

(i) Rates reviewed and rates changed :
By number
By type — merit increase, revaluation.

(ii) Job evaluation — by department or type of job.

(iii) Overtime — total hours, departments and number of employees affected, total cost.

(iv) Earnings :

Weekly average, by department; hourly rated or salary proportion in each age and salary class.

(v) Call-in and call-back pay :
By department
By cost.

J. Records and Reports

(i) Special reports released.

(ii) Personnel actions recorded.

K. Research

(i) Projects completed.

(ii) Progress reports on continuing projects.

(iii) New projects planned or undertaken.

L. Staff Administration

(i) Staff assignments by name.

(ii) Expenditure on staff activities :
By controllable vs. uncontrollable
By major activities.

at right time. It indicates how the supervisor is handling his workforce. Comparative data help in action at the time of reduced availability of manpower when more of the causal labour go for agricultural work. Comparison of similar records of previous years help highlighting specific problems of certain areas.

Essentials of a Good Report

The submission of a report on a particular issue is the responsibility of the person appointed for the purpose, who puts it up to one of the top executives. It may also be sent by an immediate supervisor to his departmental head. To be useful, a report should satisfy some conditions. These are :

(a) It should deal with a specific objective.

(b) It should dwell on the issues referred to the the person making it.

(c) The person who makes the report should collect the data and interpret it honestly.

(d) A report should contain data on all the aspects of personnel management.

(e) It should make specific recommendations.

(f) It should be timely, so that proper action may be taken on it.

(g) It should be clearly worded and easily comprehensible.

(h) It may include illustrative points to strengthen the observations made in it.

(i) It should be reader-oriented.

Types of Personnel Reports

1. Regular of Routine Reports. Regular reports are prepared and submitted by the personnel department to the top management and Government on regular basis, such as, rate of labour turnover, extent of absenteeism, etc.

2. Peroidic Reports. Peroidic Reports contain the information relating to the topes such as :

(i) Extent of absenteeism, (ii) Training programmes conduct internally and staff sent out for external programmes-follow up reports, (iii) Details of promotions, transfer and terminations, (iv) New industrial relations and policies, (v) Resignations, department-wise, month-wise, (vi) Negotiations with unions, grievances filled, grievance settled, awards, etc.

Uses of Personnel Report

Personnel reports are an index of the way manpower is being

handled within the organisation. Combined with the special reports on personnel, a manager can perform his manpower control function effectively. Control depends on feed-back in the form of reports and information. If this feedback is accurate and timely, it will greatly help to take corrective course of action.

Personnel Audit

An audit is, properly speaking, an examination and verification of accounts and records. *Personnel auditing* refers to an examination and evaluation of policies, procedures and practices to determine the effectiveness of personnel management.[1] In other words, *personnel audit* or *periodical reviews* of the effectiveness of a management are concerned with :

(a) The measurement of the effectiveness of personnel programmes and activities and

(b) The determination of what should or should not be done in the future as a result of such measurement.

The effectiveness of a personnel programme, like that of personnel research, is dependent upon available information, and its scope is as wide as the field of personnel management. "The performance of people is a complex product of personnel interest, qualifications, commitment and expectations on the one hand, and of the employment environment (including working assignments, working conditions, supervision, leadership, opportunity and challenge) on the other. Because manger-employee relationships, from recruitment to retirement, are inter-related to compose the total system, no part of that system can be ignored."

Objectives of Personnel Audit

The objectives of a personnel audit are :

(a) To review the whole system of management programmes in which a management develops, allocates, and supervises human resources in an organisation with a view to determining the effectiveness of these programmes;

(b) To seek explanations and information, that is, to get answers to such question as : "Why did it happen?" and "What happened?"

(c) To evaluate the extent to which line managers have implemented the policies which have already been initiated and

(d) To evaluate the personnel staff and employees.

---

1. Seybold, G., "Personnel Audits and Reports to Top Management", in *Studies in Personnel Policies,* No. 191, N.I.C.B., 1964.

According to Gray, "the primary purpose of personnel audit is to know how the various units are functioning and how they have been able to meet the policies and guidelines which were agreed upon; and to assist the rest of the organisation by identifying the gap between objectives and results, for the end-product of an evaluation should be to formulate plants for corrections or adjustments."[2]

Importance of Personnel Audit

In modern times, personnel and industrial relations audits have been widely accepted as tools with which managers can control the programmes and practices of the personnel and industrial relations department. The importance of a personnel audit has increased in recent years because of the following reasons :

(a) A change in managerial philosophy and theory, as a result of which a management now feels that the employee's participation in the activities of an organisation, and their identification with it, has a tremendous influence on the working of that organisation.

(b) The changing role of the government, which intervenes more often and more extensively now, to control manpower management by an organisation with a view to protecting the interests of the employees, providing them with better working conditions and ensuring their economic security.

(c) The increasing role played by trade unions and their strength, as a result of which they often question managerial competence in industrial relations.

(d) The rising wages, changes in the skills of technical and professional workers, and the increasing expenditure incurred on the industrial relations department — these are the factors which have influenced and encouraged the trend in favour of a personnel audit.

Need for Personnel Audit

According to Yoder, the need for personnel audit is largely influenced by several conditions, some of these are :[3]

(a) *The Number of Employees* : Very small units, because of the very small number of persons they employ, require comparatively little in the way of a formal audit.

---

2. Gray, R.D., "Evaluating the Personnel Department", in *Personnel*, 1965, vol. 42 No. 2.
3. Yoder, Dale, *Personnel Management and Industrial Relations,* Prentice Hall of India Pvt. Ltd., New Delhi, 1972 p. 699.

CHART 6.3

The Manpower Management Audit — Area and Levels

Major Areas	**Level 1** *Results*	**Level 2** *Programmes and Procedures*	**Level 3** *Policy*
	Levels and Examples of Audit Data		
.. **Planning** Programming, forecasting, scheduling to meet organisation and personnel needs.	Personnel shortages, over-supplies, overtime, etc.	5-year plans, cost-benefit budgets.	Explain statements of intentions to provide inclusive plans for present and future manpower.
II. **Staffing and Development** Defined requirements and careers, sources, recruitment, selection, training and promotions.	Recruitment times, costs; training times, cost; labour turnover.	In-house and out-house training programme, guidance in careers.	Let-cream rise; non-discrimination.
III. **Organising** Maintaining structures for co-ordinating, communicating collaborating.	Feedback, reader interest, extent of formal organisation, reports, records.	Job definitions for individuals, departments, crews, task forces, house organs.	Encourage flexibility, reduce resistance to change, effective three-way communication.
IV. **Commitment** Individual and group motivation, interest, effort, contribution.	Productivity, performance norms, comparative costs.	Job enlargement, wage and salary administration, morale survey, exit interviews, fringe benefits.	Gain high personal identification, insure "wholeman" satisfaction.
V. **Administration** Style of leadership and delegation, supervision and negotiation.	Suggestions, promotions, grievances, discipline, union-management relations, co-operation.	Consultative supervision, collective bargaining, union-management committees.	Style adapted to changing expectations, participative involvement, collective bargaining.
VI. **Research and Innovation** Experiments and theory-testing in all areas.	Changes, experiments, reports, publications.	R & D approach in all areas, suggestion plans.	Test old and new theories encourage activity in management.

(b) *Organisational Structure* : Continuing feedback is facilitated if an organisation has a personnel department.

(c) *Communication and Feedback* : An effective two-way communications system often reduces the need for a formal audit.

(d) *Location and Dispersion* : The need for a formal audit is directly related to the number of isolated plants.

(e) *Status of an Industrial Relations Manager* : If he participates in top management plans, reports, discussions and decisions, the need for a formal audit may be less frequently felt.

(f) *Administrative Style* : The greater the delegation of authority and decentralisation of pwoer, the greater the value of a regualr and formal audit.

The field of personnel audit includes :

(a) Job analysis; (b) Recruitment; (c) Testing; (d) Selection; (e) Training; (f) Management development; (g) Promotions and transfers; (h) Rating; (i) Labour relations; (j) Morale development; (k) Employee benefits and services; (l) employee communication; (m) Employee counselling; (n) Wage and salary administration; (o) Collective bargaining and (p) Personnel management; industrial relations and research.

Yoder has given the following useful outline of the scope of personnel audit — area-wise and level-wise :[4]

Records to be Used

The main records and statistics to be used in a personnel audit are :

(a) Time standards;
(b) Cost records;
(c) Test scores;
(d) Training scores;
(e) Interview records;
(f) Work stoppages;
(g) Medical reports;
(h) Accident reports;
(i) Grievance reports;
(j) Trunover reports;
(k) Unit labour costs and
(l) Payroll data.

4. Yoder, Dale, *op. cit.*, 1972 ed., p. 719.

In other words, both *quantitative* and *qualitative* yardsticks should be used for purposes of evaluation. Monappa and Saiyadain provide a number of yardsticks and indices, which are : "averages in the levels of employee turnover or absenteeism; cost figures for each major activity or function; accident frequencies; grievances; suggestions; internal data indicators — wage and salary surveys, employees' state insurance scheme stabilities, productivity indications for certain jobs and/or machines, staffing and manning tables, job analyses and descriptions; and evaluation data regarding selection instruments."[5]

Methods of Analysis

The methods for analysing data and information are :

(a) Comparison of various time periods;

(b) Comparisons between departments and other companies;

(c) Trend lines, frequnecy distributions and statistical correlations;

(d) Ratio analysis; for example, labour cost per unit of output;

(e) Classification of data by kinds of employees, products and departments and

(f) Graphical or pictorial displays.

Frequency and Types of Audit

It is a common practice too have an annual evaluation or audit. At the end of each calendar or fiscal year, a report is presented, covering statistical information on the activities performed, the results achieved, the costs and expenditure involved, and comparisons of objectives and accomplishments. By a perusal of this report, a great deal of useful information can be had about personnel activities.

In some organisations, however, this personnel audit is conducted periodically, generally in accordance with the needs of each organisation. For example, attitude or morale surveys on particular subjects or topics may be conducted, or special reports may be prepared on such issues as grievances, the working of seniority rules or the effects of overtime practices and collective bargaining agreements.

Two practices are generally followed while conducting a personnel audit. In some cases, the audit is conducted by those employed in the organisation istelf — generally by auditors or accountants. In other cases, the services of outside experts are engaged. The former is known as *internal audit*, while the latter is designated *external audit*.

The advantages of having an outside auditor is that : (a) he has a background of knowledge of what others are doing in similar

5. Monappa, A. and Saiyadain, M.S., *Personnel Management*, Vikas Publishing House, New Delhi, 1978, p. 278.

situations; (b) he has a professional attitude toward his work and (c) he is objective in that he personally will not become a party to recommended changes.

While appointing an outside auditor certain conditions should be kept in mind regarding his work.

(i) He cannot work miracles. He can diagnose ills and recommend treatment, but the patient must provide the will to get well.

(ii) He must receive top management's support.

(iii) He cannot and should not relieve management of its responsibility for making the decisions. He can recommend, but the acceptance of his recommendations rests with management.

The Audit Report

The report should invariably by submitted, within a reasonable time, after the audit work is over. It should avoid the journalistic style; be based solely on the findings; be presented in a factual manner that is readily available for future reference; make use of graphic techniques where appropraite; and not be any longer than is necessary.

The following items should be contained in the report :

1. Table of Contents.
2. Summary and conclusion, in which the entire report is summarised for the top executives. (This may be the only part of the audit that some of the important executives will read. It should be short — not to exceed five to seven pages).
3. Preface giving a brief statement of the objectives.
4. The report proper, is which a major division is covered as a special section. (It is desirable to have this so typed that any section may be removed and sent to the persons concerned). Each section should be complete, and should contain as many supporting data as are practical without making it too voluminous. Other data should be included in the appendix.
5. Summary. This is more complete than summary and conclusions at the beginning of the Report.
6. Appendix. This includes supporting data that would be too voluminous to appear in the body of the Report.
7. It should be signed by all members making the audit.

Certain aspects of an audit report (such as a morale survey, a safety survey and similar special items of wide general interest) may be made available to the employees. Other phases of the audit may be appropriate to give only to top management.

PERSONNEL RESEARCH

Meaning and Characteristics

According to Yoder, "research is a shortcut to knowledge and understanding which can replace the slower, more precarious road of trial and error in experience......."[6]

"It implies," he points out, "searching investigations, re-examinations, re-assessments and revaluations. It is a purposive and systematic investigation designed to test carefully considered hypotheses or thoughtfully framed questions."[7]

Personnel research, according to Jucius, "is the task of searching for, and analysing, facts to the end that personnel problems may be solved or principles and laws governing their solution derived."[8]

In other words, *research is purposive*; that is, it seeks to answer specific questions and is not merely an accumulation of unstructured observations.

It is objective, that is, it recognises and limits bias and prejudice in every step of the process.

It is systematic, that is, it begins with a comprehensive design or plan, and the investigation is conducted in terms of that design.

It is parsimonious, that is, it identifies methods and techniques for the solution of problems with the minimum cost.

It is repeatable, that is, it can be used independently by several researchers at the same time.

'Research' is different from 'casual observation' in that it uses systematic investigation and objective analysis instead of any casual or informal means. The essential characteristic of research is its method or point of view. Its other characteristics are :

1. It is a planned and designed investigation and analysis.
2. It is conducted in a systematic manner to check, verify or disprove clues, assumptions or hunches.
3. It supplements knowledge and extends the frontiers of understanding.

---

6. Yoder, Dale, *op. cit.*, 1972 ed., p. 719.
7. *Ibid.*, p. 721.
8. Jucius, M.J., *Personnel Management*, Richard D. Irwin, 1975, p. 488.

Objectives of Personnel Research

Research is a multipurpose tool whcih is used to help solve a variety of organisational problems. The concept of research can be applied to all organisational studies, be they large or small, descriptive or analytical, major or minor, human or non-human, broad or narrow in perspective, dimension and scope.[9] In fact, it is useful for everyone who is concerned with personnel problems — labour, management, the general public, governmental agencies and consumers.

Research is immensely valuable in developing more effective personnel practices. Surveys and analysis of the statistics of a company's internal functioning, for example, are so vital to the effective operation of an enterprise that they are conducted almost as a mattter of course. Research, moreover, provides the most efficient relationships which otherwise might never have been observed or verified, or which sometimes are discovered after decades.[10]

More specifically, research is related to the following aspects of personnel management, human relations and labour-management relations :

(a) To measure and evaluate present conditions;
(b) To predict future conditions, events and behavioural patterns;
(c) To evaluate the effects and results of current policies, programmes and practices;
(d) To provide an objective basis for a revision of current policies, programmes and practices;
(e) To appraise proposed policies, programmes and activities;
(f) To keep the management abreast of its competitors by replacing old products by new products, old techniques by new techniques and old organisational practices by new organisational practices and
(g) To discover ways and means of strengthening the abilities and attitudes of employees at a good or a high level and on a continuing basis.

It is obvious, then, that the need for personnel research stems from the requriement of finding the most efficient manner of handling people-related employment concerns. Personnel research is the means

9. Block, Carl E., "Industrial Relations Research : Needs and Suggestions", in *Personnel Journal*, Vol. 47, No. 4, 1968, pp. 233-241.
10. French, Wendell, *Personnel Management Process : Human Resources Administration*. Houghton Mufflin Co., Boston, 1970, p. 581.

of bringing about the "end-state" of improved performances. Its fundamental purpose is to improve the philosophy and practice of personnel administration and manpower management.[11]

Coverage of Personnel Research Area

Reserarch in manpower and human resources covers all those specific areas which are the subject matter of personnel administration. The scope of such research may vary from the very simply to the very complex, or from the short and inexpensive to the long and costly. Most studies reveal that the four most dominant areas of research are selection; training and development; attitudes and leadership; and measurement devices.[12]

The personnel researcher seeks to discover the basic relationships which may lead to improved personnel decison-making in such areas as trunover, absenteeism, compensation levels and structure, job satisfaction, employee morale, assessment of managerial potential, training effectiveness, grievance handling, labour relations and collective bargaining.

Personnel research areas are often identified in terms of high or low appearance : selection, opinion measurement, training and development, appraisal, motivation, organisational effectiveness, managerial obseloscence, counselling and retirement.[13] Managerial selection and development and general employee motivation have generally been identified as the two main human resources areas which are in the greatest need of additional research.

Types of Personnel Research

1. Basic or Exploratory Personnel Research. It is concerned with the discovery of knowledge for its own sake. Under it the researcher builds conceptual models and tests various hypotheses against them. Many to the published result of such research are of little practical applicability to the business managers. Yet these generalisations mark advances in the field of personnel management, both in theory and in practice. This research is accomplished generally by Government agencies, Colleges/Universities, professional initiations and individual researchers.

---

11. Sikula, A.F., *Personnel Administration and Human Resources Management*, John Wiley & Sons, New York, 1976, p. 443.
12. Block, Carl E., *op.cit.*, p. 240.
13. Lake, Dale G.m, Miriam, R. Ritvo, and O'Brien, Gregory M., "Applying Behavioural Science : Current Projects", in *Journal of Applied Behavioural Science,* Vol. 5, No. 3, 1969, pp. 367-369.

2. Operational or Applied Research. This is directed towards the solution of particular business problems. Its pay off is immediate, observable and tangible. It provides instant solution to any selected problem in any operative area of personnel management such as manpower planning, recruitment and selection, absenteeism, turnover, compensation, motivation, job-satisfaction, grievance procedure etc. It may be conducted by any individual corporate manager on behalf of the company.

Benefits of Personnel Research

1. All Areas. Benefits of personnel research are numerous. It is used effectively in every area of personnel management. The potential benefits far exceeds the costs. Recently, Organisations have begun to realise the significance of the human element upon the firm's ability to achieve its goals. Competitive nature of business is making it increasingly difficult to obtain and retain individuals. Many of the traditional concepts regarding human resources management have been questioned. New ideas are needed to accomplish tasks effectively.

2. Applied to Varying areas. The specific applications of personnel research depend upon the organisation's needs. The areas of personnel research vary from organisation to organisation depending upon such factors as size, goals and particular problems of the individual organisation. It is used in selection, test validation, turnover reasons, turnover costs, improving performance appraisal, interviewing management training, surveys of employee attitudes, identification of high potential employees for accelerated promotion, opinion and motivation surveys, organisation climate and organisation development, management styles and organisation structure etc. It may provide the means by which people may learn to accept change more readily and thereby continue to be productive employees.

Procedure of Personnel Research

1. Identification of the Problem. One of the most difficult tasks in the research process is to recognise that a problem exists. The problem may be caused by an inadequate selection process, insufficient management training, or a multitude of other reasons. Or, there may be on problems. Openness on the part of the manager is the cornerstone of problem recognition.

2. Statement of the Problem. This means to clearly state the purpose of the research. For this one should not focus upon sysmptoms but concentrate upon solving problems. As you might expect, this may prove difficult. For example, a manager might maintain that the cause of decreased production is low employee morale while research may determine that dictatorial supervisors have been exerting so much pressure upon employees that they could care less about productivity. A clear definition of the problem is essential for effective research.

3. Choice of the Method of Inquiry. This depends to a large extent upon the nature of the research. The case study, the survey, and the experiment are all viable alternatives as methods of inquiry. However, most personnel researches use either the case method or the survey.

4. Selection and use of the Appropriate Research tool. Numerous quantitative tools are available for use by the personnel researcher. The selection of a tool depends upon the particular purpose for which the research is being conducted. If managers are to adequately perform research, they should know available quantitive tools, circumstances under which these tools should be used, strength and weaknesses of each method and the ability to interpret the results.

5. Interpretation of the Results. This should be done by the person closet to the problem. Strange conclusion have been reached when outsiders have attempted to interpret the results. A person who is not close to the situation might unjustly assign the problem to a wrong cause.

6. Implementation of the Necessary Action. This is the most difficult phase of the research process. The research results may identify areas where changes should be made. Personnel departments is the catalyst to convince management that a change is necessary. This takes is quite difficult since telling a manager that his managerial style is causing excessive turnover may be a tedious matter.

Methods of Personnel Research

1. Historical studies;
2. Case studies;
3. Survey research;
4. Statistical studies;
5. Mathematical models;
6. Simulation and
7. Field or action research.

1. Historical Studies. In historical studies past records and documents are systematically investigated and interviews are conducted with former employees. Almost all big organisations maintain records of the various personnel problems — absenteeism, turnover, accident rates, wage structures, etc. This method is systematic investigation, utilising an extended time span or longitudinal dimension.

2. Case Studies. These consist of analytical investigation of the relationships significant in a particular situation or set of circumstances. Although the precise meaning of the findings of a case study is limited to its unique past situation, a careful analysis and thoughtful generalisation may be derived from it, giving it a broader significance and application. Individual case studies may lead to the formulation of general hypotheses useful in laying a foundation for additional or more intensive future research. This method enables the researcher to make a thorough, in-depth investigation of key incidents or situations. It is historical in nature and does not necessarily represent general conditions.

3. Survey Research. In a survey research, concentrates attention on the collection of original data by administering a questionnaire or conducting a structured interview. While research hypiotheses are established, survey questions are designed to collect data. The correlation among observed phenomena, possible causes and related efforts is now computed, and conclusions are drawn. This method is time-consuming and costly. Its application may emphasise the importance of the collection of data and not that of analysing these data and formulating a theory on their basis.

4. Statistical Studies. These studies deal with the collection, analysis, calssification and interpretation of mathematical data and quantitative information. They lay emphasis up on the importance of quantification, mathematical manipulation and statistical inference. They use averages, means, medians, modes, measures of dispersion, trends, regressions and correlations. Their use is becoming increasingly widespread due to the development of high-speed modern electronic data-processing equipment.

5. Mathematical Models. These are generally used to explain the relationships among the variables that are to be examined. They help to develop and test the designs and sequences of equations which tentatively describe the behaviour of interacting variables in terms of mathematical notations. These also help us to examine comparatively simple and extremely complex relationships and evolve decision-rules of wide applicability.

6. Simulation. Computers have popularised designs which involve simulation. The process begins with the statement of a hypothesis. Which is used to study problems of production and inventory control, of marketing, purchasing, hiring and training of personnel, and of collective bargaining.

7. Field or Action Research. This method has been most effectively used in understanding group behaviour in communities and working organisations. It involves difficult design problems since the observer himself becomes a variable in the process of obervation. This self-involvement gives new insights to the researcher gained from an active interaction which would not have been possible under passive observation.

Following personnel researchers, utilise these methods or tools :

(i) *Academic bodies* : universities, bureaux of business research, social research institutions or centres;

(ii) *Government agencies* : departments of labour and employment;

(iii) *Private consultants* : individuals or sophisticated research organisations;

(iv) *Personnel departments* : commercial and industrial undertakings and

(v) *Time departments* : either independently or in conjunction with personnel departments.

Responsibility for Research

Research is not the sole responsibility of any one particular group or department in an organisation. It initial responsibility is that of the personnel department assisted by line supervisors and executives at all levels of management. The assistance that can be rendered by trade unions and other organisations like educational institutions, private research groups, and governmental agencies should be properly made use of. Psychologists, sociologists, economists, mathematicians, and specialists in business administration, political science and other areas should also make contribution in so far as research is concerned. To conclude with Jucius, "The field of research requires the resources of several types of researchers and different kinds of tools. To seek answers through the methodology and principles of a single speciality is to build upon a weak foundation. Rather, research calls for a cosmopolitan attitude and inter-disciplinary co-operation. The specialists who try to build a fence around all aspects of research do themselves and industry a serious disfavour."[14]

QUESTIONS FOR EXERCISE

1. What is Personnel Record? Explain its uses, types and objectives. What are the essentials of an effective record system?
2. What is Personnel Report? Explain its traits, types and uses.
3. Define personnel audit? Discuss its objectives, scope and types.
4. What is Personnel Research? Describe its types, major benefits.
5. Explain methods and procedure of Personnel Research.

---

14. Jucius, Michael J., *op. cit.*, p. 494.

7

Manpower Planning

MEANING OF MANPOWER PLANNING

Manpower Planning is synonymous to personnel planning. Objectives of manpower planning are to ensure proper linkage of economic planning with manpower and education so that no plan programme suffers due to lack of trained manpower.

1. *Eric W. Velter* : "The process by which a management determines how an organisation should move from its current manpower position to its desired manpower position. Through planning management strives to have the right number and the right kind of people, at the right places, at the right time, to do things which result in both the organisation and the individual receiving maximum long run benefit."[1]

2. *Flippo* : "A manpower planning programme can be defined as an appraisal of an organisation's ability to perpetuate itself with respect to its management as determined necessary to provide the essential executive talent."

3. *Dale S. Beach* : "It is a process for determining and assuring the organisation to have an adequate number of qualified persons, available at the proper times, performing jobs which meet the needs of the enterprise and which provide satisfaction for the individual involved."

4. *Coleman Bruce P.* : "Manpower planning is the process of determining manpower requirements and the means for meeting those requirements in order to carry out the integrated plans of the organisation."[2]

5. *Macbeth* : "Manpower planning involves two stages. The first stage is concerned with the detailed planning of manpower requirements

---

1. Velter, Eric W., *Manpower Planning for High Talent Personnel,* 1967, p. 15.
2. Colemn, Bruce P., "An Integrated System for Manpower Planning," *Business Horizon,* Vol. 13, 1970, pp. 89-95.

for all types of levels of employees throughout the period of the plan. The second stage is concerned with planning of manpower supplies to provide the organisation with the right type of people from all sources to meet the planned requirements."

6. *G. Stainer* : Manpower planning the "strategy for the acquisition, utilisation, improvement, and preservation of an enterprise's human resources. It relates to establishing job specifications or the quantitative requirements of jobs determining the number of personnel required and developing sources of manpower."[3]

7. *W.S. Wickstrom* : Human-resource planning consists of a series of activities, viz.,[4]

(a) *Forecasting* future manpower requirements, either in terms of mathematical projections of trends in the economic environment and development in industry, or in terms of judgemental estimates based upon the specific future plans of a company;

(b) *Making an inventory of* present manpower resources and assessing the extent to which these resources are employed optimally;

(c) *Anticipating* manpower problems by projecting present resources into the future and comparing them with the forecast of requirements to determine their adequacy, both quantitatively and qualitatively and

(d) *Planning* the necessary programmes of requirements, selection, training, developing, utilization, transfer, promotion, motivation and compensation to ensure that future manpower requirements are properly met.

Thus, *manpower planning consists in projecting future manpower requirements and developing manpower plans for the implementation of the projections.*

CHARACTERISTICS OF MANPOWER PLANNING

1. A continuous and never ending process. As the manpower needs of an organisation change from time to time, it is a continuous and never ending process.

2. A comprehensive process. Manpower planning includes various aspects of manpower management which ensure the availability of right type of people in sufficient number in the organisation.

---

3. Stainer, G., *Manpower Planning,* William Heinemann Ltd., London, 1971, p. 3.

4. Wickstrom, W.S., *Manpower Planning : Evolving Systems,* Conference Board, New York, 1971, p. 2.

3. Determination of future needs. Determination of future needs of manpower in the organisation includes forecasting of demand for and supply of human resources. Determination of manpower needs in advance helps management to take up further actions. Suitable actions can be taken to make the existing manpower suitable for the future positions.

4. Utilisation of manpower. By indicating the various factors which should be considered like working environment, suitable performance appraisal, promotion etc, manpower planning helps in utilisation of manpower.

5. Fixing responsibility of management. Manpower planning is the responsibility of management as a whole and not only of the personnel department. The personnel department only guides and assists operating managers in framing manpower plans.

BASES OF MANPOWER PLANNING

1. Existing stock of manpower. The first basis of manpower planning and the starting point of all planning processes is the existing stock of manpower. Analysis of the existing stock of manpower requires studying the position of total stock of manpower by dividing it into groups on the basis of function, occupation, level of skill or qualification. A group-wise detailed statement is prepared giving the number of workers in the group, their age, qualification date of retirement and chances for promotion. etc.

2. Checking wastage. For a good manpower planning, appropriate adjustment in the existing stock of manpower should be made for the possible wastage of manpower caused by any foreseeable changes in the organisation. Rate of labour turnover and the period of active management etc., should be studied in order to analyse the wastage of manpower. Other reasons of wastage may be expansion and modernisation of plant, retirement, promotion, transfer and training of workers etc. These factors should be taken into consideration to make the necessary adjustment in the requirement of personnel.

3. Future manpower requirement. After evaluating the existing stock of manpower and analysing the various factors of wastage caused by any foreseeable change in the organisation, one may easily assess the future requirement of manpower in an industry taking into account the future plans of the company, government plans and programmes, employment policy, demand and supply of manpower in future, productivity of labour and other factors of production and replacement needs. Care should be taken of the possible changes in the techniques and methods of production in the near future.

NEED FOR HUMAN RESOURCE PLANNING

(i) To carry on its work, each organisation needs personnel with the necessary qualifications, skills, knowledge, work experience and aptitude for work. These are provided through effective manpower planning.

(ii) Since a large number of persons have to be replaced who have grown old, or who retire, die or become incapacitated because of physical or mental ailments, there is a constant need for replacing such personnel. Otherwise, the work would suffer.

(iii) Human resource planning is essential because of frequent labour turnover which is unavoidable and even beneficial becaust it arises from factors which are socially and economically sound such as voluntary quits, discharges, marriage, promotions; or factors such as seasonal and cyclical fluctuations in business which cause a constant ebb and flow in the work force in many organisations.

(iv) In order to meet the needs of expansion programmes (which become necessary because of increase in the demand for goods and services by a growing population, a rising standard of living — which calls for larger quantities of the same goods and services as also for new goods; the comeptitive position of a firm which brings it more business arising from improvements effected in the slump period; and the rate of growth of the organisation), human resource planning in unvoidable.

(v) The nature of the present work force in relation to its changing needs also necessitates the recruitment of new labour. To meet the challenge of a new and changing technology and new techniques of production, existing empoloyees need to be trained or new blood injected in an organisation.

(vi) Manpower planning is also needed in order to identify areas of surplus personnel or areas in which there is a shortage of personnel. If there is a surplus, it can be redeployed; and if there is shortage, it may be made good.

Strategies for Manpower Planners

Stainer recommends the following nine strategies for the manpower planners :[5]

(a) they should collect, maintain and interpret relevant information

5. Stainer, G., *op. cit.*, p. 9.

regarding human resources; (b) they should report periodically manpower objectives, requirements and existing employment and allied features of manpower; (c) they should develop procedures and techniques to determine the requirements of different types of manpower over a period of time from the stand point of organisation's goals; (d) they should develop measures of manpower utilisation as component of forecasts of manpower requirements along with independent validation; (e) they should employ suitable techniques leading to effective allocation of work with a view to improving manpower utilisation; (f) they should conduct research to determine factors hampering the contribution of the individuals and groups to the organisation with a view to modifying or removing these handicaps; (g) they should develop and employ methods of economic assessment of human resources reflecting its features as income-generator and cost and accordingly improving the quality of decisions affecting the manpower; (h) they should evaluate the procurement, promotion and retention of the effective human resources and (i) they should analyse the dynamic process of recruitment, promotion and loss to the organisation and control these process with a view to maximising individual and group performance without involving high cost.

Responsibility of Line and Staff Manager

Human resource planning is the responsibility of both the line and the staff manager. The line manager is responsible for estimating manpower requirements. For this purpose, he provides the necessary information on the basis of the estimates of the operating levels. The staff manager provides the supplementary information in the form of records and estimates. The staff manager is expected to : [6] (i) report about manpower utilisation in the present and the past; (ii) provide help and advice managers on the assessment of manpower utilisation and to develop sources of information and techniques for purposes of comprison; (iii) administer the procedure of forecasting or objective setting; (iv) present the overall forecasts of departmental managers and (v) to advice line managers on forecasting techniques.

Levels of Uses

Human resource planning is practically useful at different levels, as stated by Narayanrao. According to him : [7]

(i) *At the national level* : It is generally done by the Government and covers items like population projections, programme of

---

6. *Ibid.*, p. 110.
7. Narayan Rao, U.S., Manpower planning in companies, *Indian Management*, Vol. 19 No. 12, 1971, pp. 17-31.

economic development, educational facilities, occupational distribution, and growth, industrial and geographical mobility of personnel.

(ii) *At the sector level* : It may be done by the Government — Central or State — and may cover manpower needs of agricultural, industrial and service sector.

(iii) *At the industry level* : It may cover manpower forecast for specific industries, such as engineering, heavy industries, consumer goods industries, public utility industries, etc.

(iv) *At the level of the individual unit* : It may relate to its manpower needs for various departments and for various types of personnels.

PROCESS OF HUMAN RESOURCE PLANNING

The process of human resource planning is one of the most crucial, complex and continuing managerial functions which, according to the Tata Electrical Locomotive Company, "embraces organisation development, management development, career planning and succession planning." The process has gained importance in India with the increase in the size of business enterprises, complex production technology, and the adoption of professional management techniques. It may be rightly regarded as a multi-step process, including various issues, such as :

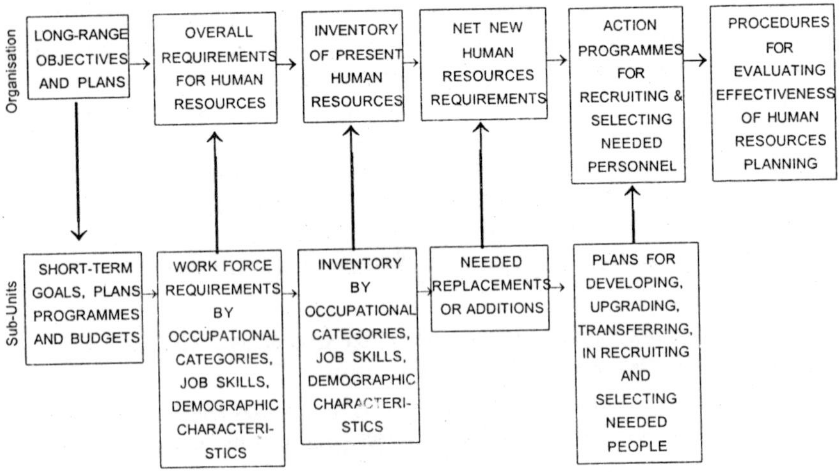

Chart 7.1 : Human Resource Planning System.

(A) Deciding goals or objectives;
(B) Estimating future organisational structure and manpower requirements;
(C) Auditing human resources;
(D) Planning job requirements and job descriptions and
(E) Developing a human resource plan.

OBJECTIVES OF MANPOWER PLANNING

1. To increase the size of the business. A number of workers are required to be recruited in expansion of the plant. A stock of the existing manpower should be taken and future needs of the personnel should be assessed at the time of taking the decision. It is essential to know whether new responsibilities should be assigned from among existing personnel or they should be recruited afresh from outside to meet the challenges of the new responsibilities. It should be decided whether persons are to be trained within the organisation to take charge of the new responsibilities or fresh well qualified personnel should be recruited. All this requires manpower planning.

2. To achieve effective recruitment and selection policy. Future needs may be predicted by manpower planning for which only right man on the right job at the right time may be recruited and selected. An enterprise has not to invest much amount on the training of workers who are recruited and placed after proper scrutiny. Effective manpower planning reduces the rate of labour turnover.

3. To reduce cost of labour. To maintain the supremacy over the other competitive firms, it is necessary for any organisation to control the cost of labour by effective use of manpower and thus reducing the wastage. This may be well done by manpower planning.

4. To avoid disruption in production. Manpower planning may help the organisation in producing the skilled and qualified workers. Through manpower planning future needs of personnel may be estimated and they are recruited and trained on the basis of a well-developed recruitment and training policy thus lowering the amount of expenditure on training. This production is carried on uninterrupted.

5. To follow national policy on employment. National policy on employment does not permit any employer to dismiss the worker once recruited by the organisation. Therefore, care should be taken in recruiting the worker according to the needs of the enterprise and to develop a recruitment policy of the organisation to avoid any unnecessary hardship in the near future. Here manpower planning alone can help the organisation.

6. To provide effective employee development programme. No effective employee development programme can be worked out without linking it with the manpower requirements of the organisation. While executing the employee development the talents, abilities and motives of the individuals as well as the organisational objectives in relation to the manpower should be taken into consideration thus making employee development programmes effective.

7. To maintain good industrial relations. An effective manpower planning helps the management in developing the good employer-employee relationship. For example, redundancies of workers caused by automation or any other technical change in methods and machines may be estimated well in advance with an effective manpower planning. It will help management consider the ways and means to avoid the anticipated untoward situation. Management may plan to absorb the redundant workers to some new job after proper training. Thus, good industrial relations may be maintained by an effective manpower planning.

FACTORS IN MANPOWER PLANNING

A. Quantity of Personnel or Workforce Analysis

In many companies, steps are taken to find replacement only after vacancies occur or are likely to occur. This method aggravates interruptions to production and tends to result in hurried and hence poorly evaluated selection of replacements. The effectiveness of hiring can be increased by forecasting manpower requirement of different categories of personnel, operative, technical and executive on the basis of the following factors :

1. Economic forecasting. The economic forecasting relating to national economy, international economic scene and future perspectives are made to determine future manpower requirements. If prospects of future economic situation are good, the future sales and production prospects will also be good resulting into more hands to obtain that level of activities. Hence, inflation, deflation, increase in costs of inputs and raw materials are the economic contingencies which influence the short-term and long-range plans of all business organisations.

2. Production estimates. Manpower requirements in some cases change with fluctuations in production. Hence, production forecast depends upon sales forecast. Thus, sales forecast are the basis upon which the estimates of manpower requirements are built. How much manpower is needed in a given department of a company depends upon factory and storage policies.

3. Departmental schedules. Most companies do not produce strictly to the sales curve. In its place a production schedule is prepared which levels out somewhat the peaks and valleys of sales estimates. The degree to which the production schedule is stabilized in comparison with sales curve is largely dependent upon the storability of the products and their non-susceptibility to the style factor. Departmental workloads can be established after factory schedules are computed. These department schedules provide the basis for determining future manpower needs of the department.

4. Expansion programmes. If expansion programmes are on the anvil, it will create needs of different types of personnel. Therefore, expansion programme should also be taken into account while calculating future manpower requirements.

5. Work standards. A change in work standards due to a negotiation between trade unions and management also creates demand for labour. For example, if standard production per worker is at present 50 units per day and it is reduced to 40 per worker under a settlement it will require 25 per cent more workforce in order to maintain the same level of production.

6. Manpower inventory. After making economic forecasts and production estimates, total manpower requirements may be determined keeping in view the work standards. It is necessary to ascertain how much manpower of various kinds is available to produce the output scheduled for the period of time in question. These two classes of information can be compared to compute the manpower to be added to or removed from the payroll. It may be put as following :

Total manpower requirements existing or available manpower
= Manpower to be added or to be removed from the payroll

7. Labour turnover rate. An old device of estimating future manpower requirements in any company is through the computation of labour turnover in the company, it is wise to estimate statistically how many are likely to leave. It may be possible to learn about the number of job vacancies, even though it cannot be ascertained as to who will specifically leave. Such estimates are best made in terms of past turnover. Labour turnover rates may be calculated either by separation method, replacement approach or flux method. In every case knowing the trends of turnover is an excellent means of calculating how many vacancies are likely to occur in the future.

8. Estimate of retirement and resignations. In estimating future manpower requirements, the expected losses should also be taken into account which are likely to occur through retirement, deaths, transfers, promotions, demotions, dismissals, disability, resignations, lay off etc. Changes in the human quality resulting from the experience gained in the jobs during the period and the training achieved should also be considered. The real shortage or surplus may be found out after making adjustments for wastages, anticipated and expected losses and separations.

9. Estimates of changes in management. Changes in the quality or quantity of productive services require a change in the organisation structure. Changes in management philosophies and leadership styles, the use of mechanical technology such as the introduction of automatic controls or the mechanisation of materials handling functions necessitate changes in the skills of workers as well as a change in the number of employees needed.

B. Quality of Personnel or Work-load Analysis

Work-load analysis is the technical aspect of human resources planning which involves the study to nature and composition of existing workforce, *i.e.*, auditing of human resources, study of work standards, demand analysis etc.

1. Auditing of human resources. Auditing initiates the preparation of a skill inventory. A skill inventory contains data about each employee's skills, abilities, work preferences and other items of information. It assists in examining the nature and composition of existing workforce and estimating the future type of requirements of different categories of personnel. Some organisations prepare organisation charts for it while others compile and maintain Employee Information Card for this purpose.

2. Study of work standards. The study of work standards is essential for determining the quality and type of personnel required. It is necessary to prepare a job analysis which records details of training skills, qualifications, norms, abilities, experience and responsibilities, etc., needed for a job. Job analysis includes the preparation of job description and job specifications. Study of work standards also removes the possibilities of underestimation of the quality and number of employees required leading to shortfalls in performance.

IMPORTANCE OF MANPOWER PLANNING

According to Dr. Ram Tarneja, "Management can ensure control of labours costs by avoiding both shortages and surpluses of manpower through proper manpower planning." Failure in planning and in developing personnel proves a limiting factor in achieving the organisational objectives. There will be disruptions in the flow of work and the pace of production will also be low if the number of persons in an organisation is less than the number of persons required to carry out the organisational plans. On the other hand, if some persons are surplus in the organisation, they will have to be paid remuneration if they are retained or compensation if their services are terminated. A sound personnel policy requires that there should be adequate number of persons of the right type to attain the organisational objectives. For this the manpower planner should be concerned with the timing and the scheduling of planning of personnel and persuading the management to use the result of manpower planning studies in the conduct of the business. Manpower planning can prove to be important to frame the training and development programmes for the personnel because it takes into account the effects of anticipated changes in technology, markets and products on manpower requirements and educational and training programme requirements.

FORMS OF MANPOWER PLANNING

A. Short-Term Manpower Planning. It involves the matching of present employees with their present jobs so that they may perform their functions efficiently. It is wrong to expect a perfect match between jobs and individuals. In the short-run, only jobs can be adjusted or modified to adjust with the individuals due to many constraints — legal, organisation and social. It is very difficult to throw an employee out of job. Hence, some adjustments have to be made in the job itself in the short-run. Short-term manpower planning is influenced by the following factors :

1. Employees less qualified than the requirements. The following steps should be taken :

(i) Providing training, (ii) Change in the job, (iii) Providing assistant to the man, (iv) Change of incumbent such as transfer or demotion, (v) Separation of the incumbent.

2. Employees more qualified than the requirement of job. The following adjustments may be made :

(i) Job enlargement. (ii) Additional charge. (iii) Promotion of higher position (if vacant). (iv) Seeking council and advice from him. (v) Temporary assignments.

B. Long-term manpower planning. In this management has sufficient time gap to take necessary steps and making this matching process a calculated exercise. It is a planning for 10-15 or more years in respect of manpower requirement for the organisation. In the long-run the management may take the following steps in the direction :

1. Projecting manpower requirements. This is required to meet future needs of the organisation. As environment in which an organisation operates is constantly changing, the whole job structure should keep pace with such changes. The present organisation structure may continue to be the best. The management must predict as accurately as possible what jobs will be needed in future. However, such prediction is neither easy nor always possible. As Flippo has observed 'that some firms claim that executive manpower needs are too intangible to forecast, that management cannot be defined or planned for in any constructive manner'. Three problems can be identified under projecting manpower needs :

(i) Can one predict a rate of loss of manpower and thus predict the need for its replacement?

(ii) Can one predict the need for new manpower over and above the need for replacement?

(iii) Can one determine the abilities necessary to man these jobs so that requirement and training processes can be facilitated? An analysis of these problems may help in protecting the manpower needs.

2. Manpower inventory and analysis. It involves the appraising of present key personnel and cataloguing their characteristics without reference to specification to a particular position. Inventory in a term used in relation to the counting of tangible objects such as raw materials, goods in progress, or finished product. In manpower inventory, however, the items involved are intangible. It is not simply the counting of number of persons available presently, but it includes a cataloguing of present and potential abilities and aptitudes. The inventory should include young men who have good potential, as well as present executives, because a good deal of shifting from position to position will undoubtedly occur in future. The manpower inventory requires the following :

(i) Determination of personnel to be inventoried.

(ii) Cataloguing of factual background information on each individual.

(iii) Systematic and detailed appraisal of those individuals.

(iv) Detailed study of those individuals deemed to possess potential for development.

Thus, manpower inventory provides information about present and future executives in the organisation. It may be more complete and accurate than any unsystematic impression of the general status of the organisation. The existing and future gap in number of managerial personnel and their ability may be ascertained through this inventory. It will form the basis for recruitment, selection and training process.

3. Recruitment and selection of suitable persons. After making manpower inventory, the next step in the direction is the recruitment and selection of suitable persons. These activities involve various functions of long-term nature.

4. Training and development. Training and development is the process of developing men to cope with the new responsibilities. The efficiency of any organisation depends on how well its members are trained and developed.

STEPS IN MANPOWER PLANNING

1. To Prepare manpower inventory (current manpower position). Manpower planning seeks to avoid the situation of over — and understaffing. The stock of existing manpower is to be assessed for this purpose. It requires a critical assessment of present manpower. Manpower inventory refers to the assessment of the potential capabilities of present employees — qualitatively and quantitatively. Not simply a head count of existing staff it is cataloguing of their present and potential talent. It reveals the degree to which these capabilities are employed optimally. It helps to reveal the undeveloped potential, if any, and also the gap that exists or that is likely to arise in the firm's human resources. Preparation of manpower inventory involves the determination of personnel to be inventoried, cataloguing of factual background information such as level, skill, work experience, number, job history, date of recruitment etc., of each individual, systematic appraisal of each individual and listing the present and potential abilities and aptitudes of each. It helps in designing the selection and training programmes for the future. Present manpower should be evaluated according to age groups, skill groups, level groups, potential-wise and cost effectiveness.

2. To Forecast manpower needs. Manpower planning determines the future manpower needs of the organisation. These can be projected on the basis of production and sales budgets, workload analysis and workforce analysis, taking into account the objectives, size, area of operations, expansion schemes, technology of production processes, future changes in organisation etc. Absenteeism and rate of loss of personnel on account of retirement, discharge, resignation, death, disability, etc., should also be estimated. Again, the future manpower requirements should be estimated qualitatively and quantitatively. The quality of manpower is determined with the help of job description and job specification on the basis of information collected from job analysis.

(i) *Job description.* Job description describes the details about the title of the job. It involves nature of the job to be performed, duties involved, authority, relationship, working conditions, tools and techniques, responsibilities etc. The details of the job are required, not only for selection of personnel but also for preparing training and development programmes.

(ii) *Job specification* : Job specification summarises the man specification *i.e.* the characteristics of man required to perform the job. It lays down the educational qualification, technical qualification, experience, mental ability, skills, aptitude etc. required to perform the job efficiently. The contents and requirements of a job provide an objective guide for determining the quality of personnel needed in future. While job description describes the details of the job, job specification describes the quality of the person required to perform the job.

3. To identify manpower gaps. A comparison of future needs of personnel and the person's manpower inventory reveals the gap in terms of number and quality of personnel which points out the additional personnel required in future. It also identifies the improvement to be made in the present personnel to prepare them for the jobs in future.

4. Manpower programme. Programmes and strategies are developed for recruitment, selection, training, transfer, promotion and appraisal. If the nct requirement reveals the need of additional staff, development plans are designed to ensure a continuing supply of trained people to take over job as they fall vacant either by promotions or by recruitment or through training. On the other hand, if the existing staff is in excess of future needs, plans must be prepared to absorb them in the organisation against future vacancies as it is now-a-days not easy to discharge or lay off a person due to trade union pressure. Thus, persons may be trained to fill the future vacancy so that the shortage and redundancies can be avoided in the long-run.

RESPONSIBILITY FOR HUMAN RESOURCE PLANNING

Human resource planning is the responsibility of the personnel department. In this task, it is aided by the industrial engineering department, the top management and the team of directors of different departments. It is mostly a staffing or personnel function. The overall responsibility lies with with Board of Directors because, as the manpower planning scheme of Hindustan Lever indicates, "these members are in a position to direct the future course of business, set sappropriate goals for the management concerned in the formulation of personnel policies." The personnel department's responsibility is "to recommend relevant personnel policies in respect of manpower planning, devise methods of procedure, and determine the quantitative aspects of manpower planning."

The responsibilities of the personnel department in regard to manpower planning have been stated by Geisler in the following words :

(i) To assist, counsel and pressurise the operating management to plan and establish objectives;

(ii) To collect and summarise data in total organisational terms and to ensure consistency with long-range objectives and other elements of the total business-plan;

(iii) To monitor and measure performance against the plan and keep the top management informed about it and

(iv) To provide the research necessary for effective manpower and organisational planning.

Precautions in Manpower Planning[8]

The Personnel Department/Director must first decide on a plan period, *i.e.,* the time span for which the plan is to be made. A plan period of less than three years or more than five years would be unrealistic. The process of recruitment, training and placement often takes three or more years.

Having decided on the time span (say five years), it should be seen that it runs span of five years and in blocks. Only then the plan can be kept realistic and functioning.

The plan should be worked out in sufficient detail. Its implementation should be evaluated and controlled properly. *This requires a great deal of tenacity, persistence and vigilance on the part of personnel managers.*

Every component of the plan has to be compatible with policies regarding recruitment, promotion, termination, inter-departmental transfers, retirement and training. *Policy formulation is an essential pre-requisite for manpower planning.*

Whatever plan is made, it has to be realistic. A plan has to be put into operation and, therefore, *whatever is not feasible should be excluded.*

For every part of the plan, allowances should be made for lead time, otherwise the result will be adversely affected. A balance between conflicting requirements of standards and time available has to be achieved. In other words, *practicability has to be given precedence over perfection.*

Finally, the paramount consideration should be to make the plan an integral part of the corporate plan. *It has to mesh with plans in other functional areas.*

Manpower Plan Component

The manpower plan can be broken down into three components :

8. Basu, K.S., *New Dimensions in Personnel Management,* The Macmillan Co., of India Ltd., New Delhi, 1979, pp. 40-42.

(i) *Forecasting* : Estimating future needs and stock taking of available resources in the organisation; (ii) *Recruitment plan* : To meet the gap between the internal resource and estimated need by external recruitment; (iii) *Training and Development plan* : To utilise fully the human resources of the organisation and to develop the potential resources.

In practice it has been found that short-term (under 2 years) and medium-range plans (2 to 5 years) are easier to formulate with greater degree of uncertainity.[9]

Fig. 7.1 summarise factors related to two major forms of human resource planning.[10]

FIG. 7.1

Three Ranges of Manpower Forecasting

	Short Range (0-2 years)	Intermediate Range (2 to 5 years)	Long-range (beyond 5 years)
Demand for	Authorised expansion, technological changes; new legislation; Employee turnover; lay-offs, and contractual restrictions	Operating needs from budgets or plans. Expansion or Contraction or adjustments.	Geographical Capacity; size of the organisation and system; product lines; services offered; load anticipated. Changes in environment and technology essentially judgemental. Labour saving equipment, efficiencies, productivity, etc.
Supply of Labour; Internal	Departmental, divisional roasters; promotions. expected losses; quits, death;	Merger or acquisition plans; managerial and supervisory development programmes.	Management expectations of changing characteristics of employees and future available man power.
Supply of Labour; External	Area employment levels; Number of employees needed.	Labour Market projections, business development plans, general institutional plans to hire.	Management expectations of of future conditions affecting immediate decisions.

9. Walker, J.W., "Forecasting Manpower Needs", *Harvard Business Review,* March-April, 1969, p. 156.

10. Burack, Elmer H., and Smith, Robert D., *Personnel Management — A Human Resource Systems Approach*, West Publishing Company, New York, 1977, p. 123.

Short Range Analysis

Short range forecasts usually grow out of normal budgetary processes. Fig. 7.2 illustrates the key steps in the short-term forescasting planning process.

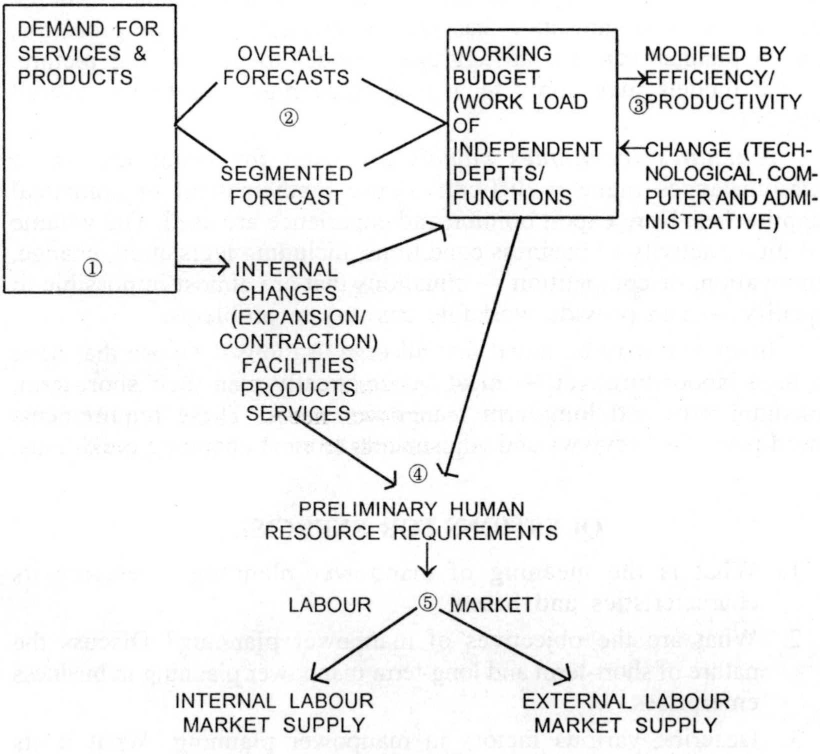

Fig. 7.2 : Short-Range Human-Resource Forecasting Organisational Perspective.

Long Range Analysis

The parameters of short-range forecasting usually are fairly well-defined. They are handled in the normal course of budget preparation and require simple arithmetic calculations. Long-range planning is more complex and is dependent upon mathematical and statistical models, as knowledge of demand variables and appropriate measurement techniques.

Two general kinds of forecasting techniques are used : indirect and direct methods. *Indirect methods* involve the forecasting of general rules — production figures, for example — that must be translated into specific requirements or measures. *Direct techniques* involve the use of methods of estimate (directly) labour hours, number of supervisors or particular occupational needs.

Aggregate models are based on several key variables that are known to directly affect the organisation's overall human resource needs. Every organisation has special characteristics or problems, and a planner can use an aggregate model to get the big picture. These models may apply to a geographic region or to the overall system.

Estimates techniques models are used for situations where circumstances make it difficult to use mathematical or statistical approaches. Here expert opinion and experience are used. The volume of future activity of business conditions, including legislation, change, innovation, or competition — situations that are almost impossible to qualify — can provide workable answers to problems.

In sum, it may be noted that all organisations — those that have a high labour turnover — must systematically plan their short-term, medium-term and long-term manpower needs. These requirements need periodical reviews and adjustments to meet changing conditions.

QUESTIONS FOR EXERCISE

1. What is the meaning of manpower planning? Describe its characteristics and bases.
2. What are the objectives of manpower planning? Discuss the nature of short-term and long-term manpower planning in business enterprises.
3. Describe various factors in manpower planning. What is its importance?
4. Distinguish between various forms of manpower planning.
5. Explain the steps in the process of manpower planning in industry.

8

Job Analysis, Job Description and Job Specification

Job analysis is a systematic procedure for securing and reporting the information which defines a specific job. It determines the qualifications required for a job; provides guidance in recruitment and selection; evaluates current employees for transfer or promotion and establishes the requirements for training programmes. It is a foundation for job evaluation. It helps in employee development by means of appraisal and counselling. By establishing improved methods of analysing problems of health, safety and fatigue; it functions as a guide in connection with discipline and grievances and as a basis for transfers, lay-offs and comparison of the pay rates obtaining in other organisations. It establishes workloads and job assignments.[1] It helps in redesigning the jobs to improve operational performance or to enrich job content and employee improvement. Managers may develop ways of providing their employees an increased sense of personnel accomplishment and control over themselves and their work.

The following figures shows areas of application of job analysis.

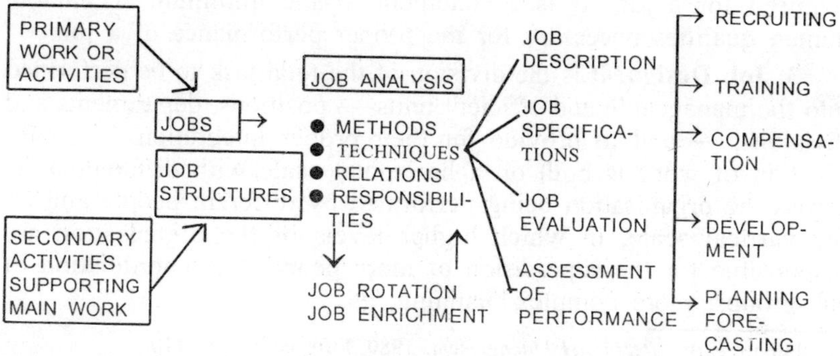

Fig. 8.1 : Area of Application of Job Analysis.

1. Calhoon, R., *Managing the personnel,* 1964, p. 133.

Documentation

Job Analysis produces four kinds of documentation and procedures crucial to personnel activities : (i) Job descriptions; (ii) Job specifications; (iii) Job evaluation and (iv) personnel assessment. These are basic inputs for diverse personnel functions.

Definition of Job Analysis

Job Analysis : It is a procedure by which pertinent information is obtained about a job. It is a detailed and systematic study of information relating to the operations and responsibilities of a specific job.[2] According to U.S. Dept. of Labour Employment service, job analysis is "the process of determining, by observation and study, and reporting pertinent information relating to the nature of a specific job...It is the determination of the tasks which comprise the job and of the skills, knowledge, abilities and responsibilities required of the worker for a successful performance and which differentiate one job from all others."[3]

1. Job Description. Job Analysis includes job description, job specification and job design. It is a written record of the duties, responsibilities and requirements of a particular job. According to W.D. Scott, it "is concerned with the job itself and not with the work."[4] It is a statement describing the job in such terms as its title, location, duties, working conditions and hazards. It tells us 'what is to be done' 'how it is to be done' and 'why'. It is a standard of function. It defines the appropriate and authorised contents of a job.

2. Job Specification. It is a standard of personnel which designates the qualities required for an acceptable performance. It is a written record of the requirements sought from an individual worker for a given job. It refers to a summary of the personal characteristics required for a job. It is a statement of the minimum acceptable human qualities necessary for the proper performance of a job.

3. Job Design. It is the division of the total task to be performed into the manageable and efficient units — positions, departments and divisions, — and to provide for their proper integration. The sub-division of work is both on a horizontal scale with different tasks across the organisation being performed by different people and on the vertical scale, in which higher levels of the organisation are responsible for the supervision of more people, the coordination of sub-groups, more complex planning, etc.

---

2. Flippo, E.B., *Personnel Management,* 1980, Fifth edition, p. 110.
3. U.S. Department of Labour, Employment Service, *Training and Reference Manual for Job Analysis*, Washington, 1944, p. 1.
4. Jones, Jean J. and Decothis, Thomas A., Job Analysis National Survey Findings, *Personnel Journal,* October, 1969, p. 805.

Job Analysis is a procedure and a tool for determining the specified tasks, operations and requirements of each job. According to Jones and Decothis, "It is the process of getting information about jobs : specially, what the worker does; how he gets it done; why he does it; skill, education and training required; relationship to other jobs; physical demands; environmental conditions."[5] *It refers to the anatomy of the job*. It is a complete study of job, embodying every known and determinable factor, including the duties and responsibilities involved in its performance, the conditions under which the performance is carried on, the nature of the task, the qualities required in the worker, and such conditions of employment as pay, hour, opportunities and privileges. It also emphasises the relation of one job to others in the organisation.

Meaning of Job Analysis

1. *John A. Shubin* : "Job analysis is the methodical compilation and study of work data in order to define and characterize each occupation in such a manner as to distinguish it from all others."

2. *Dale Yoder* : "Job analysis is the procedure by which the facts with respect to each job are systematically discovered and noted."

3. *Scott, Clothier and Spriegel* : "Job analysis is the process of critically evaluating the operations, duties and relationship of the job."

4. *Flippo* : "Job analysis is the process of studying and collecting information relating to the operations, duties and relationship of the job."

5. *Michal J. Jucius* : "Job analysis refers to the process of studying the operations, duties and organizational aspects of jobs in order to derive specifications or as they are called by some job descriptions."

6. *United States Department of Labour* : "Job analysis is defined as the process of determining, by observation and study and reporting pertinent information relating to the nature of a specific job. It is the determination of the tasks which comparise the job and the skills, knowledge, abilities and responsibilities required of the worker for successful performance and which differentiates the job from all others."

7. *Blum* : "A job analysis is an accurate study of the various components of a job. It is concerned not only with an analysis of the duties and conditions of work, but also with the individual qualifications of the worker."

---

5. Scott, W.D., Clothier, R.C. and Spriegel, W.R., *Personnel Management*, New Delhi, 1977, sixth ed., p. 127.

8. *J.H. Hackett* : "In the process of job analysis, the fundamental elements of a job are established and clarified, while simultaneously the abilites desirable in the worker are known, the abilities that will help him to perform his function skilfully. Thus, job analysis has two aspects, one the analysis of duties and conditions of work, and the other, the analysis of qualities desired in the worker or employee".

Contents of Job Analysis

The basic data provided by the job analysis is classified under the suitable sub-heads. Dale Yoder has classified these sub-heads as follows :

(i) The job identification : its title and code number, etc.

(ii) Distinctive features of the job : its location, physical setting supervision, hazards and discomforts, if any.

(iii) Duties and responsibilities of the workers.

(iv) What materials and equipments are needed.

(v) How the job is performed.

(vi) Required personal qualities.

(vii) Job relationship.

Procedure of Job Analysis

1. Collection of Factual Material. Various approaches are utilised in studying a job and the four currently most popular are (i) questionnaires, (ii) narrative descriptions, (iii) observations and (iv) interviews. Two types of informations are collected, *i.e.*, (i) information regarding job such as its physical environment (temperature, noise, dirt, comforts and dangers etc.), its socal environment (whether job is in teams, shifts or isolated), financial conditions (wages, bonus, incentive schemes or fringe benefts etc.), and (ii) information relating to qualities of persons holding the job, *i.e.,* his physical demands (muscular energy, hours of work, travel etc.), intellectual demands (university, technical or professional degrees and problems solving abilities required), skills, experience and personality factors required on the job.

2. Completion of Job description Blank. After collecting information the job analyst puts it in a standard job description form as a comprehensive draft. It is a statement showing full details of the activities of the job. There may be used separate job description forms for various activities in the job and may be compiled later on. The job analysis forms may be used as references for the future.

3. Job specification. Job specifications are prepared on the basis of information collected. It is a statement of minimum acceptable qualities of the person to be placed on job. It specifies the standard by which the qualities of the person are measured. Job analyst prepares such statement taking into consideration the skills required in performing the job properly. This statement is used in selecting a person matching with the job.

4. Preparation of Report. On the basis of information collected mentioning the analysis of various activities on the job and qualities of the individual to be placed on the job analyst prepares a report. Such report will be presented before the supervisor and the personnel manager for suggestions and comments. The analyst should revise the original report in the light of the suggestions or comments given by the supervisor or the personnel manager to make it more correct and informative.

5. Preparation of Final draft. The complete draft presented by the analyst and approved by the supervisor and personnel manager may now be received by the top executive. The office-bearers of the trade unions may also be taken into confidence before approving the draft finally. It union officials have ideas for making changes, the management should consider them as suggestions and incorporate them in the job description and job specification. The final draft should be approved by the top line executive or by the personnel manager who is responsible for making final decisions on the matter.

Significance of Job Analysis

1. Achieve manpower planning. Job analysis is the qualitative aspect of manpower requirements. It determines the demands of the job in terms of responsibilities and duties and then translates these demands in terms of skills, qualities and other human attributes it determines the quantum of work which an average person can perform on the job in a day. It facilitates the division of work into different jobs. Thus, it is an essential element of manpower planning as it matches jobs with men.

2. Helps recruitment, selection and placement. In order to hire the right person on a job, it is essential to know the requirements of the job and the qualities of the individual who will perform it. The informations regarding these two are procured from job description and job specifications respectively. These help the management in matching the job requirements as closely as possible with workers' aptitudes, abilities, interests etc. It facilitates the execution of employment programme.

3. Determines training and development. Job analysis determines the levels of standard of job performance. It helps administering the training development programmes. Job descriptions and job specifications are written documents. It the contents of these two documents are known to the employees, they will try to achieve the skills and knowledge required to perform the task assigned to them efficiently. They may also prepare themselves for the higher post in the light of the job description and the job specifications. The same information may be used by those who administer the training and development programmes by determining the contents and subject matter needed in such programmes.

4. Determines job evaluation. Job evaluation aims at determining the relative worth of the job which helps in determining the compensation of job. These jobs are evaluated in terms of money. An accurate and comprehensive set of job descriptions and the job specifications forms of factual basis for evaluating the worth of the job.

5. Provides data for performance appraisal. Job analysis data provide a clear-cut standard of performance for every job. The performance of employee can be appraised objectively with the standard of job performance so established. A supervisor may very easily compare the contribution of each man with the set standards.

6. Helps job designing. Industrial engineers may use the job analysis information in designing the job by making the comprehensive study of the job elements. It helps in time and motion study, work-specifications, methods and work-place improvement and work-measurement. Human engineering activities such as physical, mental and psychological are studied with the help of job analysis information.

7. Ensures safety and health. The job analysis process uncovers the hazardous and unhealthy environmental factors such as heat, noise, fumes dust etc. The management may take corrective measures to minimise the chances of risks to ensure safety to workers and to avoid unhealthy conditions.

8. Maintains discipline. Job analysis provides the information regarding characteristics of various jobs and the job-holders. It studies the failure of the workman to meet the required standard of performance. Corrective measures may be taken in time to avoid untoward situation. In this way it helps in maintaining the discipline in the industry.

METHODS OF GATHERING INFORMATION

1. Questionnaire or Survey Method. In this method a questionnaire is prepared to get the job information and it is circulated among all job holders. The questionnaire asks the job holder to supply the several types of information sought in job analysis. It may, in addition, ask the immediate supervisor to examine and comment on the replies provided by the job holders.

No single questionnaire is appropriate for all types of jobs. However, most of them follow an outline that first identifies the job, seeks information on the principal tasks involved and then ask questions design to discover the mental skill and physical requirements of a satisfactory job holder. In one section, information is requested on any usually working conditions. The job holders are told the objective of such survey so that they may fill up the questionnaire property.

A specimen of a questionnaire is given on next page.

Defects of Questionnaire Method

(i) Time consuming method.

(ii) Workers are more trusted.

(iii) Cannot be used for all jobs and illiterate workers.

(iv) Workers may not be interested or competent in filling these questionnaires.

2. Interview Method. In this method the job analyst interviews the job holders and ask questions from them observing the following rules :

(i) *Leisure Time* : Interview should be taken in leisure time.

(ii) *Introduction* : Job analyst must introduce himself to the job holder first and tell him the purpose of the interview.

(iii) *Interest* : Job analyst must take interest in job holder and his work.

(iv) *Job Centred* : He must concentrate on the job and not on the personnel matters.

(v) *Motivation* : The job holder should be motivated to speak more.

(vi) *No Instruction* : No instruction are issued to the other holder.

(vii) *Atmosphere* : As far as possible, the atmosphere of interview must remain informative and conversation must be held in the language of the job holder.

(viii) *Average Worker* : An average job holder should be selected for interview. The information will not be useful if the best job holder is contacted.

QUESTIONNAIRE FOR INDIVIDUAL JOB

Important Note. Please read all the questions before making any entries, then answer each one as briefly as possible. Return this questionnaire within one week to the Personnel Department.

Title of Position..
Department.....................Section..
Division...........................Date...

Description of Duties :

(i) What is the general purpose of your work?...................
(ii) What are your routine duties?...
(iii) How many employees do you supervise?........................
(List job names and number of people in each job)..................
....

Performance of Duties :

(a) Mental Requirements..
(b) Skill Requirements...
(c) Experience Requirements..
(d) Physical Efforts...

Responsibility :

(i) What is your responsibility?..
(ii) What is the nature and extent of your responsibility for the employees under your supervision? ....
(iii) Give the nature and extent of any responsibility you may have for men and money. ....
(iv) Roughly what proportion of your time is spent in dealing with customers?..

Working Conditions :

(i) What are your usual working hours?....................................
(ii) What are the disagreeable features of your work?....................
(iii) Any suggestion...

Other Information :

(i) Your name...
(ii) Length of service in this position (in years)............................

3. Observation Method. Here the job analyst observes the work and worker while the worker is involved with the work. Experienced and expert analysis combine interviewing and on the job observation to provide a more accurate reply than is usually secured by the use of questionnaire of unspecialized interviewers.

Defects of Observation

(i) It gathers the job information relating to only simple and repetitive nature of work.

(ii) If any work is to be done by week, fortnight or a month, it is difficult to observe it with this purpose.

4. Record Method. In it, various job information are received from the old records of the personnel department. The job analyst goes through the records and notes the relevant aspects of information.

Defects of Record

(i) Many things are left unknown such as worker-supervisor relationships, the nature and description of the implements and tools being at present used to do the job current working conditions.

(ii) If the records are old then the very purpose of job analysis will be defeated.

5. Individual Psychographic Method. In this method, the mental peculiarities of an individual successful in a particular kind of job are examined, a list of these peculiarities is prepared and this list transcribed in figure form on graph. This provides some standard of judgement in future recruitments for the same job.

6. Job Psychographic Method. According to Viteles, follows three things are essential to job psychographic method :

(i) Accurate classification of mental qualities.

(ii) Valid method of evaluation.

(iii) Driect examination or analysis by trianed examiners.

In this method, some specialist analysts study the work, and they evole a valid and standard method of evaluation. They prepare a very accurate list in which the various mental qualities required for the job are properly and reliably classified. A graph of these qualities is prepared so that selection of candidates for the job may become easier.

7. Job Analysis by Test. In the test method, some relaible and valid tests are performed on the basis of essential qualities and abilities; the candidates are tested for selection and suitability by these tests.

8. Motion Study Method. Under this method, the speed of an individual worker in performing some job and time consumed therein are both noted. Similar examinations being performed on other individuals doing the same work, the results obtained are compared. Such a study of speed and time helps in job analysis and classification of the workers.

CHART 8.1

Job Analysis Record Form

Name of Company		Job Analysis Record		
For Division's Use :	Present Job Title	Staff Division		Date
	Proposed Job Title	Organisation Components	Employee Report	Supervisor Report to
For Central Staff Use	Position Title	Position Code		Date

Description of Duties

(i) **General Summary Statement**. Indicate the extent of supervision received or exercised; summarise the basic and distinguishing characteristics of the nature of work, and show the general level of responsibility.

(ii) **Typical Duties**. When describing duties, be as detailed as possible in outlining the main duties of a position, considering what is done and how it is done, and list them in order of their importance. Indicate whether work is performed as a regular routine or intermittently.

Factors

(i) **Previous Experience Required.** Indicate the periods of time required in lower or related jobs, measured from the time when the qualification level of education, cited in factor (ii) is acquired, that are essential for starting on, and a proper performance of, a work.

(ii) **Specialised or Technical Edcuation Required.** Indicate in definite terms the minimum level of academic education essential for a proper performance of a job, citing specific qualifications and/or recognised levels of attainment.

(iii) **Manual or Physical Skill Required.** What kind of manual or physical skill is required in the performance of the duties?

(Examples : Typing, Shorthand, Comptometer, Book-keeping machine).

(iv) **Physical Efforts Required.** Waht kind of physical effort is required and what is the duration of such exertion? Examples : Continuous, walking, standing, lifting of heavy objects, etc.

(v) **Complexity and Difficulty of Work.** **Assessment**

Divisonal Central Staff

(a) The extent to which decisions made and action taken are controlled by precedents, prescribed work practices, regulations or other guidelines;

(b) The degree of originality, judgement and development work invovled;

(c) The variety and the scope allowed by timing schedules.

(vi) **Seriousness of Errors.** What type of errors are possible in a job; and what would be the consequences of such errors in terms of additional expense to the company, rework or loss of goodwill?

(vi) **Hazards.** What type of hazards and risks to health are involved in the performance of duties? State frequency.

(viii) **Adverse Working Conditions.** Are there any physical conditions surrounding the work that are definitely disagreeable or uncomfortable? (Such as dirt, noise, weather, etc.)

(ix) **Contacts with Customers, the General Public or other Companies.** Indicate the organisational level of persons in other companies dealt with; the type, difficulty and importance of transactions handled; and the potential effects of such contacts on company goodwill. How contact is made — by telephone, personal contact or correspondence?

(x) **Contacts with Other Departments.** Indicate type, volume, importance and difficulty of transactions with other department of the company. How contact is made — by telephone, personal contact or correspondence?

(xi) **For the Safety of Others.** Show the extent of responsibility of protecting, safeguarding or eliminating hazard to fellow employees or the general public.

(xii) **For Company Funds or Property.** Does a job involve actual custody of, or personal accountability for, any company funds or portable tools and equipments? If so, state the amount of money or type of tools and equipment involved.

(xiii) **For Confidential Information.** Does the work involve contact with any confidential data? Does a job involve descretion to reveal this data? If so, explain the nature of data and extent of discretion.

(xiv) **For performance of Work Without Immediate Supervision.** Who assigns the work to an incumbent? How is the progress of work assignments checked by the supervisor? How frequently? What is the average duration of an assignment?

(xv) **For the Supervision of Others.** Does the work involve supervision or direction by others? If so :

(a) Describe the type of work and indicate the number of employees;

(b) The percentage of time spent on work similar to that to the subordinates involved.

Analyst Approved by

Notes

JOB DESCRIPTION (JD)

"Job description" is an important document basically descriptive in nature. It contains a statement of job anaysis. It provides both *organisational information* such as (location in structure, authority, etc.) and *functional information* (What the work is). It defines the sccope of job activities, major responsibilities, and positioning of the job in the organisation. It provides the worker, analyst, and supervisor with a clear idea of what the work must do to meet the demands of the job. Job Description describes 'jobs,' not 'job holders.' The movement of employees due to promotion, quits, etc. would create instability to job descriptions if people rather than jobs are described.

Job Description and Performance Assessment

Job description is different from performance assessment. It concerns such functions as planning, coordinating, and assigning responsibility; while the performance distance concerns the quality of performance itself. Though job description is not assessment, it provides an important basis for establishing assessment standards and objectives.

Job Description and Job Specification

Job description and job specification are the names given to the written and specially designed summary of significant findings from job analysis. Actually these are the by products of job analysis process. Though both are the descriptions but they give different information. While job description contains the main characteristics of the job, job specification is the outline of personnel qualifications regarded as essential to perform the job. Following are the main points of difference between these two :

(i) Job description describes in full about the job while job specification describes person's ability and qualifications required to perform the job.

(ii) Job description is the standard of job while job specification is the reflection of the ideal person required to do the job.

Thus, both these documents are distinct and different in nature but both are complementary. Both help in the proper selection, training and development programme as well as in job evaluation.

Definition of Job Description

1. *Edwin B. Flippo* : "The first and immediate product of the job analysis is the job description. As its title indicates, this document is basically descriptive in nature and constitutes a record of existing and pertinent job facts."

2. *Pigors and Myres* : "A pertinent picture (in writing) of the

organisational relationships, responsibilities and specific duties that constitute a given job or position. It defines a scope of responsibility and continuing work assignment that are sufficiently different from those of other job to warrant a specific title."

Contents of Job Description

1. Proper job title. The job title should be short, definite and suggestive of the nature of the job. The desirable qualities of job-holder should be clear from the title so that everty job should be distinguished from one another. Commerce and industry nomenclature, wherever applicable should always be sued in phrasing meaningful job titles.

2. Job summary. The findigns of the job analysis should be descriptively summarised so that all the necessary facts may be incorporated in paragraphs to make it convenient to identify the job. Primary, secondary and job other duties to be performed on the job should clearly be indicated separately.

3. Job location. Job location should be given in the description. It is where *i.e.,* in what department the job is to be performed.

4. Duties and responsibilities. The duties and responsibilities to be performed on the job arranged in chronological order with proper classification as primary, secondary and other duties should clearly be written in the job description. Time taken in performing the job and sub-jobs should also be mentioned.

5. Degree of supervision. Certain job like unskilled jobs require close supervision while other jobs like skilled or supervisory or managerial jobs require less supervision or no supervision. The degree of supervision, required on each job should be mentioned in job description.

6. Required machines, tools and materials. The machines, tools, equipment and materials required in the performance of each job should also be included in job description to indicate the nature and complexity of the job and help devising the training programmes.

7. Description of relation to other jobs. Description of relation to other jobs intensifies the vertical relationship of promotion and horizontal relationship of work-flow and procedures.

8. Description of working conditions. The working conditions, the job hazards and physical surroundings within the working area should be described. It will be helpful in job evaluation.

9. Description of amendments. Job description should be elastic enough as to incorporate all necessary amendments from time to time to make it up-to-date.

10. Mention of policies. The policies for the job-holder should be mentioned in the job description.

Preparing Job Description

Job description provides the data of the job in terms of duties and responsibilities. As the name suggests it is a descriptive document mentioning each and every aspect of the job in detail. In other words, it is a precis of the details collected by the job-analyst. In may be used in evaluating the job and determining the wage structure. It is a record for future reference and guidance.

Characteristics of a Good Job Description

(i) *Uptodate* : It should be kept uptodate, *i.e.,* necessary amendments and adjustments should be made from time to time.

(ii) *Short Tile* : Job title should be short, definite and suggestive as to indicate the nature of the work.

(iii) *Clear definition of Duties* : Primary, secondary and other duties and responsibilities should clearly be defined.

(iv) *Clear job specifications* : Job specifications should clearly be mentioned.

(v) *Short* : It should be descriptive but short.

Uses of Job Description

Job description has following uses :

1. Preliminary drafts can be used as a basis for productive group discussion, particularly if the process starts at the executive level.
2. It aids in the development of jobs specifications, which are useful in planning recruitment, in training and in hiring people with required skills.
3. It can be used to orient new employees toward basic responsibilities and duties.
4. It is a basic document used in developing performance standards.
5. It can be used for job evaluation, a wage and salary administration technique.
6. A job description enables the manager to frame suitable questions to be asked during an interview. It is particularly helpful when the application form is used as a tool for eliminating the unfit personnel. According to Zerga, who analysed 401 articles on job description about 30 years ago, a job description helps us in :

(i) Job grading and classification;

(ii) Transfers and promotions;

(iii) Adjustments of grievances;

(iv) Defining and outlining promotional steps;
(v) Establishing a common understanding of a job between employers and employees;
(vi) Investigating accidents;
(vii) Indicating faulty work procedures or duplication of papers;
(viii) Maintaining, operating and adjusting machinery;
(ix) Time and motion studies;
(x) Defining the limits of authority;
(xi) Indicating case of personal merit;
(xii) Facilitating job placement;
(xiii) Studies of health and fatigue;
(xiv) Scientific guidance;
(xv) Determining jobs suitable for occupational therapy;
(xvi) Providing *hiring* specifications and
(xvii) Providing performance indicators.

Job description helps top executives, in jointly discuss one another's responsibilities. Overlapping or confusion can then be pointed out; questions can be raised about the major thrust of each position, and problems of structure can be identified. *A job description becomes a vehicle for organisational change and improvement.*

Some companies have more than one job description for each job. A detailed version may be used in training and in evaluating a job, while a shorter version may be used in planning and hiring of management.

Guidelines for Writing a Job Description

Job descriptions are written by Personnel Department or its representatives. Following pattern is fairly typical, and used by many companies :[6]

1. A paragraph is allocated to each major task or responsibility.
2. Paragraphs are numbered and arranged in a logical order, task sequence or importance.
3. Sentences are begun with an active verb, *e.g.*, "types letters," "interviews the candidates," "collects, sorts out, routes and distributes mail."
4. Accuracy and simplicity are emphasised rather than an elegant style.

---

6. Valerie, Grant J., and Smith, G., *Personnel Administration and Industrial Relations*, Longmans Group Ltd., London, 1977, pp. 10-20.

5. Brevity is usually considered to be important but is largely conditioned by the type of job being analysed and the need for accuracy.
6. Examples of work performed are often quoted and are useful in making the job description explicit.
7. Job descriptions, particularly when they are used as basses for training, often incorporate details of the faults which may be encountered in operator tasks and safety check-points.
8. Statements of opinion, such as "dangerous situations are encountered," should be avoided.
9. When job descriptions are written for supervisory jobs, the main factors (such as manning, cost control, etc.) are identified and listed. Each factor is then broken down into a series of elements with a note on the supervisor's responsibility.

The British Institute of Management Publication adds four more guidelines :[7]

1. Give a clear, concise and readily understandable picture of the whole job;
2. Describe in sufficient details each of the main duties and responsibilities;
3. Indicate the extent of direction received and supervision given;
4. Ensure that a new employee understands the job if he reads the job description.

Limitations of Job Description

Job descriptions are not prefect reflections of the job. The object of a job description is to differentiate it from other jobs and set its outer limits. Exclusives tend to carry work patterns with them into new jobs, thus modifying the job drastically. Hence, care must be exercised in writing a job description to make it as accurate as possible. At the managerial or professional level, it should be reviewed and discussed after the job. *Jobs tend to be dynamic, not static, and a job description can quickly go out of date. Therefore, jobs should be constantly revised and kept up-to-date.* The personnel and the other departmental heads should be apprised of changes. Both supervisors and subordinates should understand the uses of job description. The relevant parties should agree that a job description fairly reflects the job.

---

7. British Institute of Management, *Job Evaluation : A Practical Guide for Managers* 1970.

Chart 8.2

A Specimen of a Job Description for a Supervisor

Job Title.................................... Supervisor...........................

JOB

Factor	*Elements*	*Supervisor's Responsibility*
(i) **Manning**	(a) Requisition for instructors	Act
	(b) Preparation of advertisements	Recommended
	(c) Interviewing candidates or instructor jobs-Accept/Reject	Act
	(d) Assessment of instructor's performance/ merit for pay purposes	Recommended
	(e) Discharging for misconduct	Recommended
	(f) Supervision of training centre instruction and ensuring that established performance standards are met	Act
	(g) Supervision of clerical and secretarial duties of training centre secretary	Act
(ii) **Equipment**	(a) Developing a system for safeguarding and distributing tools	Act
	(b) Operating a system for safeguarding and distributing tools	Delegate
	(c) Authorising within the budget limitations the purchase of small items of capital equipment, *i.e.,* tools	Act
	(d) Purchase of major items, *i.e.,* machines	Recommended
(iii) **Safety**	(a) Ensuring compliance with training centre safety regulations	Act
	(b) Preparation of accident reports	Act and Delegate
	(c) Requisition and issue of protective clothing	Act
	(d) Ensuring the use of protective clothing	Act and Delegate
(iv) **Cost Control**	(a) Preparation of annual cost budget for training Centre	Prepare and Recommend
	(b) Submission of reports on reasons for monthly budget variances to superiors	Act
(v) **Inspection**	Receipt of inspection reports on below standard work	Advise instructors
(vi) **Apprentice Trainees**	(a) Instruction of apprentices in training school	Delegate
	(b) Placement of apprentices in appropriate course	Act
	(c) Examination of reports on apprentices and allocation of apprentices today; Release for subsequent sessions	Act

(d) Assessment from apprentice feedback of the value of specific courses	Act
(e) Selection of alternative courses if the existing ones are inadequate	Recommended
(f) Preparation of documentation for rates for age rewards	Act
(g) Authorisation of rate for age rewards	Act
(h) Assessment from the reports of instructor and foreman for additional annual merit awards	Recommended
(i) Placement of apprentices on completion of training	Act with appropriate line supervisor
(j) Raising and processing documentation for those apprentices who resign	Act
(k) Discharge of apprentices failing to meet 80 per cent performance level	Recommended
(l) Maintenance of apprentice records	Delegate
(m) Preparation of work rotation for apprentices	Act

JOB SPECIFICATIONS

Job specifications translate the job description into terms of the human qualifications which are required for a successful performance of a job. They are intended to serve as a guide in job evaluation. As a guide in hiring, they deal with such characteristics as are available in an application bank, with testing, interviews, and checking of references. *It tells what kind of person to recruit and for what qualities that person should be tested.*

Kinds of Specification

The items to be included in job specifications vary according to the nature of an organisation and the uses to which they are put. However, items like age, sex, experience, skill, education, dexterity and personality and invariably included in job specifications; for example, 5 years experience; ability to lift 30 kgs; versatility in languages and fluency in speech; ability to type 100 words per minute and take shorthand dictation at 120 words per minute. The personnel department co-ordinates the writing of job descriptions and job specifications and secures agreement on the qualifications required.

These specifications relate to the following :

1. Physical characteristics. These include health, strength, endurance, age-range, body size, height, weight, vision, voice, poise, eye, hand and foot co-ordination, motor co-ordination, and colour discrimination.

2. Psychological characteristics. These include such qualities as manual dexterity, mechanical, aptitude, ingenuity, judgment, resourcefulness, analytical ability, mental concentration and alertness.

3. Personal characteristics or traits of temperament. These include personal appearance, good and pleasing manners, emotional stability, aggressiveness or submissiveness, extroversion or introversion, leadership, co-operativeness, initiative and drive, skill in dealing with others, unusual sensory qualities of sight, smell, hearing, adaptability, conversational ability etc.

4. Responsibilities. These include supervision of others, responsibility for production, process and equipment; responsibility for the safety of others; responsibility for generating confidence and trust : responsibility for preventing monetary loss.

5. Other features of a demographic nature. These include age, sex, education, experience and language ability.

Job specifications are based on the educated guesses of supervisors and personnel managers. They give their opinion as to who do they think should be considered for a job in terms of education, intelligence, training etc.

Definition of Job Specification

1. *Edwin B. Flippo* : "A job specification is a statement of minimum acceptable human qualities necessary to perform a job properly."

2. *Dale Yoder* : "The job specification as such is a summary popularly described, thus a specialised job description, emphasising personnel requirement and designed especially to facilitate selection and placement."

Contents of a Job Specification

1. Physical characteristics. These include height, weight, sight, physical structure, health etc.

2. Psychological characteristics. These include decision making ability, analytical view, mental ability, etc.

3. Personal characteristics. These include behaviour, mental stability, enthusiasm, leadership qualities, etc.

4. Personnel characteristics. This means the sense of responsibility in a person to be appointed on the job.

5. Qualifications and experience. These include academic qualification, experience, training, etc.

Both job description and job specification are interrelated as well as important tool in the job study they are important by products of job analysis. Both serve as a basis for scientific selection, promotion, training and development programmes. A job description is the standard description of the job while a job specification is the main specification. Job description tells what it to be done and what is the natrue of job;

on the other hand job specification tells us what qualities are needed in the prospective job holder.

JOB OF PERSONNEL MANAGER

According to the Dictionary of Occupational Titles, published by the U.S. Training and Employment serivce the description for a Personnel Managers job is as follows :[8]

He is Director personnel; manager, employee relations; Personnel supervisor.

"Plans and carries out policies relating to all phases of personnel activities :

"Organisations, recruitment, selection and training procedures, and directs activities of sub-ordinates directly concerned. Confers with company and union official to establish pension and insurance plans, workmen's compensation policies, recreational, and educational activities. Studies personnel records for information, such as educational background, work record and supervisor's reports, to determine personnel suitable for promotions and transfers. May represent — company in negotiating wage agreements with labour representatives. May act as liasion between management and labour within organisation."

CHART 8.3

Specimen of Personnel Specifications of Works Manager

Personnel Specifications

(Interpretation of job description in terms of the kind of person suitable for the job)

(i) **Physical Characteristics**

Essential	Good health.
	No significant disabilities in voice, hearing and eyesight.
Dress	Neat conventional dress.
	Well groomed and takes trouble with details of personal appearance.

(ii) Attainments

Essential	At least a Bachlor of Science or engineering; evidence of occupational success in previous employment; production management experience — minimum of 5 years. Age, not above 30 yrs. Knowledge of work study, work programming, quality control and stock control techniques and experience of negotiating with trade unions at plant level.
Desirable	A degree in business, management.
(iii) Essential	Top 10 per cent.
	An intelligent approach to the solution of business problems.

8. U.S. Training and Employment Service, *Dictionary of Occupational Titles*, Washington, third edition, 1965, p. 448.

(iv) **Special Aptitudes**

Essential	Fluency in speaking and writing; analytical skills; ability to prepared and understand basic statistical information; competence in arith metic; ability to read B/S and P & L A/c. and understand their significance; high degree of listening skill; evidence of ability to plan ahead and organise the work of others.

(v) **Interests**

Essential	Evidence of some interest outside work but nothing specific.

(vi) **Disposition**

Essential	Acceptability to other people and previous occupational evidence of influencing others : ability to accept responsibility without undue strain; co-operative in relations with others.

(vii) **Motivation**

Essential	Ambitious-evidence of fairly rapid promotion and the acheivement of high but realistic goals; must be willing to control output to meet vigorous performance standards/targets.

(viii) **Circumstances**

Essential	Ability to work long hours if required.

Based on Statistical Analysis

Job specifications may also be based on statistical analysis to determine the relationship between : (1) some *predictor* or *human trait* (as height, intelligence, finger dexterity, etc) and (2) some *indicator* or *criterion* of job effectiveness (such as performance as rated by the supervisor.

The statistical analysis comprises five steps : (i) analysing the job and determining criteria of success; (ii) selecting personnel traits which should predict successful performance; (iii) testing candidates for these traits; (iv) measuring these candidates' subsequent job performance and (v) statistically analysing the relationship between the 'human trait' and 'job performance.

Job Performance Standard

While job descriptions essentially set *what is to be done as a job,* performance standards describe *how much and how well a job* is performed. Job performance induces "goal-consciousness" among superiors and subordinates. It is a means for performance review based on actual accomplishment. Performance standard may be in the form of a job description expanded to include a statement of job goals for some period; or it may be separate statements supplemental to a job description. These should be written in quantitiative terms, whenever possible.

According to Schlech, the advantage of written job performance standards is that each person knows specifically what is expected of him in terms of goals and targets. But, in actual practice, some job aspects are difficult to reduce to quantitative terms. When this is so, qualitative statements must be made.[9]

Targets for safety, reduction in waste, increase in sales, the building of new plants, and the starting of new production are all performance standards implicit in jobs.

According to Schlech, job performance standards should be based on overall objectives and should spread from the top throughout the entire organisation. However, such standards should not be imposed upon members in an autocratic and dictatorial manner, for that would generate resistance. If subordinates participate in setting their own standards, they are likely to set them high and be committed to achieving them.[10]

Standards must be within the capabilities of the person involved in a job; and the motivational system of an enterprise must result in a willingness of a person to attain them. Unrealistically high standards are likely to be a source of friction between supervisors and subordinates, and lead to low performance.

Group discussions of targets and standards do result in getting things done, besides enhancing creativity and team effort. Likert says : "The salesmen in the offices using group methods of supervision sell more on the average than do men in the other offices, and they have more favourable attitudes towards their work."[11]

Zero Defects Programmes

"Zero-Defects" programmes have been developed especially in the armed services, jet aircraft, aero-space, the defence industries, etc. where reliable products are needed and for this special programmes are designed to encourage the commitment of employees to high quality standards and to "do it right the first time." Such programmes are also known as *PRIDE* and *Targer-Zero*. They are based on the basic assumption that most people want to do 'quality' work provided they are given the proper support and recognition. The recognition may be given in the form of plaques, certificates, letters, news items, etc.

Work Rules

Work rules are essential in organisational life. They are pre-

---

9. Schlech, E.C., *Management by Results*, McGraw Hill Book Company, New York, 1961.

10. Schlech, E.C., *Executive Management of Personnel,* Prentice Hall, Englewood Cliffs, 1958, p. 22.

11. Likert, Rensis, *The Human Organisation,* McGraw Hill Book Co., New York, 1967, pp. 57-59.

determined decisions that a certain course of aaction will be taken if certain contingencies arise. They are an integral part of the systems designed to facilitate all broad operational processes because they are adjuncts of job description and performance standards. They are the minimum standards of conduct or performance which apply to groups of persons. They serve the following purposes :

(i) They canalise the process of an enterprise in the direction of its goals.

(ii) They serve as control devices, since the management uses them as standards against which to apply sanctions in order to ensure a reasonable level of conformity.

(iii) They ensure predictability of behaviour so that an organisation may function without undue disturbance, and its total performance is achieved.

Violation of Work Rules

Rules are framed by the chief executive and implemented by the personnel manager. Once these rules are endorsed by the top management or are negotiated into a Labour Agreement, all the managers are responsible for their enforcement.

Any violation of rules usually results in punishment or penalty. Offences considered serious enough to warrant immediate discharge are dishonesty, insubordination, drunkenness on duty, and deliberate damage to material or property. Lesser penalties include oral or written warnings, demotions, transfers or disciplinary lay-off.

following partial list of the offences, which may lead to disciplinary action, has been compiled by the American Management Association.

— Absence without leave;
— Dishonesty, deception, fraud;
— Drunkenness or possession of liquor on the job;
— Deliberate damage to material or property;
— Fighting on the job;
— Stealing;
— Falsification of accounts;
— Failure to meet work standards;
— Smoking in prohibited or hazardous areas;
— Use of abusive, threatening, or profane language;
— Insubordination;
— Repreated tardiness;
— Carrying concealed weapons;

— Immoral conduct;

— Sleeping on duty;

— Erratic work schedule.

Work rules should be reasonable otherwise they are laible to be circumvented, and lead to subterfuge and resentment. If they are too lax they may lead to non-completion of the work in time. If they are arbitrary, they may be resented and ignored. If they are reasonable they assist in the attainment of an organisation's need for security, order, predictability, and avoidance of physical harm. Rules should have a definite organisational purpose, and must not conflict with the employees' interest.

QUESTIONS FOR EXERCISE

1. What is job analysis? Describe its procedure and significance in personnel management.
2. "Job analysis is the process of critically evaluating the operations, duties and relationship of the jobs." Evaluate this statement and give meaning of job analysis.
3. What are the different methods of gathering job information for job analysis?
4. What do you know about questionnaire or survey method of job analysis?
5. What is your idea of interview method for job analysis?
6. What is the significance of observation method for job analysis? In what way is record method useful for the job analysis?
7. Explain the meaning and contents of job description. How is it prepared and by whom? Explain the characteristics of a good job description.
8. "Job description is the extensive discussion of objective, scope, duties and responsibilities of a specific job." Discuss this statement.
9. Define job specification and give its contents. Distinguish it form job description.

9

Recruitment, Personnel Selection and Placement

According to Kempner, recruitment is the first stage in the process which continues with selection and ceases with the placement of the candidate.[1] It is the next step in the procurement function, after the manpower planning. It makes it possible to acquire the number and types of people necessary to ensure the continued operation of the organisation. *It is the discovering of potential applicants for actual or anticipated organisational vacancies.* Thus, it is a 'linking activity' bringing together those with jobs and those seeking jobs.

Definition of Recruitment

1. *Yoder and others* : "Recruitment is a process to discover the sources of manpower to meet the requirements of the staffing schedule and to employ effective measures for attracting that manpower in adequate numbers of facilitate effective selection of an efficient working force."[2]

2. *F.B. Flippo* : "It is a process of searching for prospective employees and stimulating and encouraging them to apply for jobs in an organisation. It is often termed *positive* in that it stimulates people to apply for jobs to increase the 'hiring ratio,' *i.e.,* the number of applicants for a job. Selection, on the other hand tends to be *negative* because it rejects a good member of those who apply, leaving only the best to be hired."[3]

Factors Affecting Recruitment

Large or small all organisations engage in recruiting activity, though not to the same extent. It differs with : (i) the size of the organisation;

---

1. Kempner, T. (ed.), *Handbook of Management*, Weidenfield and Nicolson, London, 1971, p. 310.
2. Robbins, Stephen P., *Personnel : The Management of Human Resources*, Prentice-Hal Inc., Englewood Cliffs, New Jersey, 1978, p. 75.
3. Flippo, Edwin B., *Personnel Management,* McGraw-Hill Kogahusha, Ltd., New Delhi, 1980, p. 131.

(ii) the employment conditions in the community where the organisation is located; (iii) the effects of past recruiting efforts which show the organisation's ability to locate and keep good performing people; (iv) working conditions and salary and benefit packages offered by the organisation — which may influence turnover and necessitate future recruiting; (v) the rate of growth of organisation; (vi) the level of seasonality of operations and future expansion and production programmes and (vii) cultural, economic and legal factors, etc.

Theories Regarding Recruitment

Just as the recruiter has a choice whom to recruit and whom not, so also the prospective employee has to make the decision if he should apply for that organisation's job. According to Behling and others, the individual makes this decision usually on the basis of following three different theories :[4]

1. The objective factor theory. It views the process of organisational choice as being one of weighing and evaluating a set of measurable characteristics of employment offers, such as pay, benefits, location, opportunity for advancement, the nature of the work to be performed, and educational opportunities.

2. The critical contact theory. It suggests that the typical candidate is unable to make a meaningful differentiation of organisation's offers in terms of objective or subjective factors, because of his limited or very short contact with the organisation. Choice can be made only when the applicant can readily perceive the factors such as the behaviour of the recruiter, the nature of the physical facilities, and the efficiency in processing paper work associted with the application.

3. The subjective factor theory. It emphasises the congruence between personality patterns and the 'image' of the organisation, *i.e.*, choices are made on a highly personal and emotional basis.

Constraints on the Freedom of Manager to Recruit

1. The image of the organisation. A prospective candidate may not be interested in getting job in a particular organisation either because its reputation or goodwill is not good in the community, or because the conditions of work are unsafe or it is indifferent to the need of the community. These factors reduce organisations ability to attract the best personnel available.

2. The unattractive job. If the job is regarded as boring, hazardous, anxiety creating or lacking in promotion potentional, people would not be attracted to such an organisation.

4. Behling, O, Labovitz, G. and M. Gainer, "College Recruiting : A Theoretical Base," *Personnel Journal*, No. 47, 1968, pp. 13-19.

3. Internal organisational policies. If the policy aims at providing promotion to its employee from within, people would be attracted to it. Such a policy enjoys several advantages such as that of creating good public relations, building high morale, encouraging good people who are ambitious and improving the probability of a good selection.

4. Union requirements. These can also restrict recruiting sources as some unions emphasise recruitment to members of the unions only. In such a situation management has to recruit from a restricted supply.

5. Constitutional influence. According to national constitution, an employer cannot distinguish any individual, on the basis of physical appearance, sex or religious background, for purposes of recruitment.

Chart 9.1 shows the place of recruitment in the entire selection process.

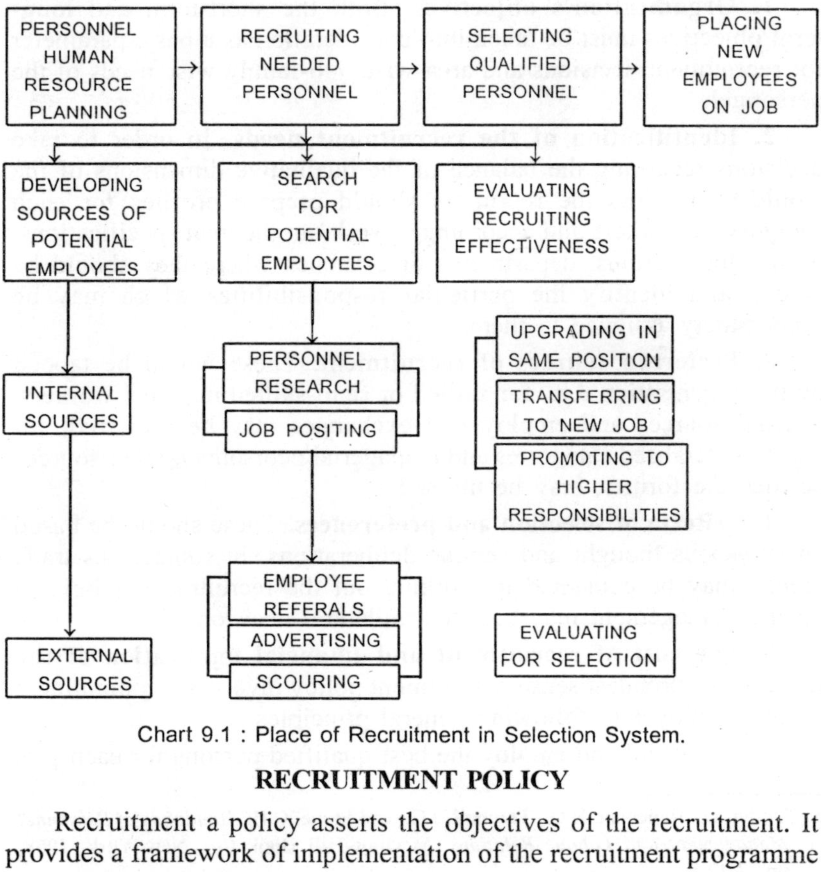

Chart 9.1 : Place of Recruitment in Selection System.

RECRUITMENT POLICY

Recruitment a policy asserts the objectives of the recruitment. It provides a framework of implementation of the recruitment programme in the form of procedures. As Yoder and others oberve :[5] "Such a policy may involve a commitment to broad principles such as filling vacancies with the best qualified individuals. It may embrace several issues such as extent of promotion from within, attitudes of enterprise in recruiting its old employees, handicaps, minority groups, women employees, part-time employees, friends and relatives of present employees. It may also involve the organisation system to be developed for implementing recruitment programme and procedures to the employed."

A well considered and pre-planned recruitment policy, based on corporate goals, study of environment and the corporate needs, avoiding hasty or ill-considered decisions may go a long way to man the organisation with the right type of personnel.

Elements of good recruitment policy

1. Organisation's objectives. Both the short-term and long-term objectives must be taken into consideration as a basic parameter for recruitment decisions and area-wise, job-family-wise needs of the personnel.

2. Identification of the recruitment needs. In order to take decisions regarding the balance of the qualitative dimensions of the would-be recruits the recruiters should prepare profiles for each category of workers and accordingly work out the man specifications, decide the sections, departments or branches where they should be placed and identify the particular responsibilities which may be immediately assigned to them.

3. Preferred sources of recruitment. These would be tapped by the organisation *e.g.,* for skilled or semi-skilled mannual workers, internal sources and employment exchanges may be preferred; for highly specialised categories and managerial peorsonnel, other sources besides the former, may be utilised.

4. Criteria of selection and preferences. These should be based on conscious thought and serious deliberations. In some cases trade unions may be consulted in working out the recruitment policy. In others, management may take the unilateral decision.

5. The cost of recruitment and financial implication of the same. In its broadest sense, recruitment policy involves a commitment by the employer to following general principles :

(i) To find and employ the best qualified persons for each job;

---

5. Yoder, D., Heneman, H.G., Turnbull, J.G., and Stone, C.H., *Handbook of Personnel Management and Labour Relations*, McGraw-Hill Book Co., New York, 1968, pp. 7.27.5

(ii) To retain the best and most promising of those hired;

(iii) To offer promising opportunities for life-time working careers and

(iv) To provide programmes and facilities for personal growth on the job.

BROAD GUIDELINES FOR STAFFING

According to Dale Yoder, "the recruitment policy is concerned with quantity and qualifications (*viz.*, and Q1 and Q2) of manpower." It establishes following broad guidelines for the staffing process :[6]

(i) To carefully observe the letter and spirit of the relevant public policy on hiring and, on the whole, employment realtionship;

(ii) To provide individual employees with the maximum of employment security avoiding frequent lay-off or lost time;

(iii) To provide each employee with an open road and encouragement in the continuing development of his talents and skills;

(iv) To assure each employee of the organisation interest in his personal goals and employment objectives;

(v) To assure employees of fairness in all employment relationships, including promotions and transfers;

(vi) To avoid cliques which may develop when several members of the same household or community are employed in the organisation;

(vii) To provide employment in jobs which are engineered to meet the qualifications of handicapped workers and minority sections and

(viii) To encourage one or more strong, effective, responsible trade unions among the employees.

PREREQUISITES OF A GOOD RECRUITMENT POLICY

1. It should be in conformity with its general personnel policies;
2. It should be flexible enough to meet the changing needs of an organisation;
3. It should be so designed as to ensure employment opportunities for its employees on a long-term basis so that the goals of the organisation should be achievable; and it should develop the potentialities of employees;

6. Yoder, Dale, *Personnel Management and Industrial Relations*, Prentice-Hall of India, New Delhi, 1972, p. 263.

4. It should match the qualities of employees with the requirements of the work for which they are employed and
5. It should highlight the necessity of establishing job analysis.

RECRUITMENT ORGANISATION

The most commonly adopted practice is to centralise the recruitment and selection function in a single office. All employment activity should be centralised if the policies of the top management are to be implemented consistently and efficiently. There a possibility of maximum efficiency and success in hiring only when personnel requisitions go through one central source and all employment records are kept up-to-date.

Advantages of centralisation of recruitment and selection.[7]

1. It reduces the administrative cost associated with selection by consolidating all activity in a single office;
2. It relieves line officers of the details involved in hiring workers, which is common under a decentralised plan;
3. It tends to make the selection of workers scientific;
4. It makes possible the development of a centralised manpower pool in a company;
5. It provides a wider opportunity for placing an applicant in several departments of the company;
6. It ends to reduce favouritism as a basis for selection.

Employee Office

This centralised department is generally known as the *Employee Office*, or the *Recruitment Section.* The staff personnel is attached to it. Thus specialists concentrate upon the recruitment function; and soon become very efficient in the use of various recruitment techniques.

Employee office should be properly equipped with furniture. Its waiting room should be roomy, clean and well ventilated. It should have lighting facilities and drinking water, and it should be comfortable. It should also have a table or a counter so that candidates may fill in their application blanks conveniently. The personnel records should be filled in a room accessible to the interviewer.[8] Employee's office is concerned with the following functions :

1. Establishing employment standards;
2. Making initial contact with prospective employees;

---

7. Keith, L.A., Gubeline, C.E., *Business Management*, 1958, p. 197.
8. National Industrial Conference Board, "Organisaiton of Facilities and Personnel," *Studies in Personnel Policy,* No. 144, 154, p. 1.

3. Conducting final interviews;
4. Testing;
5. Conducting physical examinations;
6. Conducting final interviews;
7. Filling out necessary forms and record keeping;
8. Introducing the employee to his superior and
9. Following up the employee.

Recruiting procedure is merely informal in small organisaton generally the "line official" may be responsible to handle this function. But in larger organisations, it is entrusted to a staff unit with Personnel or Industrial Relations Department.

IMPORTANCE OF RECRUITMENT METHOD

The method of recruitment that an origination uses directly affects the efficiency of its selection and placement programme in, at least, three ways :

1. It determines the number of qualified applicants applying for a particular position.

2. It influences how well the organization meets its obligation to hire minority group members and women. This usually entails advertising in minority newspapers, sending recruitment to minority colleges and high schools, and cooperating with such agencies as the Urban League that specialize in working with the minority community. It also involves actively searching for qualified women when filling positions not traditionally held by women.

3. It can sometimes affect the subsequent turnover, rates of employees. Several studies have shown that when recruiters give applicants realistic expectations about a particular job by pointing out both the positive and negative aspects of it, lower turnover rates result. This is particularly true when the job is fairly complex in terms of the psychical and mental demands placed on the incumbents, as in the case of managerial and sales positions. Often recruiters give applicants unrealistic expectations regarding the company and their future jobs, thereby resulting in frustration, dissatisfaction, and early termination. One possible solution to this problem used by several companies is a work sample preview, which gives the prospective employee a realistic picture of what will be expected of him or her. This involves providing films, videotapes, printed booklets, or job visit to realistically depict training and work.

SOURCES OF RECRUITMENT

Sometimes organisations recruit internally by using computerized data banks that store information about the skills, knowledge and abilities of each employee. When a new position becomes available, the computer can survey the entire work force in a matter of minutes. Quit rates (number of hired persons who subsequently quit) by recruitment sources has been investigated. If an organisation limits its recruiting to its best sources, it can reduce its quit rates — thereby resulting in substantial cost savings. In general, employee referrals have been found to be among the best sources of applicants.

Among the many external sources that organizations use to actively recruit new employees are the following : (1) advertising in newspapers, radio, professional magazines and local television; (2) visits to the college and high school campuses; (3) government and private employment agencies; (4) word-of-mouth recruiting by current employees, who are given incentives for doing this; (5) labour unions and (6) professional organizations and societies.

A. Internal sources of recruitment. Internal sources of recruitment means promotion of workers from the lower rank to the upper rank. Most of the companies have a policy of promotion from within. Vacancies other than at the lowest level are filled up by promoting the personnel to the higher office. Thus, there is a chain of promotions that can be filled from those lowest in ranks by giving them training to make them eligible for higher position in the organisation. Practice of internal recruitment leads to a healthy and progressive atmosphere, lower cost of training and a high rate labour turnover. This source of recruitment is generally adopted to fill vacancies of middle and top personnel. Lowest recruitment is generally from external sources.

B. External sources of recruitment. Vacancies at lowest level or recruitment of the time of expansion of the firm or where job specification cannot be met by the present employees, require external sources of manpower supply. Following are amongst the most commonly used outside sources.

1. Recruitment of present employees. Sometimes, the present employees recommend their friends and relatives to the organisation. It is expected that the present employees will command only such candidated who have the potential and qualification to meet the company's standard of expectation. However, in order to avoid nepotism a great care should be taken in selecting a person among those recommended by the present staff.

2. Recruitment of former employees. Former employees are persons who have ever worked in the enterprise and have been laid off or have left the organisation for personnel reasons and now wish to return. These former employees having good record on their credit may be prepared for filling up new vacancies. These will require less initial training to bring them up to the standard of production than strangers to the enterprise.

3. Contracts of intermediaries. This system of recruitment is most current in Indian industries. Intermediaries are generally known as jobbers, Mukaddams, Choudhary or contractors. Management consult intermediaries at the time of their requirements. This system of recruitment has many disadvantages.

4. Recruitment at the gate. Direct recruitment of unskilled and semi-skilled workers is generally made at the gate of the factory or office. The number of vacancies, nature of work and time of interview are notified by the personnel department on the blackboard at gate. Prospective candidated attend the interview at the appointed time and get the appointment.

5. Use of unsolicited applications. Nowadays an organisation of repute draws many unsolicited applications at the company's office. These applications are examined off and on whenever needed to locate suitable candidates for the job.

6. Advertisement in newspapers and journals. This is the most popular source of recruiting staff. Though employers resort to advertising for all types of vacancies, but it is the most suitable source for filling the vacancies of technical and senior personnel. Particulars regarding the job and the qualifications of the prospective candidate are given in the advertisement in newspapers, journals and magazines. Candidates possessing the requisite qualifications apply for the job in reference to the advertisement. This system attracts the applicants of requisite calibre.

7. Visit to schools, colleges, universities and technical institutions. These are a very useful source of recruitment for a full range of jobs. The employment managers of the enterprises maintain a close liaison with the universities and schools of technology particularly for recruiting officer Apprentices or Management Trainees. Universities and technical institutions also empanel the promising young talents for employment and refer their names to the prospective employers as and when asked for.

8. Notification to Employment Exchanges. Employment Exchanges are the most popular source of recruitment for unskilled, skilled, or semi-skilled operative jobs. The job seekers get their names registered with employment exchanges, managed and operated by the Central and State Governments. The employers notify the vacancies to such exchanges and the exchanges refer the names of prospective candidates to the employers.

9. Recruitment through private agencies. Some private agencies also do recruit the technical and professional personnel for a company. They provide a nation-wide service in attempting to match the demand and supply of personnel. Many private agencies tend to specialise in a particular type of work like sales, office, engineers, etc.

10. Recommendation from professional bodies. Some professional institutions like Institute of Charted Accountant, ICWA, Institute of Company Secretary etc. maintain a register of qualified persons from which they recommend the names of the job seekers to the employers when asked for.

11. Assistance by personnel consultants. Nowadays consultants who specialise in the recruitment of managers and other senior officials are also called upon to assist the management in filling of these posts. At the time of recruitment of the senior officials companies hire the services of these consultants. On receiving requisition from the client companies, these consultant agencies advertise job descriptions in leading newspapers and periodicals without disclosing the names of the employers. The applications received are passed on to the concerned employers. If asked by the company these firms may screen, interview and select the candidates for the company.

12. Assistance of trade unions. Trade unions assist in recruiting the staff in some companies. This cooperation helps in developing better labour relations. However, this source of labour supply is not reliable since sometimes trade unions support a candidate who is not fit for the job and is not acceptable to management. This worsens the labour relations.

13. Making part-time employees full time. Sometimes, persons are employed to dispose off heavy seasonal work or the arrears of work temporarily on part-time basis. These part-time employees are a good source of labour supply as and when vacancies occur. If they fulfil the requisite qualifications to suit the jobs, vacancies are filled up among them.

14. Leasing of personnel. Short-term fluctuations in personnel needs are sometimes stabilised through leasing of personnel for some specified period from other industries, offices and units. This system of leasing is well adopted by the public sector organisations. The acute shortage of managerial personnel, particularly at higher levels in public sector leads them to borrow the personnel of requisite calibre from the Government departments. They are given an option to choose either their parent services or the present organisation at the end of their term.

No source is good or bad in itself in all circumstances and for all employees. No single source of recruitment can suit all the companies for filling up the posts of different nature and at different times. Fore recruiting the unskilled workers, direct recruitment at gate of friends and relatives of existing employees or casual workers may be the best sources of recruitment. For the recruitment of managers and high officials at various levels, consultants, professional bodies, universities and technical colleges may be the good sources of recruitment for skilled or semi-skilled operative personnel. Finally, the suitability of the source of labour supply depends upon the size of the company, nature of job and the supply of qualified personnel.

CHART 9.2

Recruiting Practices and a Firm's Position in the Labour Market

Degree of Tightness in the Labour Market	*Source Used for Recruitment*	*Area Covered for Recruitment*
1. Most loose	Direct hiring	Immediate vicinity
2. Intermediate	Unions, friends and relatives; private and public agencies	Part of an urban industrial area
3. Tight	Advertising, nearby special sources (colleges, private agencies)	The whole urban industrial area
4. Most tight	Labour scouting	Regional and national

According to Flippo, the present tendency among most business firms is to "home grow" their executive leaders.[9] Koontz and O'Donnel rightly observe that the policy should be to "raise" talent rather than "raid" for it.[10]

Recruitment Practices in India

I.I.P.M. has classified the different sources for recruitment in India as follows :[11] (i) Within the organisation; (ii) *Badli* or temporary workers; (iii) Employment agencies; (iv) Casual callers; (v) Applicants introduced by friends and relatives in the organisaiton; (vi) Advertisements and (vii) Labour contractors. The following methods were used to recruit employees[12] according to a survey of public and private sector employers by Prof. Basavaraj.

1. In the public sector (steel units), the major sources of

9. Flippo, E.B., *op. cit.*

10. Koontz and O'Donnel, *Principles of Management*, McGraw-Hill Book Co., New York, 1972 p. 418.

11. I.I.P.M. *op. cit.,* pp. 219-221.

12. Rudrabasavaraj M.N., *Personnel Administration Policies in India*, V.M.N. Institute of Cooperative Management, Pune, 1969, pp. 105-107.

recruitment in order of preference. (i) Casual callers or employment seekers; (ii) Newspaper advertisements; (iii) Scheduled tribes and scheduled cates; (iv) Employment exchanges; (v) Other public undertakings; (vi) Internal advertisement; (vii) Displaced persons; (viii) Relative and friends; (ix) Employee recommendations and (x) Institutions.

In the public sector (heavy engineering), the sources for non-supervisory staff. (i) Employment exchanges; (ii) External advertisement; (iii) Internal advertisement; (iv) Central training institute; (v) Introduction by the liaison officer of a corporation; (vi) Deputation personnel and (vii) Transfers from other public undertakings.

2. In the private sector. The survey disclosed that the procedures, though formulated, were not institutionalised in character. In some organisations, preference was given to sons and relatives of employees and to local people. In order of preference, the major sources are :[13] (i) Advertisements; (ii) Employment exhanges; (iii) Relatives and friends; (iv) Casual callers and (v) Employee recommendations.

The Problem of the "Sons of the Soil"

In recent years a controversy has arisen over giving preference to "Sons of the Soil" in recruitment. In this connection the National Commission on Labour has observed : "The solution has to be sought in terms of the primacy of common citizenship, geographical mobility and economic feasibility of locating industrial units, on the one hand, and local aspiration on the other." It has suggested that :[14]

1. Young persons from families whose lands are acquired for industrial use should be provided training opportunities for employment in jobs which are likely to be created in new units set up on these lands;

2. To remove unjustified apprehensions among local candidates, the following steps should be taken to supervise the implementation of the directives of the Government of India on recruitment for public sector projects :

(i) While recruiting unskilled employees, first preference should be given to persons displaced from the areas acquired for the projects. The next to be preferred should be those who have been living in the same vicinity.

(ii) The selection of persons to posts in lower scales should not be left entirely to the head of the unit. It should be made

13. *Ibid.*, p. 109.

14. *Report of the National Commission on Labour*, New Delhi, 1969.

through a recruitment committee, with a nominee of the government of the state in which the unit is located.

(iii) In the case of middle level technicians whose recruitment has to be on an all-India basis, a member of the State Public Service Commission should be associated in making selections in addition to the State Government official on the Board of Directors.

(iv) Apart from the report sent to the concerned Ministry at the Centre, the undertaking should send a statement to the State Government at regular intervals, preferably every quarter, about the latest employment and recruitment position.

The Commission has suggested these steps for employment in the public sector. It is of the opinion that they should apply equally to recruitment in the private sector, though the mechanism to regulate this recruitment would necessarily differ from that in the public sector. In India traditional methods for recruitment of industrial labour such casual or *badli* workers on lists maintained by the factory; the use of jobbers, *sardars, mukadams*, etc., employees' relatives and dependants and undertaking's own labour force, etc., and contract labour are still used for getting labour in textile industry, for building and construction industry, digging of canals, building of roads and dams, etc.

Large industrial complexes have developed a more 'committed' labour force. There are a number of Crafts Training Schools — Industrial Training Institutes; Advanced Vocational Training Institutes at Bombay, Calcutta, Hyderabad, Kanpur, Ludhiana and Madras; Seven Craft Instructors Training Schools; and an Institute for Training of Foremen at Bangalore for supplying skilled operatives.

PERSONNEL SELECTION

Selection (Hiring) Procedure

The selection procedure is concerned with securing relevant information about an applicant in a number of steps or stages. Its objective is to determine whether an applicant meets the qualifications for a specific job. It seeks to choose the applicant who is most likely to perform well in that job.

Successive Hurdles Technique

The hiring procedure is essentially a series of methods or steps or stages by which additional information is secured about the applicant. It may be compared to a series of successive hurdles or barirers which an applicant must cross. These are intended as screens, and designed to eliminate an unqualified applicant at any point in the process. This known as the *successive hurdles technique.*

Non-Random Process

Accroding to Dale Yoder, "the hiring process is of one or many 'go, no-go' gauges. Candidates are screened by the application of these tools. Qualified applicants go on to the next hurdle, while the unqualified are eliminated." According to the Blum and Nylor an effective selection programme is a non-random process because those selected have been choosen on the basis of the assumption that they are more likely to be "better" employees than those who have been rejected.[15] Chart 9.3 gives the hiring requirements as outlined by Yoder.[16]

Selection processes or activities typically follow a standard pattern, beginning with an initial screening interview and concluding with the final employment decision. According to National Industrial Conference Board the traditional selection process includes : preliminary screening interview; completion of application form; employment tests; comprehensive interview; background investigations physical examination and final employment decision to hire.[17]

PERSONNEL SELECTION POLICY

While formulating a selection policy, due consideration should be given to organisational requirements as well as technical and professional dimensions of selection procedures. Yoder and others have suggested golas, technology issues, cost factors, extent of formality, etc. In other words, an effective policy must assert the "why" and "what" aspects of the organisational objectives."

Essentials of Selection Procedure

1. Nature of selection. It should be safe, because a faulty selection affects not only the training period that may be needed, but also results in heavy expenditure on the new employee and the loss that may be incurred by the organisation in case the job-occupant fails on his job.

2. The Policy of the company and the attitude of the management. As a practice some companies usually hire more than the actual number needed with a view to removing the unfit persons from the jobs.

---

15. Blum, M.L., and Nylor, J.C., *Industrial Psychology — Its Theoretical and Social Foundations,* Harper and Row Publishers, New York.

16. Yoder, Dale, *op. cit.,* p. 229.

17. National Industrial Conference Board, "Organisation of facilities and personnel, *Studies in Personnel Policies* No. 144, 1954 p. 1.

CHART 9.3

Hiring Requirements

Types of Qualifications or Specifications	*Types of Gauges*
1. Arbitrary	1. Application blank
Security	2. Security check
Sex	3. Police records
Age	4. Personnel records
2. Physical health and adequacy	Physical Examination
3. Skills (including specialised knowledge)	1. Application blank
	2. Education, training, apprenticeship
	3. Grades
	4. Exployment records
	5. References
	6. Biography
	7. Trade tests
4. Experience	1. Application blank
	2. Biography
	3. Employment records
	4. References
	5. Interviews
5. Aptitude (including intelligence.	1. Employment records
	2. Personnel appraisals
	3. References
	4. Tests
6. Interests	1. Application blank
	2. In
	3. Reference
	4. Biography
	5. Test in
7. Emotional maturity, moods, motivations	1. Biography
	2. Employment records
	3. Tests
8. Attitudes	1. Interviews
	2. References
	3. Personnel appraisals
	4. Attitude-Morale scales.

3. The length of the probationary or the trial period. The longer the period, the greater the uncertainty in the minds of the selected candidate about his future.

Preliminary requirements of the hiring process :

1. *Authority to hire* : This authority comes from the employment requisition, as developed by an analysis of the work-load and work force.
2. *Standard* : There must be some standard or personnel with which a prospective employee may be compared, *i.e.*, there should available, beforehand, a comprehensive job description and job specifications as developed by a Job Analysis.
3. *Sufficient number of applicants* : There must be a sufficient number of applicants from whom the required number of employees may be selected.

Thus, selection process is a tool in the hands of the management to differentiate the qualified and unqualified applicants by applying various techniques such as interviews, tests, etc. Thus, selection is a negative process of employment in which only a few qualify for the job and offered employment while all others are denied the opportunities. It is a decision-making process where the management decides certain norms and principles to adhere to standards on the basis of which, a discrimination between qualified and unqualified candidates may be made. A sound selection policy ensures the selection of a suitable candidate.

Procedure of Personnel Selection

1. Scrutiny of application forms. Selection procedure starts only after the applications are received by a concern. Considering the standards set out by the organisation these applications are scrutinised. The applicants are screened out at each step.

2. Priliminary interview. Its purpose is to eliminate the unqualified or unsuitable candidate. It should be brief to have an idea of general education, experience, training, appearance, personality and salary requirements of the candidate etc.

3. Application Blank. A Blank Application Form or Application Blank is a weeding out device in the selection procedure. It is supplied to the successful candidates in preliminary interviews. Application Blanks give a written record of the following informations :

(i) *Identification* : Such as family background, date and place of birth, age, sex, height, citizenship, marital status etc.

(ii) *Education* : It includes information about academic career, subjects taken at various school certificate and degree levels, grade, division or place awarded in school and college, technical qualification etc.

(iii) *Experience* : Giving full details of past jobs such as nature of work, job responsibilities, periods involved, designations, salaries with allowances, reasons for leaving the present assignment etc.

(iv*) Expected salaries* : Allowances and other fringe benefits.

(v) *Community activities* : These consist of details regarding extra-curricular activities, hobbies, position held in social organisation such as clubs, management association etc.

(vi) *References* : These may be gathered from reliable persons.

4. Employment Tests. These days psychological and other tests are becoming increasingly popular, as a part of the selection process. The personnel department may guide and help in the selection of types of tests appropriate for a particular position.

(a) *Trade Tests* : Technical jobs require trade test. The purpose of trade test is to assess the capabilities of the candidates for the type of job which is being offered to them. For example, for recruitment of a stenographer in an office, a test can be taken to check his speed at dictation and typing.

(b) *Psychological Tests* : As the individual differ from one another the industrial psychologists have devised certain tests to assist the management in evaluation the expected performance on the task relative to that of the other candidates. Some of these tests are the following :

(i) *Aptitude Tests* : These are designed to measure the aptitude of applicants and their capacity to learn the skills required on a particular job. These are more useful for clerical and trade positions.

(ii) *Intelligence Tests* : These aim at testing the mental capacity of a person with respect to various things. It measures the individual learning ability to grasp or understand instructions and also ability to reason and make judgement. There are verbal and non-verbal individual and group intelligence tests.

(iii) *Interest Tests* : These determine the preference of the applicants for occupations of different kinds.

(iv) *Knowledge Tests* : These are devised to measure the depth of the knowledge and proficiency in certain skills already achieved by the applicants such as engineering, accounting etc.

(v) *Projective Tests* : In Projective techniques the applicant projects his personality into free responses about pictures shown to him which are ambiguous.

(vi) *Personality Tests* : These determine personality traits of the candidate such as co-operativeness against dominance or the emotional balance the temperamental qualities of a person.

(vii) *Judgement Tests* : These are used for evaluating the ability to apply knowledge judiciously in solving a problem.

(viii) *Dexterity Tests* : These are used to discover the ability to use the different parts of body in a coordinated manner. These are useful in identifying accident prone candidates for certain manufacturing jobs. Psychological tests are simply a step and not a replacement for the other phases of the selection process.

5. Employment interview. It must be conducted in a friendly atmosphere. The candidate must be made to feel at easy. The questions should better be asked on the basis of job specifications. Unwarranted questions should be avoided. A verification of the information furnished by the candidate in Application Blank may be made. An additional information may be sought for future record. The candidate should be given a chance to ask questions to satisfy himself regarding the history of the concern, future prospects, salary offered and nature of job, etc.

6. Reference check. If the applicant crosses all the above hurdles, an investigation may be made on the references supplied by the applicant regarding his past employment, education, character, personnel reputation etc. Referees may be called upon on telephones. They may be contacted through mail or personal visit. Additional material may also be recorded by asking the question from referees.

7. Medical examination. It is a part of selection process for all suitable applicants. It is conducted after the final decision has been made to select the candidate. A thorough physical examination is also essential to ensure that the candidate is able to handle the job efficiently.

8. Final selection. If a candidate successfully passes through an appointment letter may be given to him mentioning the post on which selected, the terms of appointment, pay scales, etc. When he joins the organisation, the personnel manager should introduce him to the company and his job.

Whatever may be the procedure the personnel department play an important role in the selection of a candidate. Though the decision to recruit the personnel is not taken in the personnel department but it assist the top executives in selecting the candidate by devising the form of Application Blank and preparing job description and setting the job specifications.

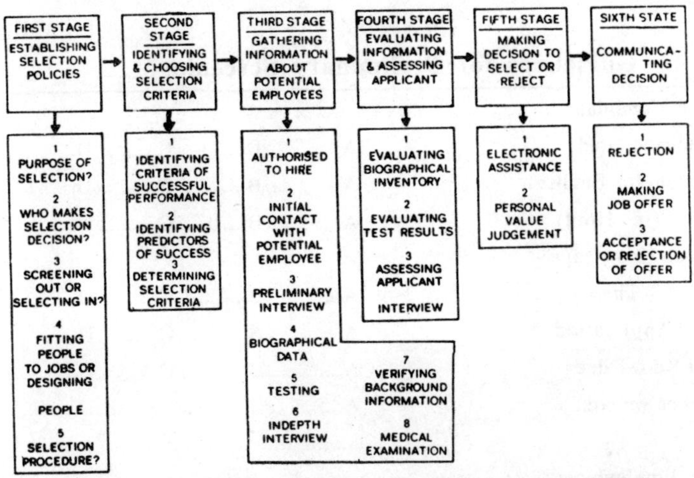

Fig. 9.1 : Model Procedure for Effective Personnel Selection.

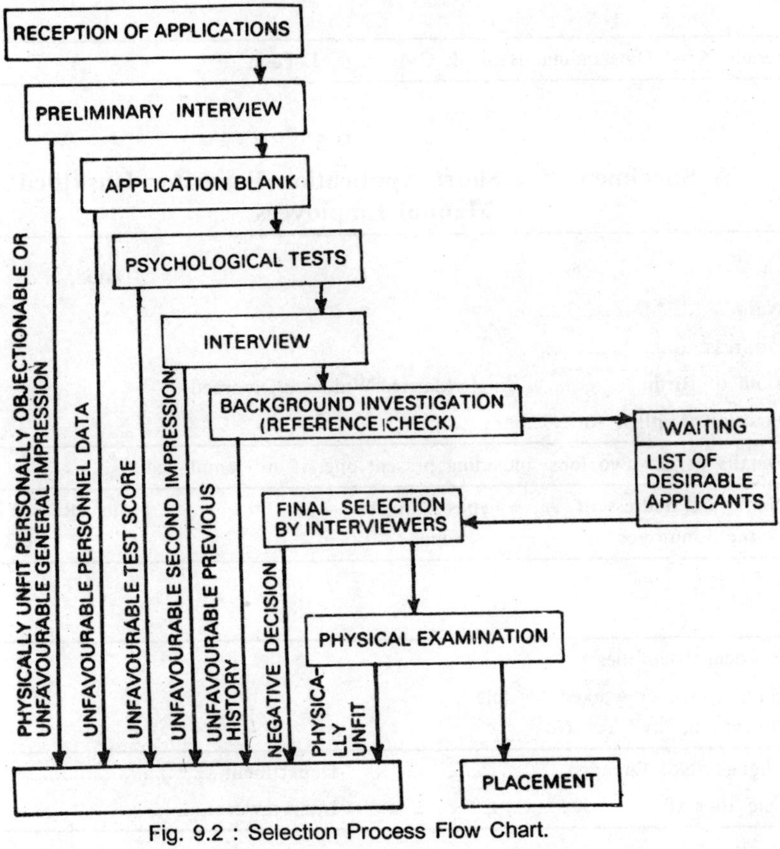

Fig. 9.2 : Selection Process Flow Chart.

CHART 9.4

Guidelines for Preliminary Screening

Name of the Candidate :..

(a) Personality : Grade	A...........B.......... C..........D..........
(b) Expression (in English)	A...........B.......... C..........D..........
(in Hind)	A...........B.......... C..........D..........
(c) Technical Knowledge	
Theory :	A...........B.......... C..........D..........
Application :	A...........B.......... C..........D..........
(d) General Knowledge	A...........B.......... C..........D..........
(e) Any other remarks	A...........B.......... C..........D..........
	....
Selected for Employment Test	..................Yes..............No............
Date of Interview.........................	Signature of the Interviewer
	....

Grade A — Outstanding; B-Good; C-Average; D-Poor.

CHART 9.5

A Specimen of a Short Application Form for Unskilled Manual Employees

Date..................

Name:................................

Address:.............................

Date of Birth.................... Single/Married/Widowed/Divorced

Position Applied for......................

Details of last two jobs, including present one, if still employed

Name and address of the Employer	Types of work done	To	From	Reason for leaving
1.				
2.				

Physical disabilities :

Have you ever worked for this concern before? Yes No

Engaged/Not Engaged................................ Department.....................................

Due to start.. Interviewer......................................

CHART 9.6

Long Application Blank

Post...........................

FORM FOR APPLICATION

Note : 1. Any entries must be made in candidate's handwriting.

2. Any subsequent change in the particulars given in the application must be intimated to the Personnel Department within a week of such change.
3. If space against any query is not adequate a separate sheet should be attached.
4. Canvassing in any form will disquality a candidate.
5. The candidate will render himself liable to summary dismissal if it is found that any information given by him is incorrect or any relevant information has been supressed.

1. Full Name with surname in Block Letters :
2. Nationality : Caste Religion Sex
3. Father's Name and Occupation :
4. Present Address :
5. Permanent Address : Village Mohalla
   H.No. P.O. Dist. State
6. Age : Date of Birth Place of Birth
7. Academic/Technical Qualifications (stating examinations passed from High School SLC/Hr. Secondary onwards) :

Name of University	Examinations Passed	Subjects Offered	Year of Passing	Division Class (Mark obtained if there is no division or class)
1.				
2.				
3.				

8. Apprenticeship/Practical Training

Nature of Apprenticeship/Training	Organisation in which served	Duration Form (Date)	To (Date)	Result

9. Languages : (a) Can Speak : Hindi, English, Gujarati, Marathi any other.

   (b) Can Speak, read and write :

10. Physique :.. Games played :

(a) Height : (in cms).. Hobbies :

(b) Weight : (in kgs) ....

(c) Strength of glasses of worn : ....

(d) Any disability : (current) : ....

(e) Any major disability or ailment suffered in the past :

(f) Identification Marks :

11. Past Experience :

Name Employer with complete address	Total Number of Staff and Workers	Post held and Exact Nature of Duties	Period Date of jointing	Date of leaving	Salary : basic and allowances at start and leaving	Reasons for leaving
1.						
2.						
3.						
4.						
5.						

Information regarding specilization in a particular subject and other matters of interest

....

12. (a) Have you ever been removed from your job., If so, state where and why.....

....

(b) Have you ever been convicted by a court of law? If so give particulars.........

....

13. (a) Have you ever applied to, been interviewed by this Company before?.............

....

(If yes, please state the name of the post and the date of interview)..............

....

14. References (other than relations) (Name and full address to be given) :

....

....

....

15. Minimum salary acceptable (including all allowances) : ....

....

16. Time required for joining (if selected) : ....

17. Number of dependants : .... Male ....Female

18. Marital status : Married Bachelor Divorced/Widowed/Separated

19. (a) Children ....

(b) Ages of children : ....Sons ....

Daughters ....Name of relative...............................

Department ....Relationship ....

20. Any acquaintance in our Company or at Udaipur. If so, give name and full particulars of each acquaintance : ....

....

21. Copies of Testimonials attached :

1.

2.

3.

4.

5.

Place

Date Signature of Applicant

(TO BE FILLED IN BY THE PERSONNEL DEPARTMENT)

Examined by 1.................................. (on date)

2..................................

3..................................

Remarks :

....

....

....

Appointed by : ....

Date of Appointment : ....

Salary Fixed : ....

Post of which appointed : ....

Nature of vacancy : Temporary/Permanent : ....

Period of Probation : ....

For Company
Chairman

To be filled in by the selected candidates only.

I have read and understood the Company's Service Rules and agree to abide by them, including any changes made therein by the Management from time to time.

Specimen Signature :

Specimen Initials :

According to Pell Arthur four types of information can be gathered[18] from the analysis of the above Application Blank

1. One can make judgements on *substantative matters,* such as "does the applicant have the education and experience to do the job?"

2. One can draw conclusions about the applicants' previous *progress and growth* (especially in the case of management candidates).

3. One can also draw tentative conclusion concerning the applicant's *stability* based on his previous work record.

18. Pell, Arthur, *Op.cit.*, pp. 96-98.

4. One may be able to use the data in the application to *predict* which candidates will succeed on the job and which would not.

WEIGHTED APPLICATION BLANK

The information on an application blank is analysed to determine statistically its relation to latter success in the job. The answers are weighted according to the extent of job success. Such application blanks are known as weighted application blanks.

CHART 9.7

Weighted Application Blank for the Post of Secretary[19]

Item	Percentage		Weight
	Short-term	Long-term	
Age			
20 or under	10	0	0
21-25	50	12	–4
26-30	20	12	0
31-35	10	23	0
Over 35	10	53	5
Marital Status			
Married	20	47	2
Single	63	41	1
Widowed	0	0	0
Divorced	10	6	0
Separated	7	6	0
Education			
Attended Grade School	0	0	0
Grade School Graduate	0	0	0
Attended High School	0	12	0
High School Graduate	33	41	0
Attended College	40	41	0
College Graduate	27	6	1
Business School	10	29	0
Years on Last Job			
Less than 1	50	0	–5
1 to 1½	7	35	2
1½ to 2½	37	12	–1
2½ to 3	0	6	0
More than 3	10	35	2
Years of experience			
0	3	18	0
Less than 1	20	0	–1
1 to 2	20	0	–1
2½ to 3	30	0	–3
Over 3	27	71	5

19. Novack, Stanely R., "Developing an Effective Application Blank," *Personnel Journal*, Vol. 49 No. 5, May 1970, pp. 421-422.

A weighted application form should be used with caution. Its objectives should be clearly determined. The factors that bring about success may also be taken into account. The varying conditions in an organisation should be noted. The blank should be continually up-dated. No firm should try to select an employee solely on the basis of one or two important facts.

BIO-DATA

If a management wants to appoint an existing employee to a higher position, it may ask him to submit his necessary bio-data for consideration at the time of selection or interview. The employee need not fill in an application blank. Bio-data may also be procured from different organisations having good employees for whom changes of advancement in their own organisation are very bleak.

CHART 9.8

Bio-Data on Mr. X

Name : .... Sex : ....

Date of Birth .... Age : ....

Father's Name : .... Address : ....

Education Qualifications : ....

Exams Passed	Institution	From	To	University	Marks Obtained	Subjects offered	Division Obtained
1	2	3	4	5	6	7	8

Previous Experience :	Employed in	Capacity	– During	Reasion for Leaving	Salary & Grade

Extra-curricular activities/hobbies : ....

Salary expected : ....

References (Three) : 1 ....

2 ....

3 ....

Any other fact ....

....

....

Place :

Date : Signature of the applicant

BIOGRAPHICAL INVENTORIES

These are specially constructed for the purpose of predicting success in a given type of work. Its items are those which the person, who a conducts an analysis, believes to have some potential as predictors. A typical inventory contains a large number of items. It utilizes a multiple-choice formal exclusively. It deals with those matters that are normally not covered in application blank. Such items deal with experiences in early life, hobbies, health, social relations, values and opinions, etc.

CHART 9.9

Typical Biographical Inventory questions[20]

Classification Data

What is your present marital status?

1. Single
2. Married, no children
3. Married, with one or more children
4. Widowed
5. Separated or divorced

Habits and Attitudes

How often do you cut jokes?

1. Very frequently
2. Frequently
3. Occasionally
4. Seldom
5. Cannot remember jokes

Health

Have you ever suffered from?

1. Allergy
2. Asthma
3. High blood pressure
4. Tuberculosis
5. Ulcers
6. None of these

Human Relations

What are your relations with your neighbours?

1. Not interested in them
2. Like them but seldom see them
3. Visit each other's homes occasionally
4. Spend a lot of time together

Parental Home, Childhood, Teens

With whom did you live for most of the time before you were 18?

---

20. Glennan, J.R., Albright, L.E., and Owens, W.A., *A Catalogue of Life History Items*, American Psychological Association, Washington.

1. Parents
2. Relatives
3. Hostel

Personnel Attributes

How creative do you think you are?

1. Highly creative
2. Somewhat more creative than most in your field
3. Moderately creative
4. Somewhat less creative than most in your field

Present Home, Spouse and Children

Regarding moving from location to location, my wife

1. Would go willingly wherever I do
2. Would not move under any circumstances
3. Would move only if it were absolutely necessary
4. Has not told me how she feels about moving
5. Not married

Self-Impressions

Do your generally do your best?

1. At whatever job you are doing
2. Only in what you are interested
3. Only when it is demanded of you

Recreation, Hobbies, Interest

How do you pass your leisure time?

1. Going to a movie
2. Visiting friends
3. Playing games
4. Reading light material
5. Gardening
6. Stamp collecting

Values, Opinions and Preferences

Which one of the following seems most important to you?

1. Having a pleasant home and family life
2. Getting a challenging and exacting job
3. Foreiging ahead in the world
4. Making the most of your particular ability

Work

How do you feel about travelling on business?

1. Would you enjoy it tremendously?
2. Would you like to do some travelling?
3. Would travelling be troublesome if it were necessary?
4. Do you definitely dislike travelling?

PHYSICAL EXAMINATION

A physical examination reveals whether or not a candidate possesses these qualities. It brings out deficiencies, not as a basis of rejection but as a positive aid to selective placement and as indicating restrictions on his transfer to other positions. Candidates are medically examined either by the company's physician or by a medical officer approved by the company for the purpose.

Purposes of Physical Examination

1. It gives us an indication whether a candidate is physically able to perform the job. Those who are physically unfit are rejected.
2. It discovers existing disabilities and obtains a record of the employee's health at the time of hiring so that the question of the company's responsibilities (both legal and ethical) may be settled in the event a workman's compensation claim for an injury is preferred.
3. It prevents the employment of those who suffer from some type of contagious diseases.
4. It places properly those people who are otherwise employable but whose physical handicaps may necessitate assignment only to specific jobs.
5. The basic purpose of a physical examination is to place persons in jobs which they can handle without injury or damage to their health.

Contents of Medical Report

Usually a medical check-up invovles a quick examination of the eyes, ears and throat. Bronchial weakness is looked for as an indication of nervousness, tuberculosis and hernia. Heart and lungs may also be thoroughly examined.

Stone and Kendall have outlined the following contents of physical examination :[21]

1. The applicant's *medical history* is obtained by interviews between the applicant and the medical officer.
2. *Physical measurements* such as height, weight, chest and the abdominal circumferences.
3. *General examination*, including an examination of the skin, masculature and joints.

21. Stone, Harold C., and Kendall. W.E., *Effective Personnel Selection Procedures,* 1956, p. 198.

4. *Examination of special senses* of the applicant — visual and auditory activity to be checked closely.
5. *Clinical examination* of eyes, ears, nose, throat and teeth.
6. *Examination of chest and lungs.*
7. *Check-up of blood pressure and heart.*
8. *Laboratory tests of utine, blood, etc.*
9. *X-Ray examination of chest, and other parts of the body.*
10. *Specialist's test,* such as basal metabolic rate or consulation by a specialist.
11. *A neuro-psychiatric examination* particularly when medical history or a physician's observations indicate an adjustment problem.

Chart 9.10

Specimen of a Medical Report

Name .... Age .... Sex ....
Address ....
General Appearance .... Height .... Weight ....
Eyes (R) .... Ears (R) ....
(L) .... (Hears with) (L) ....

Nose	Throat ....
Neck	Teeth ....
Pulse	Blood Pressure ....
Chest contour	Lungs ....
Abdomen	Urin ....
Spine	Stool ....
Blood Group	Skin ....

Identification Mark ....
Past Medical History ....
Notes : ....
....

Place and Date (Signature of the Doctor)

RECRUITMENT THROUGH INTERMEDIARIES

Most of the recruitment in Indian industry is done through intermediaries or brokers. These intermediaries or brokers are either in the pay of the industrialists or work as commission agents. To gather and recruit workers according to the needs and specifications of the industrialists is the job of these intermediaries or brokers. The brokers go around the villages and residential quarters of workers and offer them opportunities of employment. At times these intermediaries bring the workers to cities by enticement and offer of illusory hopes. The industrialists pay the travel and other expenses incurred by the intermediaries. They are also paid in advance under certain circumstances the rail fare and other expanses incurred by them in transporting the workers from villages to cities. All over India these brokers recruit quite a good number of workers. In different regions of India these intermediates are known by different names. The chief local names for brokers are : Dalal, Jobber, Sardar, Mistry, Thekedar, Chaudhary, Mukaddam etc. These days even lady brokers are meant for the recruitment of girls and women for various kinds of job. The packing departments have majority of women as workers. The lady brokers are known by various names in different regions. Some of these names are : Chaudharani, Mukaddamin, Thekadarni and Naikin. The functional importance of brokers have been clearly brought out by Labour Investigation Committee : "He is almost an ubiquitous feature of recruitment and labour administration in India and usually combines in himself a formidable array of functions. Thus, he is not only a recruiting agent but very often a supervisor or a foreman, even a sub-employer and a worker sharing the income with other workers." This observation makes it plain that usually these brokers are the agents of the industrialists. Generally they function as go-between the worker and the employer and are the agency or instrument whereby workers represent their grievances to employers. Besides, these brokers act as informers : they pass on to the industrialists advance information about strikes and other confabulations of the workers. The workers who get employment through brokers generally have to pay some commission to the brokers.

These brokers have sometimes the right to dismiss them from service At certain places these brokers, besides performing their usual functions; also do the job of money-lending. By this means they are able to exploit workers.

Advantages of Recruitment though Intermediaries

1. Easy availability of workers. These are certain times when workers are not easily available. Besides in certain industries environmental and working conditions are such that an average worker is repelled by them and does not want to work under those conditions at any cost whatsoever. The industrialists are unable to find sufficient workers for the running of their industries. Under the circumstances where workers are not easy to come by the industrialists feel constrained to rely upon brokers for the recruitment. These brokers go around places to persuade, entice and entangle workers. They bring workers to the industries under many pretexts and gradually gain such hold over them that the workers can ill-afford to belly them. In India the coal mines and tea gardens are the two industries where the recruitment of workers is done almost exclusively by brokers.

2. Facility in industrial management. The brokers in industries know everything about workers. They are well-informed about their background, their adaptability and above all their problems regarding word. Therefore, they are able to give to the employers from time to time correct assessment about them. Based on this assessment they are able to take advance action to rectify the genuine problems of the workers and also check the building up of frustration in workers. Thus, the brokers play a useful role in keeping the wheels of industry moving by aiding in successful management of the problems of workers. The brokers are useful to the employers in another way. They know everything about the activities of workers and are able to give advance information about strike, sabotage etc.

3. Lessening of employer's responsibility. As it is clear from the above discussion the brokers perform many functions of the employers. The overseeing of workers problems, maintenance of their attendance record and settlement of inter-factional rivalries of workers are some of the tasks which the brokers competently look after. In some places the brokers impart general training to workers. On account of all these factors the responsibility of the employers is much reduced.

Disadvantages of Recruitment Through Intermediaries

1. Exploitation of workers. The majority of industrial workers in India are illiterate and poor. Moreover India is a populous country and the supply of workers for jobs far exceeds the demand. Under these circumstances it is rather difficult to find any suitable job. Taking advantage of this situation the brokers exploit the workers and charge commission for getting them jobs. Sometimes the workers are forced to make regular monthly payments to brokers. The brokers also charge money for condoning inefficient work, granting leaves and for recommending promotions. Thus, brokers exploit the workers in every possible way.

2. Recruitment of incompetent workers. It is quite apparent from the above discussion that the real criterion of recruitment of workers is commission, graft or bribe. As can be easily appreciated, payment of commission means that preference in recruitment will be given to those who are able to give maximum bribe. Under these conditions the necessary conditions of getting employment is not efficiency of work but the ability to pay. Thus, in broker-recruitment system many an incompetent worker get entry into industry. This gradually undermines the morale in industry. Besides, the work shy workers do not put in regular hours of work but get away with their truancy by silencing the broker by greasing his palm. In this connection Textile Enquiry Committee has this to say, "It would not be out of place to say that whereas hundreds of efficient and competent workers are roaming about in the city for want of employment a large number of fresh and incompetent workers are seen working in the mills on job for which they have no qualification except their willingness to pay a price for that job to the jobber."

3. Increase in industrial conflicts. The broker, as a rule are extremely hard-hearted. In order to remain in the good books of industrialists they keep back-biting the workers and give exaggerated or false accounts about the activities of workers. Their game is not one-sided; it is dual. They not only report assist workers to the industrialist but also incite the workers against employers. Thus, they keep workers and employers in dark about the real situation and try to exploit both to their personal advantage. Thus, while acting as go-between or contract between workers and employers, they normally are instrumental to increasing of industrial conflicts.

4. Non-availability of permanent workers. By employing various forms of enticement, persuasion etc., brokers bring the innocent persons from far off villages and primitive tribal belts to cities for industrial jobs. These innocent persons are unable to adjust with the urban climate and the complexities of urban life terrify them. Therefore, they do not like to stay in the cities for any length of time and rush back to villages at the first available opportunity. Thus, the recruitment by brokers fails to get the industrialists permanent workers. The transient labour, as can be well appreciated, is a great liability.

5. Immoral exploitation of female workers. Under the system of recruitment by brokers there is immoral exploitation of female workers. The majority of jobbery in industry is in the hands of men and they indulge in immoral exploitation of the female workers. Whenever a woman needs some job, she has to approach some or the other jobber. This jobber usually demands physical satisfaction from her for getting her a job. Thus, it is difficult for ladies to get jobs without making a moral compromise. In big industries where there are female jobbers, they are of low moral calibre as a rule and they do not shirk from immoral exploitation of female workers and make money out of it.

From the above discussion the merits and demerits of the broker recruitment system become quite apparent. If we think seriously about the relative balance between merits and demerits we shall find that demerits outweigh the merits. In spite of the preponderance of faults of the system is fairly popular in industry. Even today broker-recruitment system is very much prevalent in Sholapur, Kanpur and Bombay. Indeed the Indian worker is not fully awakened and is unable to make successful effort for job in his own. Besides, the task of the employer is made much easier by this. For all these reasons this system is quite popular.

RECRUITMENT THROUGH CONTRACTORS

In India a large number of workers are recruited to industry through the medium of contractors. The industrialists make arrangement for getting any job done against a specified amount with the contractors. Now it becomes the duty of the contractor to complete the job in specified time : otherwise they could not get any payment. Once a contract is made, it becomes an exclusive responsibility of the contractor who not only engages the labour force but also provides for the raw materials, machinery, an equipment needed for the completion of the job. In Public Works Department most of the jobs are done on contract. In textile mills of Ahmedabad and Cement and Paper industry 10 to 15 per cent of the labour force is recruited through contractors. In coal mines also a substantial percentage of worker are recruited through this method. In Kolar mines where gold is dugged, about 33 per cent of workers are engaged on contract basis. Besides, in other industries some percentage of workers are engaged on contract.

Advantages of Recruitment through Contracts

1. Short notice. The contract work can be got done at short notice. With the help of contractors a every large number of workers can be arranged at very short notice. Moreover, whenever there is extreme urgency of time in the completion of any job the services of contractor prove very helpful indeed.

2. Contractor's responsibility. In contract work, the completion of a job within a specified period, becomes the responsibility of the contractor and the headache of the industrialist is off. As a rule, it is made a term of contract that if a job is completed within the specified period the contractor would compensate for the loss suffered on account of non-completion of the job. Because of this condition of the contract the industrialist becomes free from all anxiety.

3. Less cost. It is generally believed that the work done on contract is less costly. These days there is a system of inviting tenders for all big jobs. Whosoever asks for the least amount and promises to do good job gets the contract. As a result of competition among contractors the job done on contract proves to be relatively cheap.

4. Contractor's control. If a job is done on contract, the entire labour force is recruited by the contractor. These workers are the employees of the contractor. They have no concern with the industrialist. Therefore, the industrialist does not bother about the government regulation pertaining labour welfare in the case of employees of the contractor. If the recruitment of the labour is made by the industrialist himself he has to make provision for various type of facilities for these workers. Thus, the industrialist saves himself the botheration of spending money and looking after the workers if he gets a job done through the contractors. Moreover, the industrialist does not have to engage supervisors to oversee the work done by the labourers.

Disadvantages of Recruitment through Contracts

1. Denial of benefits. The workers recruited by contractors are denied various compulsory benefits available to their counterparts in the industry. Now-a-days, the industrial workers' wages, leaves, pension, maternity benefits are regulated by definite labour laws enacted by government of India and state government. Any violation of these is liable to be punished suitably. Thus, the interests of industrial workers are protected by government legislation. On the other hand, there is no such legal protection of the interest of contract labour. They are completely at the mercy of contractors.

2. Arbitrary treatment. The contractors give arbitrary treatment to the workers. They exploit the workers freely. The needy workers are engaged at very low rates and their working hours also determined by the contractor. Generally, these workers are not regularly paid. Besides, the contractor always withholds certain part of the salary of the workers so that they are constrained to work the contractor in adverse conditions and much against their will.

3. Moral exploitation. Besides monetary exploitation, the poor workers are also subjected to moral exploitation.

From the above discussion about the system of contract labour it is clear that while this system is quite advantageous to the industrialists, it is equally harmful to the workers. From time to time labour welfare associations have recommended the abolition of this system. According to the recommendations of these associations it is best to do away with this system. But under special circumstances where its abolition is not feasible, the recruitment through contractors should be governed by definite rules and regulations. From time to time the government should review the conditions of workers under contractors. In order to remove these defects U.P. Government set up 'Labour Depots' in 1951. These depots were set up with the view that the contractors would recruit all the workers they need through these depots. These labour depots impart preliminary training to the workers. However, in practice these labour depots have not proved to be very effective in solving the problems of workers.

DIRECT RECRUITMENT

Besides the methods of recruitment outlined above, the industrialists employ another method for the recruitment of workers. This is known as Direct Recruitment. Under this system recruitment is not made either through brokers or though contractors. In direct recruitment a list of type of vacancies, their number and the expected qualifications in each type is pasted on the main entrance door of the mill or factory. Sometimes a copy of this list is given to newspaper for advertisement. On the appointed day and the appointed hour numerous workers throng to the main entrance gate. From this crowd of workers those who fulfil the requirements are chosen according to the availability of vacancies. The election of suitable candidates is made by the manager or labour superintendent. These officers put some questions to the workers and if need be ask them to complete certain preliminary tasks. Besides, these officers give due consideration to the health and general efficiency of those selected.

Merits of Direct Recruitment

1. Relief from exploitation by brokers. In direct recruitment the jobber has no role and importance. Therefore, the workers recruited directly are not in any way under his shadow and are free from possible exploitation by him. The workers who are fortunate to find direct recruitment do not have to pay anything for getting the job nor are they under any pressure to pay monthly commission to the jobber.

2. Recruitment of able and efficient workers. In direct recruitment there is a possibility of finding able and efficient workers. The reason for this is that in direct recruitment the recruitment is made by the representatives of the industrialists and they see to it that able and efficient workers are recruited.

3. Increase in the productivity. In direct recruitment able and efficient workers are recruited. These workers put in their best and work with great zeal and dedication. This naturally helps to boost the production.

4. Saving of funds. In direct recruitment the industrialist does not have to make any payment to the jobbers. In recruitment through brokers the employers have to spend a lot of money. Thus, in direct recruitment there is saving of funds.

Demerits of Direct Recruitment

From the above discussion one gets the impression that the method of direct recruitment is highly meritorious but, in fact, it is not the case. This system also has its defects. As a matter of fact this method is not suitable for all types of recruitment. This method is suitable for the recruitment of unskilled and semi-skilled workers but this does not work effectively in case of skilled workers. Another defect of this system is that there is no adequate provision for the publicity of various vacancies. Many workers are unable to get the information about the vacancies. Thus, many suitable candidates are deprived the chance to be present for selection. Sometimes the defects of broker recruitment system creep in this system also. Many managers and labour superintendents are liable to accept bribe and are otherwise influenced by various pressure and recommendations. Thus, many undeserving candidates gain entry into the factories.

SELECTION IN TRAINING

"Selection in training" emphasises the selection of the qualified personnel. If there is a sound policy and procedure; there is the least possibility of being biased. If abilities, aptitudes, character and individual differences are considered the skilled and qualified personnel would be able to get the appointment in the enterprise. This will reduce the cost of placement and training. The period of training will also be reduced considerably as the person selected after proper screening shows a better performance on the job. A person placed on the job most suited to his qualifications, aptitude and interest, will be the most satisfied person in the organisation. His morale will be high and he will try to understand the work better. He will perform his duties efficiently and quickly, imparting training to person who is selected after proper screening require less efforts, cost and time.

While selecting a candidate for the job appraisal should be made not for the present job for which he is being considered but also future promises for higher job so that he may be prepared for higher positions in the organisation at little cost.

Nowadays most of the concerns select the personnel from within on the basis of their proficiency on the present job. Promotion motivates employees for better performance. It is a mode of training for higher job.

Each individual differs in nature and quality and such qualities must be developed to suit the job. A well designed selection policy will help the management train the worker. Training aims at development of individuals.

Importance of Selection

1. Procurement of skilled workers. Selection is the process in which candidates are divided into two classes — those who are to be offered employment and those who are not. Thus, the candidates fit for the job are selected from among the prospective candidates for employment. Thus, selection is a process by which only desirable candidates are hired and others are denied the opportunities.

2. Reduction of the cost of training. Proper selection of candidates reduces the cost of training because (1) qualified personnel have better grasping power. They may understand the technique of the work better and in no time; (2) the organisation may develop different training programmes for different persons on the basis of their individual differences, thus reducing the time and cost of training considerably.

3. Solution of personnel problems. Proper selection of personnel reduces personnel problems in the organisation, such as labour turnover, absenteeism and monotony etc. Labour relations are better because workers are more satisfied by their work.

PROBLEMS OF PROPER SELECTION IN INDIA

1. Defective recruitment practices. The main sources of recruitment in Indian industries is jobbers or Mukaddam or contractors who recommend or select the operative staff. This has encouraged the exploitation of workers. It has led to many abuses. Hence, several new sources of recruitment have been developed since independence such as recruitment through employment exchanges or through labour officers. However, the old method of recruiting the workers through intermediaries is still alive in some private industries.

2. Obsolete selection techniques. Obsolete selection techniques are employed in Indian industries except a few public sector undertakings. Interview is regarded as the most modern techniques of selection. Use of psychological tests is made only to select the personnel at management levels and that too in some industries of repute.

3. Untrained selectors. Selectors in Indian industries are not aware of the modern techniques of selection. They are not trained even in the techniques of interview. Their behaviour with the prospective candidates is generally unwarranted and in some cases even inhuman.

4. Prejudicial preferences. Generally no scientific procedure of selection is adopted for hiring the worker at lower levels. No emphasis is laid on the future development of the personnel. Candidates who are recommended by the relatives of the existing employees are preferred whether they are fit for the job or not. Preference, not the quality, is the basis of selection of workers in industries. Sometimes unqualified workers got appointment and suitable persons are left.

5. Lack of planning. India has no manpower planning, persons are recruited as and when the posts are vacant. Therefore, there is always a dearth of skilled workers.

6. Unfavourable attitude of employers. The attitude of Indian employers towards employees is not favourable. They recruit the workers for a short time only and deprive them of the statutory benefits. They do not select good personnel, not develop new techniques of selection or training for the development of personnel in the industry. They consider the cost of development as wastage and not an investment.

PRINCIPLES OF RECRUITMENT

1. Centralisation. Recruitment of personnel for the whole organisation should be centralised. Personnel Department may be charged with this responsibility.

2. Clear policy. Both the internal and external sources of recruitment should be given due importance. It should have clearly spelt out in the policy whether the existing employees would be given any preference in filling up the higher vacant posts and if so at what basis.

3. Comparative policy. In establishing the recruitment policy for the organisation, the recruitment policies followed in similar organisations and in Government undertakings should be considered.

4. Statutory provisions. Statutory provisions regarding recruitment of personnel should also be given proper consideration.

5. Flexible policy. The recruitment policy should be flexible so that it may be amended suitably to achieve the organisation policy.

6. Consistent policy. Recruitment policy should be within the framework of personnel policy and organisation policy.

7. Clear rules. Rules regarding recruitment of existing employees' wards should be very clear.

8. Proper qualifications. The qualifications of the applicants should be commensurate with the job specification as worked out through job analysis.

9. Merit. Merit should be the basis of recruitment of other consideration like friendship, relations etc. should be ignored.

Principles of Selection Policies

1. Selection Board. The responsibility for the selection of employees should be assigned to an efficient and qualified selection board so that only the right man can be selected.

2. Job first, man next. This should be the basis and fundamental principle for selection.

3. Proper services. Selection should be from internal as well as external sources and the management should not rely much on one single source.

4. Proper standards. Selection should be based on standards set out by job analysis. If suitable candidates is not available, the post should be allowed to remain vacant for the time being till such a right man is made available.

5. Different selection methods. The different selection methods for different levels of posts should be followed.

6. Consistency. The selection policy should not surpass the organisation's general policy. It should be within that framework.

7. Commensurate. The selection policy of the organisation should be commensurate to the employment policy of the state.

8. Flexibility. Selection policy should be flexible, not rigid so that necessary amendments may be made whenever necessary.

9. Vocational guidance. The selection policy should provide the vocational guidance for the prospective candidates.

10. Unbiased. The selection policy should be unbiased and employment-oriented.

PLACEMENT OF WORKERS

What is Placement?

"Placement" may be defined as "the determination of the job to which an accepted candidate is to be assigned, and his assignement to that job. It is a matching of what the supervisor has reason to think he can do with the job demands (job requirements) : it is a matching of what he imposes (in strain, working conditions)," and what he *offers* in the form of pay roll, companionship with others, promotional possibilities, etc.[22] A proper placement of a worker reduces employee turnover, absenteeism and accident rates, and improves morale.

According to Pigors and Myres, "Placement has an experimental element. But for most employees it is a decisive step and should consist in matching what the job demands (job requirement), imposes (in stray, working, conditions etc.), and offers (if the form of pay rate interest, companionship with others, promotional possibilities etc.)". Placement is the act of offering the job to a finally selected candidate. With the placement of worker to the job, the selection procedure ends. Personnel department evaluates the various factors required for a job. It is difficult to match all these factors for a new employee,

---

22. Pigors, Paul Myres, Charles, *Personnel Administration : A Point of View and a Method*, MeGrawjhil Kazapusha Ltd. Tokyo, 1973, p. 285.

quite unknown to the job and the environment. Therefore, the first placement generally carries with it the status of probationer. The probation period is trial period, extended from 3 months to 12 months. If the employee shows a good performance he is confirmed as a regular employee of the organisation at the end of the probation period. If the worker does not work well, the management may take a decision to discharge him. But once a worker has achieved the status of regular employee he may be discharged only for sufficient reason. Thus, the trial period is a transition period at the end of which the management has to take a decision whether the employee should be made regular or discharged from the job.

Principles of Placement

1. Job Requirements. Man should be placed on the job according to the requirements of the job. The job should not be adjusted according to the qualifications or requirements of the man. 'Job First, Man Next' should be the principle of placement.

2. Qualifications. The job should be offered to the man according to his qualifications, neither higher, not lower, except in case of interview placement.

3. Information. The employee should be made conversant with the working conditions relating to the job prevailing in the industry. He should also know the penalties if he commits a wrong.

4. Loyalty and cooperation. While introducing the job to the new employee, an effort should be made to develop a sense of loyalty and cooperation in him so that he may realise his responsibilities better towards the job and the organisation.

INDUCTION OR ORIENTATION OF EMPLOYEE

Meaning of Induction of Employee

When a candidate is finally selected, he is issued the appointment letter asking to join the organisation on or up to a specified date. Induction is a follow-up action of hiring. It is concerned with the problem of introducting or orienting a new employee to the organisation.

When a new employee reports for duty, he should be welcomed as a new member of organisation. He must be helped to get acquainted and adjusted with his fellow employees and work environment. The first day of employment is long remembered by most of the people. Initial impression counts much in the later attitude of the employee towards the job and the company.

If he has not already been introduced at the time of occupational test the new employees should be introduced to the fellow employees and to the working conditions, rules and regulations. It is a first step in the proper communication of the personnel policy. It seeks to build a two-way channel of information between management and employees.

Elements of Good Induction Programme

1. Introductory information. Introductory information regarding the history of the company and company's products, its organisational structure, personnel policies, rules and regulations of the company relating to leaves, attendance, pay etc. should be given informally or in group sessions in the personnel. It helps the candidates to understand the company and its organisational policies and standards.

2. On the job information. The department supervisor should give further information to the new employee in the department concerned where he is placed on the job about departmental facilities and requirements such as nature of the job, the extent of his liability, and employee's activities such as recreational facilities, association, safety measures, job routine etc.

3. Follow-up interviews. Several weeks after the employee has been on the job a follow-up interview should be arranged by the supervisor or a representative of the personnel department to answer the problems that a new employee may face on the job and to supplement some of the information given earlier.

Objectives of Induction

1. To promote loyalty. To promote a feeling of belonging and loyalty to the organisation among newcomers so that they may not form false impression regarding the company because first impression is the last impression.

2. To make agreement. To make an agreement between the organisation goals and the personnel goals of the newcomers.

3. To build up confidence. To build up the new employee's confidence in the organisation and in himself so that he may become an efficient worker.

4. To give information. To give the new employees information regarding company, its structure, product, policies, rules and regulations and facilities provided by the company such as cafeterias, locker room, time to break off, leave rules etc.

5. To introduce the new worker. To introduce the new worker to the supervisor and the fellow-workers with whom he has to work.

6. To create a sense of security. To create a sense of security for the worker in his job by impressing the idea that fairness to the worker is the inherent policy of the organisation.

7. To lessen cost of replacement. To lessen or avoid the cost of replacing the worker in the early impressionable period because of lack of information or incorrect business impression.

Induction Practices

1. Induction guide. Induction guide books are prepared by the personnel department with information on what induction steps have been taken and what are still to be covered. The guide book lists various steps to be taken and by whom and when the instruction are to be given. Guide book containing the informations regarding the company and its various personnel activities is distributed among the newcomers is some large concerns.

2. Counselling. The supervisor may induct the new employees working under him by introducing and counselling them by reassuring and reinforcing the confidence and guarding against false impression.

3. Follow-up interview. On the basis of follow up interview, personnel department can take action to readjust conditions, reassure the worker dispel fears, gain their confidence and promote their efficiency.

Shri B.P. Billimoria observes : "induction has a greater significance in a developing country like India, where the percentage of illiteracy is very high. The new worker finds himself completely at sea when by force of circumstances he has to shift from rural surroundings into an industrial unit. It is no use tyring to push a handbook of certified rules and regulations into his hands and expecting him to turn out into a loyal and efficient employee. He needs a short and simple induction conducted by some one who speaks his own language. This will go a long way in reducing turnover and, above all, in preventing a worker from the likelihood of falling a prey to subversive elements which thrive an creating labour unrest by misrepresenting employees to illiterate employees."[23]

Induction Procedure

There is no model induction procedure. Each industry develops its own procedures as per its needs. An Organisation must make integration of the individual into the organisation as smooth and anxiety-free as possible. Orientation programme achieved through a formal or informal placement depends on the size of the organisation and the complexity of the individual's new enviornment. Many organisations

23. Billimoria, R.P., "Induction in Industry", in *Readings in Personnel Management*, The Indian Institute of Personnel Management, Orient Longman Ltd., New Delhi, 1970, p. 95.

develop formal orientation programmes which might include a tour of the offices or plant, a talk about the history of the organisation, and short discussion with a representative of the Personnel Department who will describe the organisation's benefit plans. An informal orientation programme might include being assigned to another senior employee who will not only introduce the new worker to other workers but show him other things too.

The procedure should basically follow following steps :

1. The new person needs time and a place to report to work.

2. It is very important that the supervisor or the immediate boss meet and welcome the employee to the organisation.

3. Administrative work should be completed. Such items as vacations, probationary period, medical absences, suggestion systems should be covered.

4. The departmental orientation programme should include a get — acquainted talk, introduction to the department, explanation of the functions of the department, and job instruction and to whom he should look for help when he has any problem.

5. Verbal explanations are supplemented by· a wide variety of printed material, employee hand books, flyers, employee manuals, house-journals, picture stories, comics and cartoons, pamphlets, etc. along with short guided tour around the plant.

Orientaiton programmes usually cover things like employee compensation benefits, personnel policies, the employee's daily routine, company organisation and operations, and safety measures and regulations. The new employee's supervisor is often given an orientation checklist similar to that given in chart 9.11.

CHART 9.11

Supervisor's Orientation Checklist[24]

1. Word of Welcome.
2. Explain over-all departmental organisation and its relationship to other activities of the company.
3. Explain employee's individual contribution to the objectives of the department and his starting assignment in broad terms.
4. Discuss job conent with employee and give him a copy of job description (if available).
5. Explain departmental training programmes and salary increase practices and procedures.

24. Famularo, Joseph, *Handbook of Modern Personnel Management*, McGraw Hill Book Co., Inc., 1978, p. 238.

6. Discuss where the employee lives and transportation facilities.
7. Explain working conditions :
   (a) Hours of work.
   (b) Use of employee entrance and exit.
   (c) Lunch hours.
   (d) Coffee breaks.
   (e) Personal telephone calls and mail.
   (f) Overtime policy and requirements.
   (g) Pay days and procedure for being paid.
   (h) Lockers.
   (i) Others-safety habits and security regulation.
8. Requirement for continuance of employment — explain company standards as to :
   (a) Performance of duties,
   (b) Attendance and punctuality,
   (c) Handling confidential information,
   (d) Behaviour,
   (e) General appearance,
   (f) Wearing a uniform.
9. Introduce new staff member to manager(s) and other supervisors (special attention should be paid to the person to whom the new employee will be assigned).
10. Release employee to immediate supervisor who will :
   (a) Introduce new staff member to fellow workers.
   (b) Familiarise the employee with his work place.
   (c) Begin on-the-job training.

Employee's Signature	Supervisor's Signature
Date	Date

Orientation is generally provided on the following :

1. The significance of the job with all necessary information about it including job training and job hazards;
2. The company, its history and products, process of production and major operations involved in his job;
3. Structure of the organisation — the geography of the plant and functions of the various departments;
4. Employees' own department and job and how they fit into the organisation;

5. Many programmes include follow-up interviews at the end of 3 or 6 months with a view to finding out how the new employee is getting along;
6. Relations between foremen and personnel department;
7. Company policies, practices, objectives and regulations;
8. Personnel policy and sources of information;
9. Terms and conditions of service, amenities, and welfare facilities;
10. Rules and regulations governing hours of work and overtime; safety and accidents prevention, holidays and vacations, methods of reporting, tardiness absenteeism;
11. Grievance procedure and discipline handling;
12. Social benefits (insurance, incentive plans, pensions, gratuities, etc.) and recreation services (athletic, social and cultural activities) and
13. Opportunities, promotions, transfers, suggestions, schemes and job stabilisation.

Typical Techniques of Induction Programmes

1. General orientation by the staff of the personnel department;
2. Specific orientation by the job supervisor, or his representative and
3. Follow-up orientation by either the personnel department or the supervisor.

1. General Orientation. It be conducted by the personnel department. This is general, induction gives the necessary general information about the history and operations of the firm — t*he purpose of which is to help an employee to build up some pride and interest in the organisation.* Information is also given on specific employee services, such as pension, health and welfare plans, safety programmes, etc. *The better policy is not to give everything in one day, but to administer smaller doses over a long period.*

2. Specific Orientation. *The purpose of specific induction is to enable* an employee to adjust himself to his work and environment. *Induction is specific and requires skill on the part of the foreman.* The employee is shown the department and his place of work. He introduced to other employee. He is informed of the location of the bathrooms, lavatories, canteens, and time clock; He is told about the organisation's specific practices and customs such as whether the personnel bring their lunch or whether lunch is supplied to them at concessional rates, the timings and length of rest periods, the work dress, etc.

3. Follow-up Orientation. It takes place within one week to six months from the time of the initial hiring and orientation. Conducted either by a foreman or a specialist, *its purpose is to find out whether the employee is reasonably well-satisfied with him.* The employee may be asked whether his hours of work and his pay are as represented to him before employment; how he feels about his fellow-workers; how he feels about his boss; and whether he has any suggestions to make for changes in the induction procedure or in other company practices. The interviewer records the answers as well as his own comments on the employee's progress. The line supervisor completes an evaluation of the employee, indicating his strong and weak points, indicating also whether he is doing well.

Efforts are made to remove the difficulties experienced by the newcomer through personal talks, guidance and counselling.

The best method of induction training includes lectures plus visuals followed by printed materials. A tour of the plant and the department should be arranged to acquaint the new employee with the overall operations of the company.

QUESTIONS FOR EXERCISE

1. Define recruitment and the importance of recruitment method. Explain main sources of recruitment.
2. Explain the process of selection of employees which is generally followed in a large-scale business concern.
3. Discuss the advantages and disadvantages of recruitment through Contractors.
4. Assess the merits and demerits of direct recruitment of industrial workers.
5. "Selection is one of the most important of all functions in the management of personnel." Comment. What are the major problems in the way of proper selection in India?
6. Describe the main principles of recruitment.
7. Explain basic principles of selection policies.
8. Describe the importance and principles of placement of workers.
9. What do you mean by Induction or Orientation of Employee? Explain elements of a good induction programme. Discuss objectives and practices of induction.

10

Employment Interviews and Psychological Tests

One of the most effective and widely prevelent method of personnel selection is employment interview. Not only in India but throughout the world it is the most common procedure of recruitment.

Definition of Employment Interview

1. *J. Batty* : "It (interview) is a face-to-face encounter with a purpose : it employees conversation. The interview should aim to bring out attitudes rather than facts. The key to finding this out is through people's sentiments and feelings rather than some one's knowledge."

2. *Bingham* : *Moore and Gestaed.* "An interview is a conversation directed to definite purpose other than satisfaction in the conversation itself there is give and take between the interviewer and interviewee, and much of the interaction between these two is carried on by gestures, postures, facial expressions and other communicative behaviour. Even the words acquire a variety of meanings and values as they are spoken with different inflections or in different contexts. All of these are means of communication the spoken words, the gestures, the expressions, the reflections contribute to the purposeful exchange of meanings, which is the interview."

Thus an interview is a face-to-face conversation between a panel of interviewers and the interview which affords an opportunity to undestand and develop a clear picture of the personality of candidate.

OBJECTIVES OF AN INTERVIEW

1. To find out suitability. To find out the suitability of the candidate by affording an opportunity to the interviewer to judge the applicant's qualification as a basis for sound selection and placement.

2. To secure information. To seek more information about the candidate which are not mentioned in Application Blank or not judged by various tests.

3. To produce job description. To give the candidate an accurate picture of the job with full details of terms and conditions of the employment and to give some essential facts about the objectives and the policies of the company.

4. To promote understanding. To permit feeling of mutual understanding and confidence and to permit goodwill towards the company whether or not the interview culminates in employment.

IMPORTANCE OF INTERVIEW

1. Oldest and most common device. Interview is the oldest and the most commonly used device in selecting personnel at all levels. Although application blanks, tests and group discussions etc. provide much valuable information about the candidate yet they do not provide the complete set of informations required about the applicant. Interview may be of great help in such cases. Interview helps the organisation to secure much information about the candidate and *vice versa.*

2. Selection of a suitable candidate. The main purpose of the interview is to judge the suitability of the candidates. It is the most satisfactory way of judging temperamental qualities of the candidate such as his way of thinking on labour problems, qualities of leadership etc. It decides whether the qualities possessed by him make him suitable for the required job in the concern.

3. Collection of information. In some situations the facts and pertinent information can only be given by an individual himself or there may be occasions when the interviewees may be anxious to suppress important and related facts to protect his personnel interests. Such facts may be discovered by the interviewer during interview. He may also collect certain other relevant informations regarding the candidate for future records. These may help the organisation in designing and developing future plans or programmes.

4. Knowledge of Company's Policies and Objectives. It is the duty of the interviewer to let the candidate know about the policies and objectives of the organisation during the course of interview. Interviewer should also be given a chance to ask questions, regarding the job, company and other related matters. This will develop a sense of mutual understanding and confidence between the employer and employee.

5. Getting advice and opinions. In situations where the interviewer is not getting a solution to the problem he is facing in the organisation, interview may help the interviewer in getting advice from and opinions of the interviews for the problem from different angles. Their co-operation may be sought so that their behaviour could be influenced to accomplish the desired objectives.

LIMITATIONS OF INTERVIEW

1. No judge of skill. Interview cannot judge the skill and the ability of a candidate for the job. It can test only his personality.

2. No expert. Interviewer is not always an expert of the situation or of the job to be offered. Therefore, he may not be in a position to extract maximum information from the candidate which is one of the purposes of the interview.

3. Personnel Judgement. The result of interview depends very much on the personnel judgement of the interviewer which is not always correct. Sometimes interviewer forms a particular view about a candidate which deviates from the objective of purposeful exchange of meanings.

4. Wrong purpose. Sometimes, interviewer asks questions from the candidate only to confuse him, or to defeat him and not to get the maximum information. The questions are directed to the interviewee in such a way as to allow him ot time to answer. A correct view about the interviewee's knowledge and qualities cannot be made in such a situation.

5. Pre-determined Answers. Generally, it happens that the answers of all possible questions to be asked in the interview are predetermined. It the answer given by the candidate tallies with that of the predetermined answer, he is declared successful. The other view is rejected completely, notwithstanding the fact that it is supplemented by valid arguments. It results in the selection of an undersirable candidate.

6. Unreliable communication. Due to the above limitations, the interview is an unreliable form of communication. It should be replaced by alternative methods wherever possible.

STEPS AND PRINCIPLES IN INTERVIEW

Interview is a sound principle of personnel selection. It is a well-recognised tool for appointment. The interviewer must be trained in the art of interviewing should be supplemented by other techniques of selection such as psychological tests, trade tests etc. Thus interview is one of the techniques of selection and not the only valid tool in the process of selection.

1. Preparation for Interview. A considerable amount of preparation is needed for all types of interviews. The following principles should be emphasised in planning the interviews :

(i) *Deciding Objectives* : While preparing for the interview, some decisions must be made as to which information objectives are to be accomplished in the interview. The interviewer must know what he wants to achieve out of this interview. The nature of the interview will depend upon the objectives of the interview.

(ii) *Togathering data* : All the relevant informations about the candidate is should be assembled and summarised with the help of Application Blanks before a candidate is interviewed. The interviewer will review the summary and plan his interview accodingly. For example he will determine : (a) Whether the applicant meets the minimum standard set up for each hurdle in the selection process? And whether the applicant fulfils the requirements of the job under consideration? What background, factors and personnel qualities must be explored?

2. Setting for an Interview. (i) *Physical setting* : The physical setting for an interview should be private as well as comfortable. It will encourage the interviewee to talk frankly. On certain occasions the interviewees are interviewed in a room full of people. Numerous interruptions by telephones or by a secretary reduce the privacy and indicate the lower status of the interviewee. Setting in a comfortable padded chair an individual has a tendency to relax and talk more freely.

(ii) *Mental setting* : The interviewer should make an initial effort to establish relaxed atmosphere. He may initiate some idle some idle talks instead of plunging direct into the business at hand.

3. Conduct of the Interview. Following sound principles should be followed during the course of conduct of interview :

(i) *Demonstrating liking and respect* : The interviewer should possess and demonstrate a basic liking and respect for people. It is not only a specific rule but, rather, a fundamental philosophy.

(ii) *Encouragement to talk* : The questions should be asked in a such a way that the interviewee is encouraged to talk. Question that may be answered by 'Yes' or 'No' should be avoided because it does not reveal the true nature of the applicant. Interviewee should be allowed sufficient time to answer. He should share the greater amount of talking so as to bring about materials and ideas. Silence always implies a request for more information and the interviewee ususally continues to supply it.

(iii) *Pleasant atmosphere* : Pleasant atmosphere should be created in all interviews. The interviewer should be at ease himself and keep the interviewee at ease.

(iv) *Art of listening* : The interviewer must acquire the art of listening. The interviewee must receive full attention of the interviewer. The marginal listening of the interviewee not only prevents the interviewer from obtaining the full inforamtion but it is also insulting to the interviewee. Projective listening is required to assess the hidden feelings or meanings of the ideas and the reactions of the candidates. The interviewer must listen much faster than the interviewee can talk. He should attempt to project himself into the position of interviewee. This will require an imaginative study of the personnel background of the individual as revealed by the Application Blank.

(v) *Familiarity with job* : The interviewer should be familiar with the job specifications and job description so that he may tally the qualifications of the candidates with the job specifications and relevant informations may be gathered and facts supplied to the interviewee.

(vi) *Keeping appointments* : The interviewer must keep the appointments. In India it is a common practice to ask the candidate to appear before the interview board at an appointed time but actually the interview is started too late of the scheduled time.

(vii) *Two-way-traffic* : There should be two way traffic in interviews. While the interviewers should ask the question the interviewees should also be given an opportunity to ask the questions regarding the company and the job to be offered.

(viii) *No discrimination* : The interviewer should not give an introduction of subject matter that might be interpreted as evidence of discriminatory attitude of the employer. Reference to religious and political views should be avoided. The interviewer should not insist on the candidate to the accept his ideas, attitudes and interests.

(ix) *Art of interview* : Interview is an art like other arts and the interviewer must be trained in the art of interviewing.

(x) *Personality Assessment* : Interviewer may ask cross questions to know the personality of the candidate.

4. Closing the Interview. The following principles should be followed in closing the interview :

(i) *Courtesy* : In an employment interview, the interviewer has a responsiblity for bringing the conversation smoothly to a close and it should be indicated by some overt manner. Interviewer should be courteous and friendly whether the applicant is qualified or not. Every candidate msut be thanked for having shown interest in the organisation.

(ii) *Future action* : The interviewee should be given some type of indication of future action. What would be the next step in employment processing should be known to all applicants, if they qualify the interview. The rejected applicant should be informed by direct (face-to-face) or indirect (by letter) method of communication.

5. Evaluation of the Interview. (i) *Recording.* The interviewer should record the facts, impressions and decisions immediately after the interview in an honest manner. All important points should be considered in final judgement. It will strengthen the applicant's confidence.

(ii) *Evaluation.* In addition, the interviewer may also evaluate at this point. Interviewing is an art, the application of which can be improved through practice.

TYPES OF INTERVIEWS

Interviews may be conducted on a planned or patterned and non-directed or non-planning plane. A *planned interview* is one that follows a definite plan of action, it is, therefore, also knows as an *action interview.* A *non-directed interview* is one that is not directed by the interviewer and in which the candidate is given the freedom to speak his mind feely.

Generally, interviews fall in the following categories :

1. Patterned or highly organised interviews;
2. Non-directive, free or quite unorganised interviews;
3. Depth or discussion interviews;
4. Situational or problem-type interviews or leaderless group discussion interviews;
5. Stress interviews.

1. Patterned or Structured Interview. Such interview is also called *standardised interviews*, for it is pre-planned to a high degree of accuracy and precision. It is the msot common method of interview. It is based on the assumption that, every pertinent detail bearing on what is to be accomplished, what kind of information is to be sought or given, how the interview is to be conducted, and how much time is to be allotted to it, must be worked out in advance. Questions would be asked in a particular order, with very little deviation. If an applicant wants to discuss something else, he is swiftly guided back to the prepared questions.

Advantages of Patterned Interview

McMurray points out following advantages of the patterned interview to improve the judgement of the interviewer :

1. The interviewer works from definite job specifications; he knows what qualities each job requires.

2. He has a plan, he knows what questions to ask.

3. He has been trained in the techniques of conducting an interview, *i.e.,* he knows how to put the candidate at ease, how to make him talk, and how to extract pertinent information.

4. Prior to interview, he has checked with outside sources (previous employers, schools, etc.) and already knows a great deal about the applicant.

5. He has a series of clinical concepts, *i.e.,* that of emotional immaturity — which provides him with a yardstick for interpreting and evaluating the information obtained from the candidate, *Sixth*, the interviewer himself has been carefully selected to assure that he has adequate intelligence and is emotionally well adjust.

CHART 10.1

Excerpts from Patterned Interview Form

Domestic and Social Situation

1. Married............................Single....................Widowed.............Separated...............
Divorced.................Date of Marriage..................
2. Living with spouse? Yes...................No ....(If no) Specify....................
dependants (Members)..............................
3. Age.................................What plans do you have for children?...........................
4. Do dependants provide adequate motivation?..
5. What difficulties or serious arguments have you with your spouse?.......................

Financial?........................Social?...........................Personal?...............................
6. Have you been married previously? Yes.....................No..............(If yes)..............
how many times?....................................
7. When and what was the reason for the end of the marriage or marraiges? Death.....
.............Divorce................
8. Separation (unless death) : What were reasons?..
9. Do domestic difficulties indicate immaturity?...
10. What do you to for recreation?...................What hobbies do you have?..............
.... Will hobbies help work?............................
11. To what extent do you and your spouse entertain?.........................Does applicant seem socially well adjusted?
12. When did you last drink intoxicating liquor?..
To what extent?........................Is this sensible drinking?..............................Does not drink..............................
13. What types of persons do you actively dislike?...
14. Is applicant biased?..
15. Tell us about your most recent job. Why did you decide to change?
16. As you look back on your recent job, what did you like most about it? What did you like least about it?
17. What do you feel were your three most significant achievements in your past position?

18. Could you tell us if you have any idea about what an effective manager should do?
19. How do you feel your subordinates would describe you as a supervisor?
20. Were you satisfied with the progress you made on your job? Why? Why not?
21. What plans do you have for self-improvement during the next twelve months?
22. What does success mean to you?
23. What do people criticize about you the most?
24. Many of if improve our ability to relate to people as develop more maturity. In what way would you say you have improved over the past two years?
25. What or who has contributed most to your self-development? Think about a difficult decision you have had to make recently regarding your work. Tell us how you went about making this decision.
26. How do you plan your work?
27. What has been the heaviest pressure situation you have had to face in the past year? Describe the circumstances.
28. Give us examples of the types of problems that create the greatest stress or strain for you.
29. What goals you ahve set for the next three years?

---

2. Non-directive or Free Interview. The purpose of such interview is to determine what kind of person a candidate really is. It is unstructured and is relatively non-planned as to format. The applicant is asked some very general questions. He may reply to these in any way. The interview is not directed by questions or comments as to what the candidate should be asked. The candidate is encouraged to express himself on a variety of subjects, on his expectations and motivations, background and upbringing, interests, even political predilections, etc. The interviewers look for traits of a character and nature of his aspirations and his strengths and weaknesses, mainfest or potential.

3. Depth or Action Interview. Semi-structured in nature it utilises questions in key areas which have been studied in advance by the interviewer. Its typical subjects include the candidate's home life, education, previous experience, aptitude, recreational interests, and hobbies. The interviewer provides instructional information about his organisation, the nature of work, pay, opportunities for advancement, and demands likely to be made on the employee so that one gets a true picture of the interviewee by intensively examining his background so that a correct evaluation and decision may be made.

As this type of interview demands more mature understanding of human behaviour and development therefore, it requires more careful selection of the interviewer.

4. Group or Discussion Interview. The assumption underlying this type of interview is that "the behaviour displayed in the solution of the problem is related to potential success in the job. The object is to see how well individuals perform on a particular task or in a particular situation." Groups rather than individuals are interviewed. The inerviewees are given certain problems and asked to reach a specific decision within a particular time limit. They enter into group discussions, knowing that the interview is a test, but do not know which qualities are being measured or tested. Observers watch the activities of the interviewees — those who take a lead in the discussion, those who try influencing others, those who summarise and clarify issues, and those who speak effectively.

In this type of interview, the emphasis is laid on the analysis of the interviewers' impressions from discussions rather than a factual information.

5. Panel or Board Interview. In this type of interview, a candidate is interviewed by a number of interviewers who may ask questions in turn or in random order as they arise on any topic.

6. Stress Interview. Its purpose is to find out how a candidate behaves in a stress sitaution — whether he loses his temper, gets confused or firghtened. The interviewer assumes a hostile role toward the applicant. He deliberately puts him on the defensive by trying to annoy, embarrass or frustrate him. He asks questions rapidly, criticises the interviewee's answers, interrupts him frequently, keeps the candidate waiting indefinitely and then subjects him to a barrage of interrogations questioning whatever he might state, or too many questions are asked at a time by many interviewers, make derogatory remarks about the candidate or puts him in an awkward situation by dropping something on the floor and asking him to pick it up, accusing him that he is lying and so on. Stress interview is a highly dangerous tool. The stressful interview situation may not necessarily reveal, how a candidate will behave in real stressful life situations invovled on a job. Yet its judicial application may reveal may characteristics of an applicant.

Guidelines for Effective Interview

1. Qualifications of Interviewers. Interviewers should be of a certain status, standing and experience. They should be in the know of the requirements of the job for which interviews are conducted, and be familiar with the background of the organisation and industry which they represent. They should possess a working knowledge of such topics as individual peronality, differences, dynamics, motivation, frustration, attitudes, abilities, aptitudes and human traits, and should be sympathetic and impartial.

2. Art. Skilful interviewing is an art and like all other arts, requires training and experience. It is learnt better by practice than by reading a book. However, the necessary techniques and knowledge about the subject matter may be collected from current books, periodicals and pamphlets bearing on the larger field of management.

3. Need of Study. The interviewers should interview only after thoroughly studying the relevant data about the candidate from the application blank, and the tests and preliminary interviews through which he has gone before. They should celarly understand what the job entails and what its requirements are. This will avoid putting too much weight on irrelevant information. It will help them in reducing the chances that all candidates are compared with an erroneous "stereotype". Reliability of employment selection decision can be increased by making available to interviewers extensive information about the job to be filled (such as that provided by detailed job descriptions and job titles).

4. Knowledge of Required Traits. These traits include "intelligence," "personal relations aptitude" and especially "motivation to work", assessment of personal qualities like sincerity, ability to present ideas, emotional balance, friendliness, responsiveness, courtesy, etc.

5. The coverage of factual information. Such a coverage is of greater value than any attempt to search for personnel qualities. It should lay emphasis up on : (i) reliance of education to the job specifications; (ii) reasons for the gap in educational and employment history of the applicant; (iii) reasons for choosing special courses in schools and colleges; (iv) division or grades obtained and academic achievements; reason for failure; (v) likes and dislikes for each job; (vi) information regarding domestic, health, financial and other problems, if any; (vii) the condition of the job and work the applicant expects.

6. Routine Information. The time of the interview should be consumed in collecting routine information, which can be conveniently gathered from the application blank or verified from the applicant's former employer or from his school, institution, records and documents, certificates, etc.

7. Delimitations. The interview should be diligently delimited, for it is often the only feasible way of eliciting the required information about the candidate, and it enables the interviewers to view the total individual and to appraise his personal appearance, comments, attitudes, mannerisms, motivations, interests, adjustments, temperament and other personal attributes.

8. Reliability and Validity. The interviewers should guard against being unduly prejudiced or coloured by their own personality or pet theories. Their own feelings and standards should not be allowed to influence them. The decision should be fair and impartial. Bias, prejudices, personal likes and dislikes, perferences and general impression of the candidate should not be allowed to interfere with the process of decision-making. The interviewers should determine the positive qualities in a candidate rather than give undue weight to negative ones.

9. Extensive Talking. The candidate should be allowed to talk extensively so that he may unburden himself to the point at which nothing important or relevant is left unsaid, and a fair assessment can be made of his ability. Generally, 25 to 30 minutes are sufficient for semi-skilled or skilled applicants. For high level jobs-managerial, technical, sales — an hour or more may be required.

10. Avoid too much talking. "A good working ratio for an interviewer is to talk for not more than 25 per cent of the time and to listen for 75 per cent of the time." The best interview is usually one in which the interviewer talks the least. Information from the applicant can be elicited only when the inerviewer gives him a patient, prolonged and skillful hearing.

11. No quick judgment. The interviewer should refrain from passing too quick a judgement before all the relevant facts have been gathered and evaluated. He should avoid derogatory comments and refrain from any revealing facial or verbal expression, he should not voice criticism or moralise. He should show understanding and smoothly pass on to another topic when any unfavourable information is uncovered or if the applicant is unable to answer a question.

12. Objectivity. In order to be objective the interviewer must be careful to correct irrational feelings of a negative or positive kind. If he adopts a healthy attitude that the former has not come for the interview with a "begging bowl" in his hand. Hostitlity or nervousness on the part of the applicant may be minimised. He must realise that his organisation needs a good man just as much as the applicant wants a good job.

13. Selling during the interviews. The interviewer should be aware of the fact that the interviewee is also evaluating him. Interviewees form overall impressions of the "goodness" or "badness" of an interviewer. This in turn may affect their decision to join or not to join the company. The interviewer should try to give good impression about himself and of the company he represents. In the words of Wendell French : "Good interviewers are those which take the many needs of the interviewee into account of security, belonging, esteem, wholeness and self actualization. Orderly proceedings, cordial relationships, avoidance of unnecessary, ego-damaging events, and an understanding of the process are ingredients in the best interviews."[1]

1. Wendell, French, *The Personnel Management Process,* 1970, p. 225.

Qualities of a Successful/Good Interviewer

Researches have more or less clearly shown that effectiveness of any interview depends upon several personal qualities of the interviewer. A good interviewer must have abilities to evaluate specific as well as overall abilities of the applicant and this is rather a difficult job as ability to evaluate specific traits may differ from the ability to make overall evaluation. However, according to P.K. Ghosh and M.B. Ghorpade, a successful interviewer should have the following characteristics :[2]

1. He should usually be an elderly person (say be found 40 or 45), more mature in outlook on life, slightly or moderately egostical, and not to much extrovert.
2. He must be socially detached which makes it possible for him to make more accurate judgement of others.
3. He should have slightly more than average intelligence, emotional maturity, interest in human beings and their behaviour, sports manship and well adjusted life.
4. He should have extensive acquaintance with people similar in age and occupation to those whom he interviews.
5. He should be a man with a genuine feeling of warmth and affection so that be is able to establish rapport quickly with any individual, however, nervous he may be.
6. He should be a man who has been fully trained in the art of interview, and who knows what are the special weaknesses of this method and how to avoid them; and also the person who is focussed on continually refining his method and asking questions in the light of his experience.

According to Francis G. Drake, the other qualities of the interviewer are :[3]

1. He should read standard literature and current books, periodicals and pamphlets, bearing on the art of interviewing and on the larger field of personnel management.

2. He should be well informed and up-to-date where legislation on employment is concerend.

3. He should be a member of one or more professional management organisations which serve as clearing houses for personnel information.

---

2. Ghosh, P.K. and Ghorpade, M.B., *Industrial Psychology*, Himalaya Publishing House, 1980, pp. 112-113

3. Drake, Francis G., The Interviewer and his Art, in *The Personnel Man and this job*, D.B. Taraporewala, Bomaby, 1970, pp. 128-129.

At the least, he should attend the conferences sponsored by these groups.

4. He should have an experimental and open-minded attitude towards tests and other devices which are developed to assist the interviewers in the selection of personnel.

5. If he has little or no formal educational background or training in personnel work, he should cure this deficiency by taking courses/ coaching in psychology, personnel management, general maangement, public relations and other subjects bearing on his work.

6. The interviewer must have a thorough understanding of the organisation, of the relationships between departments and jobs, the objectives of the organisation, job content, and worker's requirements; and he should have a good undestanding of the organisation's employment policies and procedures.

7. He should be receptive and sensitive to the way his behaviour affects others.

8. He should have a working knowledge of such topics as individual differences, personality dynamics, motivations, frustrations, abilities, attitudes, and other human traits.

By continuing to improve in these and other ways, he recognizes "the challenges of his art," and goes a long way towards meeting that challenge.

INTERVIEW TECHNIQUE

A successful interview of a candidate is a specialised technique requiring a thorough grounding in the art of conducting interviews. Following are the typical sequence of functions that occur in the course of an interview : (i) Preparation; (ii) Setting; (iii) Conduct of interview; (iv) Close of interview and (v) Evaluation.

1. Preparation. For two important reasons advance preparation by the interviewer is basic to the success of an interview :

(i) As the interview is generally too short to cover all the items that should be included in it, an advance preparation for it will enable an interviewer to cover all important aspects.

(ii) An advance preparation is necessary for the interviewer if he wants to remember the facts and the main points which he wants to cover in the interview. Following decisions have to be taken and arrangements have to be made before the interview begins :

(a) The determination of the specific objective of an interview;
(b) The choosing of an appropriate method of accomplishing the interview objectives;

(c) Acquainting oneself with the known information about the interview so that factors needing emphasis may be pre-determined;

(d) Determining the number of interviewers;

(e) Looking into the administration details, such as the place of interview, its approximate duration, and other arrangements.

Interviewing Procedures for Recruitment

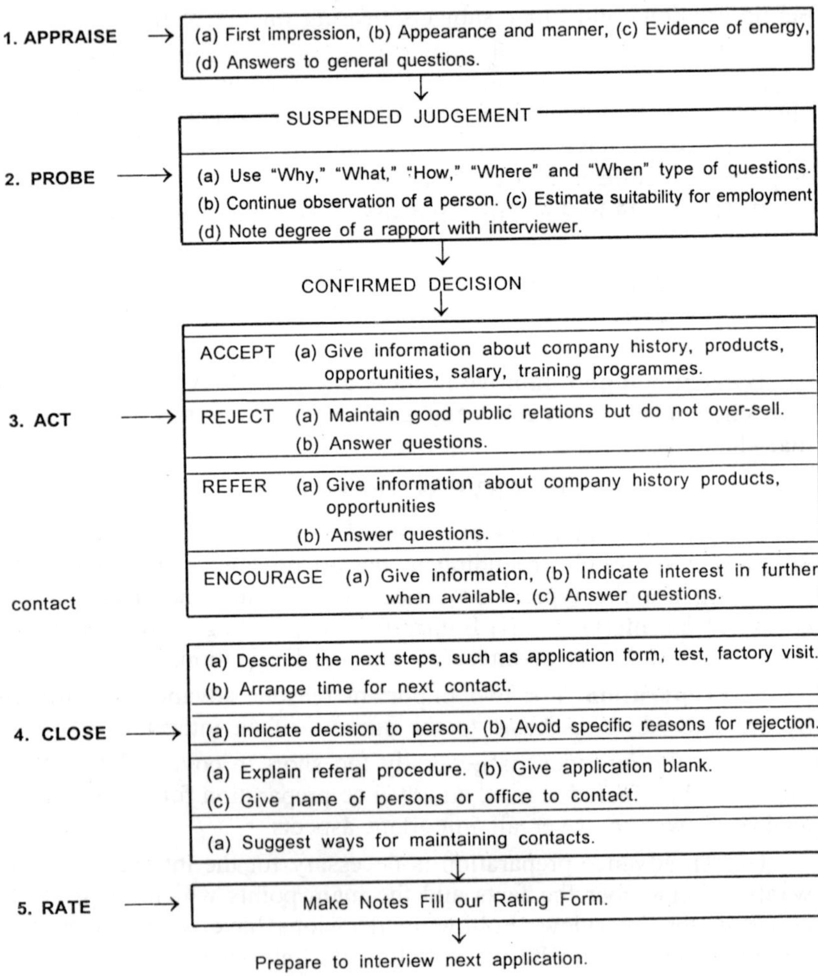

Fig. 10.1 Interviewing Procedure for Recruitment.

A. Determination of Objectives. According to the American

Management Association following are the main objectives of interviews :

(i) To afford the interviewer an opportunity to judge an applicant's qualifications.

(ii) To give the applicant the essential facts about the job and the company.

(iii) To establish a rapport — a feeling of mutual understanding and confidence — between the personnel department and the applicant.

(iv) To promote goodwill towards the company, whether the interview culminates in employment or not.

Areas of Information in an Interview

(i) *Personnel characteristics* : These include physical appearance, health, sense of humour, quickness of reactions ready-wittyness, cultural level, ability to organise thoughts, dress, poise and grooming, self-confidence, alertness, the standard the style of conversation, facial expressions, manners and general working habits. It can be found out in an interview how an applicant deports himself, whether he is out-going, an extroverted, or a well-adjusted person or whether he is very shy, introverted, and unresponsive.

(ii) *Technical competency* : These include *information about the examinations* he has passed, the grades, divisions obtained, awards and honours won, extra-curricular activities.

(iii) *Initiative, common sense and a general smartness.*

(iv) *Ability to inspire confidence by sustained effort without supervision* : The interview shows the extent of the skill or stature of the interviewee, the relevance of such skill to the post under consideration, the level attained in regard to good judgement, decision making ability, capacity for sustained hardwork, and his originality and initiative in work. These may be discovered by putting questions in regard to the jobs previously held, any special features which he likes or dislikes and why, his reasons for changing the job, his most notable achievement, the circumstances in which the existing job was secured and the kind of boss the applicant would like to work for.

(v) *Capacity of team work* : This can be gathered by knowing about the activities in which the applicant adjusted himself, his leisure-time activities, his hobbies, family circumstances and community interests, his relationship with other members of the family, the kind of persons who are his friends and the kind of people he would keep away from, his use of leisure time, the extent and nature of his general reading, the games and sports he has played and the nature and extent of his interest in these.

(vi) *Potential for growth* : The interviewer can find out about the long-range aspirations of the applicant, his reasons for applying for the particular job, his expectations about the job, the expected salary, his plans for realising his expectations, his strong and weak points, etc.

(B) Determination of the Method to be Used. Before interviewing an applicant it has to be decided. Whether it may be the *patterned interview* method, or *stress interview* method, or the *background information interview* method, or the *discussion interview* method, or the *group performance interview* method.

(C) Acquainting Oneself About the Applicant. The interviewer should equip himself with amximum information about the interviewee which may be gathered from the application blank; or verified from the applicant's former employers or from the school or institutions he attended; from referees; records and documents; certificates and testimonials; from the results of tests, etc. This prior information on various issues will make it possible for the interviewer to guard himself against any prejudices arising out of caste, religion or previous experience.

(D) Determining the Number of Interviewers. While a minimum of two interviewers may talk to candidates for a lower level position, for a higher post as many as eight or even more persons of different ages and representing different educational background, interests, and field experience may be chosen to hold a multiple interview. *Either* a panel may jointly interview each applicant *or individuals* may speak to the applicant one after the other. It is always better to interview a candidate consecutively rather than simultaneously. However, some experts believe that simultaneous interviewing is more desirable as it gives an opportunity to observe the candidate's responses to a group situation. It enables one interviewer to watch while the other is asking the questions. For example, of the three interviewers, one may ask questions on the family and educational background, another may engage the applicant in a general discussion, while the third may test his job knowledge.

Usually there is a Chairman in an interview committee along with the Personnel executive, the Department head, one or more subject experts, even a psychologist, and one or more other persons, if so desired by the Selection Committee.

2. The Physical Setting. The physical setting should be both private and comfortable. The place of interview should have cross-ventilation and proper lighting arrangements with cooling and heating devices, generally at the back of the office building where there would be no disturbance, interruptions or frequent telephone calls or noises outside the room. Properly arranged seating accommodation should also be available. The room should generally have two doors — one to be used as *entry* and the other as an *exist*. The candidates should be well-received by the receptionist, a member of the personnel department, and led into the room. Nearby, there should be privy and drinking water facilities. The room should preferably be furnished with sofas and easy chairs. A few magazines and daily newspapers and other reading material should be placed on a properly arranged table for the use of the candidates. The sitting room should be generally kept apart from the place where the actual interviews are held so that the conversation between the interviewer and the interviewee is not overheard by other prospective candidates.

All this arrangement for reception and seating give an impression to the interviewee that he is an important person the treatment of the applicant before he meets the interviewer. It may be noted that is very important. The first impressions make or mar the reputation of an organisation, its executives and interviewers.

The climate of the interview should give candidates an impression that a certain amount of preparation has been made in honour and that the interviewers do not treat the interview as an interrpution of their normal work to get over with as quickly as possible. It would be an excellent thing if a cup of tea or coffee, is offered to the candidate while he is waiting.

If a large number of people are to be interviewed for a number of identical jobs, the interviews should be so arranged all of them are not required to report at 9.00 A.M. or 9.30 A.M. in a body. The usual practice should be to interview 25 to 30 candidates in a day. These may be called in two batches one in the forenoon and the other in the afternoon. How long an interview will last will depend upon several factors like the type of position, the number of applicants, the importance attached by the company to interview as a selection device and the personality of the interviewer. While some interview for high positions may last for an hour or so; for others they may take 20 to 30 minutes. The value of interview is not so much dependent upon the time spent but the skills of the interviewer to obtain all necessary information in the *shortest possible time* without embarrassing the applicant in any way.

3. Conduct of the Interview. It aims at establishing rapport with the candidate, getting a complete and accurate inforamtion from him and recording it properly.

(i) *Establishing Rapport* : At the very beginning the interviewer should gain the confidence of the candidate by establishing rapport with him. Cheerful initial conversation about something which interests the candidate and bearing on his name, his family history, hobbies, interests, achievements; or talk on general or current topics may help to "break the ice" and establish a friendly relationship. Even a genuine smile on the interviewer's face or an offer of a cigarette or a cup of tea and exchange of pleasantries would serve the purpose. The applicant will be both physically and mentally less tense than he was before and will talk freely. The interview should proceed not on the lines of cross-examination but in the form of a conversation so that the two may get to know each other, with the specific underlying purpose of getting information in certain areas.

(ii) *Getting Complete and Accurate Information* : It is an art which calls for experience, skill and technique on the part of the interviewer. Its purpose is to know in depth the personality of the man to be hired and to evaluate his suitability for the post. During the interview the interviewer should not allow his own sense of values, feelings and prejudices to influence the course of conversation. He should use the language which is clear to the applicant. He should frame skilful questions.

Rules about Questioning

(i) Questions. Mis leading questions as well as those that reveal the interviewer's bias and prejudices should be avoided "Closed end" questions, which call for "Yes" and "No" should not be asked, for they offer little scope to the candidate to expand his answers and give more information. They limit the conversation and tend to make him tense and anxious about the next question. Therefore, preference should be given to open-end questions. Which start the conversation and keep it going.

(ii) Probing Sensitive points. In between these two types of the questions, there is a variety of ways in which sensitive points can be probed. While one interviewer asks a particular question, leading to some conversation in depth, another may ask clarifying questions based on the earlier answers, statements and responses of the candidate.

(iii) No Hogging. The interviewers should not "hog" the conversation. They should have talent, experience, natural dexterity and a genuinely sympathetic attitude so that they may draw out the applicant, who may have a considerable potential but who may be shy and reserved in the beginning. First, 'probing' questions may be asked to find out on which topics, the applicant is interested and on which he is on defensive then the topics which interest the applicant may be picked up first, but never ignoring those topics in which he has shown reluctance because they may reveal some substantial information.

(iv) No Personal questions. Highly personal questions should be omitted until one is sure that rapport has been fully established.

Devices to get Answers from the Candidate

(a) He may ask questions on different subjects at the beginning to determine which is the most provocative in getting the answer.

(b) He may repeat parts of the key sentences of an answer in a questioning tone to indicate that he wants elaboration.

(c) He may ask one question at a time.

(d) He may clarify the question without indicating what he thinks the correct answer is.

(e) He may ask a wrong question with a view to testing the common sense of the candidate.

(f) He may not ask highly personal questions until rapport has been established.

(g) He may not bring the applicant back to the point on which he disagrees.

(h) He may use the language which is appropriate for the candidate.

(iii) *Recording of Impressions* : It is necessary to "notes", "observations" and "records" of the inerviewer's impressions briefly. It indicates to the candidate that the interviewer is interested in what he is saying and, therefore, he may continue to talk freely. It provide complete information at the end of the interview to arrive at a final judgement.

4. Close of the Interview. The close of the interview is a trying situation for the candidate. It should end with the same pleasantness with which it began without creating any awkward or embarrassing situation for the interviewee. It shoud not end without the candidate being finally asked whether he himself would like to say anything on any point concerning the job and the interview. It should be closed diplomatically so that the interviewee may feel satisfied that he was given a full hearing.

5. Final Evaluation of the Candidate. In order to evaluate a candidate's suitability for the job his strength and weaknesses are critically balanced. Weightage is given to test experience, habits, behaviour and attitudes, and the acutal facts which come to the notice of the interviewers. It should be possible to know what he has done in the past and thereby gauge fairly accurately what he is likely to do or not to do in future.

Predetermined marks are allocated for requisite qualifications, division obtained at different levels, past experience and training received by the candidate. The marks are added and the position of the candidate determined.

The evaluation may be done either by giving grades ranging from

A to *E* by allocating marks. *A* may indicate excellent or outstanding : *B* very good, *C* good, *D* average, and *E* marginal/poor or below average. *B* may be given to indicate that he may be reconsidered while reaching a final decision.

The list of selected candidates may be preferably prepared in a descending order.

Following chart 10.2 provides a sample of interview evaluation form.

CHART 10.2

Interview Evaluation Form

Interviewer............................
Department...........................
Location...............................

Please complete and return immediately after interview
Name of the Candidate.......................................Date of Interview...............................

Weightage	0 Not acceptable	1 Below Average	2 Average	3 Good	4 Outstanding
1 Appearance and attitude (growing, crustesy, appropriate dress)	0	1	2	3	4
2 Personality (poise, Bearing, rapport, total impact business mannger)	0	1	2	3	4
3 Communication (ability to adequately express himself)	0	1	2	3	4
3 Education (appropraiteness of degree and course work for job)	0	3	6	9	12
3 Work experience	0	3	6	9	12
3 Technical Competence	0	3	6	9	12
2 Ambition in line with anticipated job progression)	0	2	4	6	8
2 Potential (ability and motivation to grow or advance, capable of developing scientific curiosity)	0	2	4	6	8

16 Total Points
Score
Other comments ---

Recommendation : Offer .... Reject......................
for what area(s) is applicant best suited

DEFECTS AND PITFALLS IN INTERVIEW

According to Ubrbrock, following common defects may be found in employment interviews :[4]

1. Interviewers have difficulty in establishing rapport with the applicants.
2. Interviewers do not have a clearly defined technique developed but tend to flounder looking for clue or opening.
3. Questions are not carefully formulated to elicit from the applicant freely and fully desired information.
4. Many interviewers do too much of the talking in an attempt to put the applicant at ease.
5. Many interviewers lack skill in bringing the interview to a close.

In conserving the appointment of personnel according to Scott and others the following points should be kept in mind :[5]

1. One individual differs from another in his personal aptitudes and special abilities and each contributes to the work of his company in his own way in exchange for his salary.

2. Individuals differ in interests and motives and respond best to varying stimuli.

3. Different kinds of work require different kinds of personal abilities on the part of persons who are to perform them.

4. Granting equal ability, different kinds of work are performed best by persons who, temperamentally, are particularly interested in them.

5. The work in each position changes as time goes on and duties are added or taken away. Sometimes the change is negligible, sometimees it is substantial. To the extent to which it takes place, a similar change is apt to occur in the abilities and interests which a job requires of the worker.

6. Environment, working conditions, supervision, relations with the employer and fellow-employees, and opportunity — these exercise a tremendous influence on personal efficiency and consequently on group production.

7. An individual changes from day to day from year to year in ability (both in degree and kind) and interest.

---

4. Uhrbrock, Richard S., *Analysis of Employment Interviewe,* Personnel Journal,Vol 12, No.2, pp. 98-101.
5. Scott, Clothier and Spriegel, *Personnel Management Principles, Practices and Points of View,* 1977, p. 86.

Beach has given following simple guide sheet for the beginning interviewer :[6]

1. Appearance and Mannerism. It should take into consideration dress, poise and bearing, speech and voice, facial expression, neatness and cleanliiness and nervousness.

2. Early Home and Family Background. it places emphasis on father's occupation, parents' family life, number of family members, attitude towards parents and children, economic condition of the family, activities, hobbies and interests when young and social contacts and friends.

3. Education. It deals with matters related to educational qualifications, grades and diplomas, courses liked best and least with reasons thereof.

4. Work History. It seeks information on reasons for choice of jobs, relation with and attitude to supervisors in previous jobs, reasons for changing jobs, career goals, type of work liked best, method of obtaining the previous job and salary increases, promotions obtained.

5. Personality and Social Adjustment. It deals with marital status, present interests and sparetime activities, financial responsibility, emotional stability, emotional maturity, levels of aspiration, attitude towards work associates and towards authority, sincerity, initiative, and perseverance.

6. Health. It deals with past and present health problems, observes physical limitations.

ERRORS IN INTERVIEWING

1. The Halo Effect. *The interviewers should assess the whole of the candidates personality and should not be led away by any one trait or achievement.* Good candidates come in all shape, size, ages, education, religion, case, regionality, etc. Physical appearance, his brilliant scholastic record, his fluency or lack of it in language, experience of living abroad, experience as a sportsman, etc. any one of these qualities may create a halo effect.

2. Leniency. When a candidate is rated by two raters one may show consistent leniency by giving him high scores while the other may consistently rate him by giving low scores. Leniency is usually associated with lack of confidence and interest in rating while strictness may be the result of exaggerated expectation, lack of contact with people, and general rigidity of personality.

---

6. Bearch, D.S., *Personnel Management, The People At Work,* 1975, p. 281.

3. Projection. This error arises when an interviewer expects his own qualities, skills, values in an applicant. He may select the candidates who very much resemble him in age, appearance, manners, opinion, voice and background.

4. Stereotyping. This error arises when the interviewers have already formed some mental association between a particular trait, culture or communal origin and a particular type of personality.

GUIDANCE FOR THE INTERVIEWEES

1. Prepare for a Resume. An effective, typed biographical summary — a resume or vita — includes the following :

(i) *demographic data* (name permanent address, date of birth, marital status, and telephone number, if any); (ii) *career objectives,* both for short range (such a staff assistant or labour relations) and long range (*e.g.* contract negotiator); (iii) *educational background* and *academic achievements* (iv) *leadership positions* in clubs, athletic teams, students union and social organisation and (v) *Previous work experience.*

2. Prepare for the Interview. The applicant should prepare himself fully before attending the interviews. He should study some literature about the company in order to ask specific questions about product, process, goals or competition. Questions on items that are related to job duties, the reason for joining the organisation, should be thoroughly prepared. The candidate should go in well armed with all necessary facts so that he can start off right, with a concrete, intelligent listing of his reasons.

3. Create good impression. Interviewers frequently form their final judgements within the first few minutes of the interview, and most judgements are made before half the interview is completed. The old maxim "first impressions are important" is apparently sound for the interview process. Therefore, if the interviewee enters making a good impression and starts off well, this first impression may be changed by interview, but very rarely. But if he starts off with an initial unfavourable impression if may be impossible to overcome it during the interview.

The interviewee must follow these considerations to make a good impression and "accentuate the positive" aspect.[7] (i) appropriate clothing; (ii) good grooming; (iii) a firm handshake; (iv) the appearance of controlled energy; (v) pertinent humour and readiness to smile; (vi) a genuine interest in the employers' operations and alert attention when the interviewer speaks; (vii) pride in past performance; (viii) an

7. McCormick and Tiffin, *Industrial Psychology*, pp. 269-270.

understanding of the employers' needs and a desire to serve them; (ix) the display of sound ideas; and (x) ability to take control when employers fall down on the interviewing job.

Some time, the fresh applicants, when selected, join the organisation without getting sufficient information about the organisation and the employer. They run a risk for they may not be able to fit themselves in the organisation. Therefore, it is useful for the person selected to get necessary information from different sources — acquaintances or person who work with the organisation, company manuals, brochures, annual reports, discussions with others who may have been interviewed with the same company.

Following Chart 10.3 contains a listing of questions that should be answered before accepting a position.

CHART 10.3

Questions to Answer Before Accepting a Position

I. *Promotion Criteria*

1. Does the organisation use a formal evaluation system?
2. How often is a person evaluated?
3. What are the major criteria upon which a person is evaluated?
4. Are evaluation discussed with persons being evaluated?
5. Is career counselling available?
6. Does the organisation encourage publication in professional journals?

II. *Professional Development*

1. Does the organisation offer a formal training programme?
2. If so, what is the nature and duration of the programme?
3. Is there any formal training in computers and information systems.
4. Does the organisation support travel to professional conferences/seminars?
5. Is there any form of tution refund programme for college/professional diploma programmes?
6. What type of responsibility is offered during the first year on the job?

III. *Organisational Background*

1. What are the objectives of the organisation?
2. What has been the general trend in sales, growth employment, earnings, research, expenditures, and leverage?
3. What institutions have the senior officers attended? Foreign? or Inside the country?
4. What is the nature of the organisations' affirmative action programme?
5. What is opportunity for women/handicaps/special minority groups in management?
6. How many persons left the staff during the past year?
7. What is the absentee rate for hourly personnel? Is it above the average for the industry?

IV. *Financial Considerations* (to be discussed and considered last)

1. What are the normal working hours? Is overtime pay granted for staff?
2. Is overnight stay required? If so for what period? What is reimbursement policy?
3. Is there a profit sharing plan?
4. Is retirement play vested?
5. Vacation policy? Hospitalisation? Medical benefits? Life Insurance? Pension? Provident Fund/Gratuity, etc.
6. What would starting salary be? What would be the usual allowances available?

A test has been defined both in a broad and narrow manner. Broadly, it has been defined as a "systematic procedure for comparing the behaviour of two or more persons." In a narrow sense, "it is a sample of an aspect of an individuals' behaviour, performance or attitude."[8] It may be defined *as a systematic procedure for sampling human behaviour.*

Purpose of Tests

Psychological tests are used for the following purposes :

1. To guide and counsell students seeking admission to schools and college.
2. To provide vocational guidance of adults seeking help in their careers.
3. To conduct research into human behaviour and personality.
4. To seelct candidates for an organisation.
5. To make a differential palcement or assignment of a person to the job for which he is most suitable.
6. To select candidates for promotion and transfer within an organisation.
7. To select candidates for assignment to a company training programme.
8. To assist an individual employee in solving his problems.

Psychological Tests

According to Wendell, tests are used in business for three primary purposes :[9]

(a) For the selection and placement of new employees;

(b) For appraising employees for promotional potentinals and

(c) For counselling employees. If properly used, psychological

---

8. Blum, Milton M., *Industrial Psychology and Its Social Foundantions*, Harper & Row, New York, 1956, p. 257.
9. French, Wendell, *The Peresonnel Management Process*, 1974, p. 281.

tests can be of paramount importance for each of these purposes.

According to Meyer and Bertottle, candidates are judged on the basis of their physical characteristics, their abilities and skills, their interests and personality traits. These are shown in Fig. 10.2.

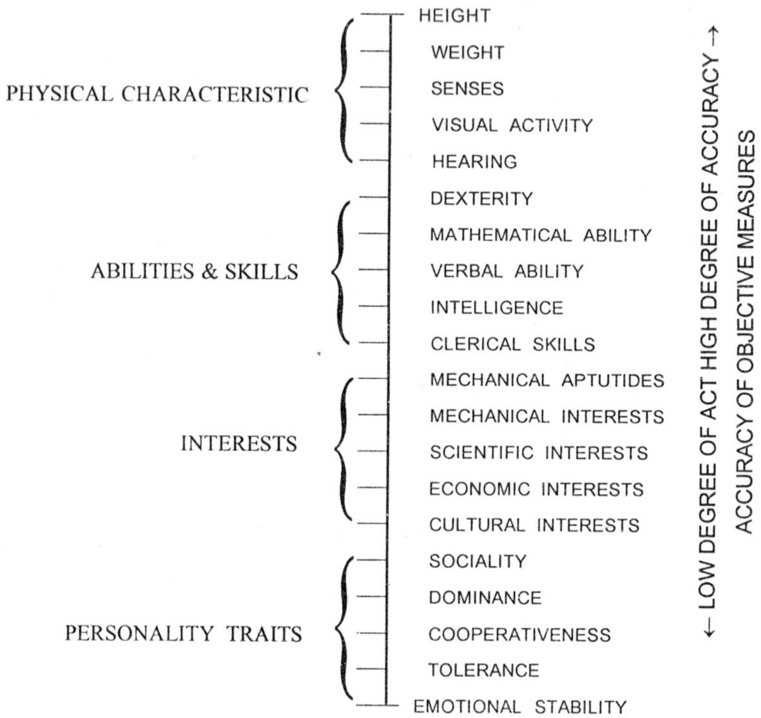

Fig. 10.2 Measures of Human Characteristics

1. *J.L. Mursell* : "A psychological test then is a pattern of stimuli selected and organised to elicit responses which will reveal certain psychological characteristics in the person who takes them."[10]

2. *L.S. Cronbach* : "A test is a systematic procedure for comparing the behaviour of two or more persons."

3. *M.L. Blum* : "A test is a sample of an individual's behaviour, performance or attitude."

Thus, psychological tests are an organisation of stimuli selected

10. Marsell, J.L., *Psychological Testing,* New York, Longman's Green, (1953), p. 1.

with some special objectives in view such as to discover psychological characteristics of the person being tested. These tests are called psycholgical tests because their main aim is to know the psychological trait such as personnel behaviour, efficiency of work and interests in work, etc.

Importance of Psychological Test

Psychological tests have proved to possess great utility in the following spheres :

1. Guidance. Psychological tests are indispensable in all forms of guidance.

2. Appropriate appointments. Psychological tests are utilised for the appointment of appropriate individuals to posts in offices, factories and government serivces. They secure proper and desirable jobs for individuals according to their interests, inclinations, intelligence and abilities. They ensure that the highest level of efficiency is achieved by the right man being in the right job. Thus both the employer as well as the employee are benefited.

3. Selection for training. An individual can benefit from training for some particular job only if he is initially in possession of the requisite intelligence, abilities and qualities, besides the necessary interest in the work involved. He should be tested in respect of these qualities before any training is imparted to him. Hence, in all civilized nations of the world all kinds of training institutes make use of psychological tests for selecting the required candidates. In India, for example, the recruitment to the Police Training Colleges, The Govt. Teacher's Training College, and other technical institutions is done only on the basis of psychological test. In public schools, the students who receive scholarships are selected on the basis of psychological tests in order to ensure that the scholarships are not wasted, as well they might be if they are provided to the wrong individuual. Psychological tests are also used for selection of candidates for Army, Navy and Air Force personnel. The use of psychological tests for the selection in training schools is constantly on the increase.

4. Classification according to the level of intelligence. The success of education depends upon the student being provided education that accords with his level of intelligence. Hence, individual students are classified and stratified according to their level of intelligence and different curicula and extra curricular programmes devised for the three categories of students the brilliant the average and the retarded. This calssification is based on intelligence tests. Intelligence tests are used to classify individuals not only in the field of education but also in various vocations, armed forces and industries.

5. Prediction. The prediction indicates the forecasting of success in the case of an individual. While guiding the individual, a psychological can normally make fairly accruate predictions as to the degree of success that one is likely to acheive. The prediction is based upon psychological tests; the greater the capacity of a psychological test to assist in prediction, the greater is its validity and its reliability.

6. Diagnosis. Before giving any guidance, the directing psychologist makes a diagnosis of the problem present before him. He gives suggestions for alleviating a certain condition only after he decides upon a dignosis, as it is only that he reaches the root causes. Without a psychological test proper diagnosis cannot be achieved.

7. Research. Psychological tests are used even in the field of psychological research. Intelligence tests, interest inventories, personality tests, tests of mental abilities and personality qualities, help in research in these specific directions.

Classification or Types of Psychological Tests

It must be noted that there is no one single and complete system of test classification, actually there are a variety of ways in which they are classified. For example,

(A) on the basis of human behaviour,

(B) individual or group tests, or

(C) on the basis of use of tests.

(A) Classification on the Basis of Human Behaviour. On the basis of human behaviour, tests have been generally classified into four categories, as depicted in the chart 10.4

CHART 10.4

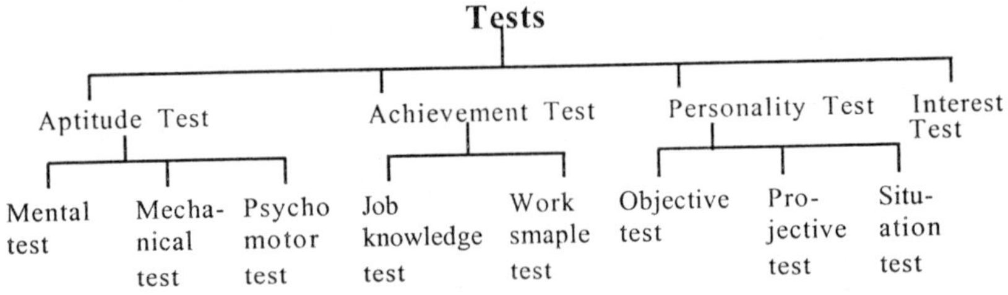

(B) Individual or Group Tests. Tests have been divided into two classes; according to method.

(i) *Individual tests* : These tests are administered to one individual at one time. They include performance tests and tests that require linguists ability. Some examples are Stanford-Binet intelligence test, Wechsler Bellevue intelligence tests, Kohez's block design test,

Rorschach's ink blot test, and T.A.T. test, etc. These are particularly appropriate for testing of individuals than they are expensive and require more expert training than in many other cases. Individual tests are less objective than group tests.

(ii) *Group tests* : These include tests performed upon a large number of people simultaneously such as the group intelligence tests of the Bureau of Psychology Uttar Pradesh, interest lists, vocational lists, etc. They are more objective and less expensive; requiring very little, if any, specialised training that may prove expensive. But in these tests there is no real rapport between the subject and the examiner of individuals, than is in the individual tests. Nevertheless, they have proved really useful in the case of educational and vocational guidance requirements.

(C) Classification on the Basis of use of Tests. From this viewpoint the psychological tests are divided into the following classes :

(i) *Verbal Intelligence tests* : These are tests in which questions are orally asked, linguistic and concerned abilities being essentially required. One of the best examples of verabal tests is Dr. Sohan Lal's intelligence test utilized at Bureau of Psychology Uttar Pradesh. These tests are no intended for and cannot be used in the case of illiterates, only slightly educated persons and small children, since such people lack linguistic ability.

(ii) *Non-verbal Intelligence tests* : These are tests which do not require the use of language, but substitue figures, pictures, blocks and other implements for it. Examples of it are Pidgon's non-verbal tests and Raven's progressive matrices. Their particular felicity lies in the fact that they can be applied to the testing of illiterates, very slightly educated individual and very young children. This category includes all non-verbal tests.

(iii) *Aptitude tests* : These depict the interest, ability, nature and reputation of the candidates. Test the nature and efficiency of the candidate for routine work.

(iv) *Interest tests* : These apply to candidate's interest in the work, his hobby and other interests. These are carried on in the questionnaire form.

(v) *Personality tests* : These tests are used to known specialities, concept, moral value and mentality self-confidence, ambition, decisivity, patience, fear, initiativeness and dominance. This procedure is applied for higher and medium status offices. The main methods of personality testing are Rorschach's Ink Blot Test and T.A.T.

Principles of Psychological Testing

The application of poorly designed tests in harmful at it might bring discredit to testing as a means of selection. There are following principles both of practical and theoretical nature that determine the functional utility of these tests in business organisations.

1. Validity. The validity of a test is the degree to which it actually measurers what it is intended to measure. In an employment situation, a valid test is one that accurately predicts criterion of job success are five different types of validity :

(i) *Content Validity* : Following shows how well the content of the test questions relate to the subject matter being measured. It is judged by a group of experts.

(ii) *Face validity* : It requires to test whether the questions in a test are related to job or otherwise. However, face validity cannot be measured in statistical terms. Moreover, it does not really test the validity of the test.

(iii) *Concurrent Validity* : It refers to the degree according to which test scores relate to the performance of employees presently on the job. A test is given to the candidates and their scores on the test are compared with their efficiency on the job. A high positive correlation shows the validity of the test.

(iv) *Predictive Validity* : It is evaluated by showing how well predictions, made by the test are confirmed at some subsequent time. If those who made the highest score at the time of selection tests also turned to be efficient later on, the test has predictive validity.

(v) *Construct Validity* : It is evaluated by determining the psychological qualities of a test measuring mental traits such as intelligence. It measures how well the test is measuring the hypotheses framed in this respect.

Of the above type of validity predictive and concurrent validity is the most important in business and industry. However, before administering the test and testings its validity, one should be sure as to what traits these tests would measure. This may done through careful job analysis and determining the standards in this respect.

2. Reliability. The reliability of the test means the consistency with which it yields the same scores throughout a series of measurements. A test possesses high reliability if a person who is tested a second or third time with the same test and under same conditions obtains almost the same result. Following are the three methods of testing reliability :

(i) *Test-retest Method* : In this method, a group of subjects is given the same tests twice after a certain interval in between. The scores at two tests are compared. The test may be called reliable if both of these are positively associated.

(ii) *Alternative form Method* : In this method, two seaprate but equivalent forms are given to the subjects. These include items that are similar in nature. Scores on these tests are associated and positive associations show the reliability.

(iii) *Split-halves method* : This method divides the whole test into two similar and equal parts and the scores on these two parts are compared. A high association indicates internal consistency of the tests.

3. Supplementing the Selection Procedure. Testing should be a supplement, not a substitute for other selection procedure. Testing is only a part of the total selection procedure.

4. Standardized Administration. Where tests are given under a variety of conditions, great variations in test scores may occur. While administering a test there should be proper control and standardisation so that results are comparable.

5. Tests must be Tested. A high test score does nt always mean a satisfactory employee. So the validity and relevance of test should be tested before its actual administration.

6. Testing to be Conducted by Experts only. Except in the simplest programmes testing should be conducted by a person who has had training in test construction, administration and analysis. Only experts can ensure good results from tests.

7. Proper Communication. As testing programmes can be made more useful by additional research, all studies of testing programmes should be reported in current professional journals. The persons incharge of psychological testing in various organisations can improve their system of testing by such communications.

8. Control. Distribution of testing materials should be carefully controlled. Misuse of tests by persons who are not familiar with thier purposes and limitations may seriously affect the interest of those tested. It may also create misunderstanding of the whole testing procedure.

9. Interpretation. Those who administer the testing programme should interpret the results to all who make use of them. Test scores can not be interpreted easily. Some of them can be desired only in terms of patterns or profits. Interpretation of scorers is essential to all who are to use them.

According to Tiffin and McCormick "It should be recognised

that psychological tests are not infalliable and that sometimes they reveal results which are not a true indication of the potential job success of the candidate.[11]

DEVELOPING A TEST PROGRAMME

The following steps are involved in developing a sound testing programme :

1. Decide the objectives of a testing programme, i.e. Whether it is meant for hiring personnel or for transfers, promotions, etc. Initially, such a programme may be set up only for some jobs, then it may be expanded to cover all types of jobs in an organisation.

2. Analyse jobs to identify those characteristics which appear necessary for job sucess. There include the need for active habits, eye-hand co-ordination, finger-and-arm dexterity, perceptual and sensory abilities and such other specific characteristics. It has to be decided as to which 'human traits and skills' are necessary for adequate performance of job. Consideration may be given to *production-related criteria, i.e.* quantity, quality etc., and this *personnel data, i.e.*, absenteeism, length of service, etc.

3. Choose tests to measure characteristics. This may be done by keeping in mind such factors as reliability, content or face validity, level of difficulty, ease of administration, and the csot involved. Battery of Test are chosen with the purpose of measuring a variety of possible predictors, such as aggressiveness, extroversion, numerical ability, etc.

4. Administer tests to an experimental group of people. For purposes of employment, a test is usually administered after an application blank has been examined and there has been a preliminary interview. Many candidates are rejected for a variety of reasons before tests are administered.

5. Establish criteria of job success. This criteria should take into account such factors as the quality and quantity of output, accident frequency, regularity or otherwise in attendance, grades obtained during training, speed of promotion in an organisation, professional achievements (published work, awards received), and formal ratings determined by the supervisor.

6. Analyse the results of tests and take decisions regarding the applications of tests. As no single test can be expected to measure all the abilities required for a satisfactory job performance, a number of tests in combination are usually administered.

---

11. Tiffin, J. and McCormick, E.J., *Industrial Psychology*, Prentice Hall of India Pvt. Ltd., New York, 1971, p. 117.

BASIC TESTING GUIDELINES

According to Hammer and Schmidt, the following are the basic testing guidelines :[12]

1. Tests are to be used as supplement rather than as a substitute for any other method. No test should be used as the sole criterion for selection, palcement, promotion or transfer. As valid tests represent a small sample of a person's total pattern of behaviour, reliance should also be palced on information derived from other procedures — from interviews, application blanks, and background checks. A reasonably complete picture of a candidate should be obtained.

2. Tests are better at predicting failure than success. Testing procedures do not necessarily determine who can or will perform such duties in a very effective and efficient manner. They determine which applicants will not or cannot perform a job satisfactorily.

3. Tests are a screening device. Tests are useful when it is necessary to pick up a small select group from many applicants. When hundreds of candidates apply for a few jobs, a test can only be a preliminary selection technique.

4. Test scores are not precise measures. As tests are samples of behaviour they cannot be totally accurate predictors of anything. A test score of 90 does not precisely reveal a 90 per cent grasp of a subject matter.

5. Test must be tested in the organisation in which it is used. It is always necessary to test the test itself. A test may be validated by undertaking research into the environment in which it is used. Besides, it must also be reliable. A person should receive the same score whenever he takes the same test, unless some significant educational development has taken place between testing dates. Following comparative chart shows the validity of various lists as predictive of job proficiency.

6. Test conditions are important. All applicants should take the test under the same test conditions is ensure that some do not get high or low scores due to differences in test conditions.

7. Invasion of privacy should be avoided. As tests are generally personal they should be held in strict confidence. It should be administered and evaluated by experts. The results should be kept confidential till they are declared.

8. Test administration, scoring and interpretation require technical competence and training in testing.

12. Hammer and Schmidt, *Contemporary Problems in Personnel*, St. Clair, Chicago, 1974, pp. 117-123.

CHART 10.5

Validity of Various Tests as Predictive of Job Proficiency[13]

	Job	Intellectual Ability	Spatial and Mechanical Ability	Perceptual Accuracy	Motor Ability	Personality Traits
1.	Exclusive	Moderate	Moderate+	Moderate	Low Moderate	
2.	Supervisor	Moderate	Moderate	Moderate	Low/ Moderate	Low
3.	Clerical	Moderate	Low	Moderate	Low	Low/
4.	Sales	Low	Low	Low	Low	Moderate+
5.	Protective Service	Moderate	Low+	Low+	Low	Low
6.	Vehicle Operator	Low	Low+	Low/ Moderate	Moderate	Moderate
7.	Trade & Crafts	Moderate	Moderate	Moderate	Low/ Moderate	Low/ Moderate
8.	Industrial	Moderate	Moderate	Moderate	Moderate	High+

(Types of Tests)

Low Predictability = 20

Moderate Predictability = .20 - .35

High Predictability = .35-.50

High = .50+

WORK SAMPLING

Based on the presumption that *the best indicator of future performance is past performance* 'Work Sampling' is another technique for screening candidates. Before selecting an employee, the personnel manager should inquire about the candidates "prior work experience" to make his judgement.

The applicants are tested on several specific tasks that are curcial to performing the job for which a candidate is being recruited. Their performance on these tasks is then used as a predictor of their performance on the job. Several advantages have been claimed for this technique as a screening tool to conclude with Gary Dessler. "The emphasis is on samples of actual behaviour so it is harder to 'fake' answers (as a person might on aptitude or interest tests). The work sample is more clearly relevant to the job you are recruiting for.

13. Ghiselli, Edwin, E., "The Validity of Aptitude Tests in Pesonnel Selection," *Personnel Psychology*, Winter, 1973, pp. 461-477.

The content of the work sample is not as likely to be 'unfair' (or to emphasise middle class concepts and values) as some psychological tests might be. And, since, you are not deliving into the applicants' background and personality, there is almost no chance of the work sample being viewed as an invasion of privacy.[14]

Limitations of Testing

Robert N. McMurry has provided an excellent summary of the limitations of testing in selection. He points out that all tests must be validated before they may be used with confidence. it cannot be assumed that becaused a given test has worked satisfactorily in selection for one job, it will be similarly satisfactory for another. Nor is it enough that the test has reliability or that repeated administrations give essentially the same results. Nor can it be assumed that the test will work simply because it appears logically related to job performance. As R.H. McMurry remarks : "It is not generally recognized that even under the best of circumstances there is a definite limit to the efficiency of a single test or a battery of tests. Actually, the validity obtained in industry for a given test or a battery of tests, rarely reaches 70."

In fact, tests are only supplements, not a substitute for other selection procedures. A good test may indicate a high co-efficient of correlation between performance on the test and job success. But it can not give hundred per cent positive results. It does not indicate the percentage of efficiency of prediction produced by the test or tests. These limitations should be kept in mind while using the tests in selection procedures.

Characteristic of a Good Test

1. Reliability. The higher the degree of reliability that results of a test have the greater is the reliability of the test. The reliability of its conclusion means that if the same test is performed upon the same individual more than once, results obtained in each individual list should be the same or commensurate with the first one.

2. Validity. The validity of test lies in the fact that it succeeds in testing the particular quality which it is designed to test.

3. Objectivity. A test has a high level of objectivity if the answer to each of its various questions is distinct and precise and if there is no difference of opinion, regarding it among the various examiners. It result is in no way influenced by the examiner's individual opinions, so that the conclusions or results are obtained no matter what the number of examiners who examine the same object.

---

14. Dersber, Gary, *Personnel Management, Modern Concepts and Techniques,* Revton Publishing Co. IMC. Revton, Virgrimia, 1978, p. 120.

4. Comprehensiveness. Comprehensive involves inclusion of all features or traits allied to the one in question. It provides information on qualities concerned with the one trait actually being tested. In a comprehensive test, questions cover the trait in question as well as allied traits so that no aspect of the measured or tested ability escapes attention.

5. Discriminating Power. This is the ability which helps to distinguish between persons with greater or less ability so that they score more or less points or marks.

6. Utility. This concerns the extent to which a particular test can be used with facility. For this it is essential that questions asked should be simple, the method easy, the time involved less and the expenses negligible.

Of the above mentioned characteristics validity and reliability are the most important characteristics.

INTELLIGENCE TESTS

The first concrete step in the direction of intelligence tests was taken by a famous French psychologist Alfred Binet. Alfred Binet was conducting some research in the mental activities of school going children. In the course of his research he observed that in order to give any useful education to the feeble-minded children it is essential to put them in special classes. In order to investigate this subject a committee headed by Binet was formed in 1904. The first difficulty concerning the study of feeble-minded children was need of a scale with which to measure the intelligence of children.

Binet Simon Test. With Simon's assistance Binet developed and published a scale in 1905, known as the Binet Simon Scale. In this scale, some 30 tasks, from the simplest to the most complex, were prescribed in a serial order. On the basis of experiments with average and feeble-minded children carried out with the help of this scale Binet-Simon intelligence tests, if a five-year old child is capable of performing tasks which an average child of three can perform, his mental age will be rate as three years and if that child fails to perform more than the first five among the thirty tasks he will be classed as idiot.

Binet and Simon made revisions in this scale from time to time. The first revised scale was published in 1908. Form the success of this revision, psychologists of other countries developed intelligence tests suitable to the environment of their own countries. Among them, Burt's London Revision, and Terman's Stanford Revision are well known. The modern revised edition was published in 1937 under the name of Terman Merrill Scale.

Terman-Meril Scale

In the Terman-Meril Scale which was a revision of the Standord-Binet Scale, some more subjects, related to intelligence tests were included. It now became useful for the age range of 2 to 18 years. In this scale, there were provisons for two types of tests, yearly and half-yearly, for children belonging to the age group of two to four years. Many other subjects were included for the adult people. For every age group there were six to eight subjects. In this scale there are tests which enable the examiner to examine the intelligence of an individual in a very short time.

Indian Scales

In Indian conditions, Binet's test was adopted for the first time by Dr. C. Herbert Rice. But its revised form is almost completely different from the Binet tests. These tests were compiled in Urdu and Punjabi. There are two types of scales in it, one having 10 tasks, the other 35 tasks, and it was the smaller scale of tests which proved dependable. In 1927, Dr. J. Munry of Christian College started verbal group tests in Urdu, English and Hindi. In 1933, Mr. Lajja Shankar developed group tests for children from 10 to 18, which adopted a revised and studied form of Terman's group tests. Besides these, the group tests started by Dr. Jalota of Lahore, in Hindi, Urdu and English proved very valuable. In Bihar, under the direction of Dr. S.M. Mohsin, a test battery was constructed to measure mental abilities and intelligence of participants in many group tests. In the nonverbal group tests for college students, important contribution have come from Dr. Lalit Kumar Shah, C.T. Phillip, H.C. Banerjee, D.H. Roy, T.P. Bhowmick and H.P. Maiti. The above description makes it quite clear that not much work has been done in the direction of non-verbal tests. There is hope of development in this direction in the future.

Types of Intelligence Tests

Intelligence tests are classified as follows according to the activities prescribed in them :

1. Verbal Individual Intelligence tests,
2. Non-verbal Individual Intelligence Tests,
3 Verbal Group Intelligence Tests,
4. Non-Verbal Group Intelligence Tests.

1. Verbal Individual Inteligence Tests. These are intelligence tests given to individuals. Language finds adequate use in them. Binet-simon tests and the various revisions are all included in this classification.

The State Bureau of psychology of Uttar Pradesh has adopted

a Hindi version of the Terman-Merrill Scale. It includes a variety of materials, from solid objects to difficult questions. The activities in the beginning are simple, like constructing a bridge or a tower of blocks or fitting irregular wooden blocks in their proper place supplied for them. At the same time, at the end of the tests there are difficult questions which need considerable thinking. This test is divided into several age groups. The higher groups use language and its use gradually declines with the age group.

2. Non-verbal Individual Intelligence Tests. These tests involve the least possible use of the linguistic ability and are similarly almost unaffected by knowledge derived from books. An example of these non-verbal tests is the Performance Intelligence Tests.

Difficulties in the Individual Intelligence Test

(i) *Requires much time* : The individual intelligence test takes an hour usually and only one person can be tested at one time. Obviously, at this rate it would be essential to have a very big number of trained examiners and in spite of that it would be difficult to test all the people.

(ii) *Requires Experienced Examiners* : In the individual intelligence tests experienced examiners are rquired because the correct result cannot be arrived at if the examiners are inexperienced. At the same time, availability of such a large number of trained personnel is almost impossible. However in come circumstances the individual intelligence tests become unavoidable because the level of accuracy reached by the individual intelligence tests, in the assessment of a person's intelligence, is beyond the reach intelligence tests.

(iii) *Verbal Group Intelligence Tests* : These owe their origin and development to the difficulties from which the individual tests suffer. These are designed to test the intelligence of a group and not of an individual. All the people in the group are given the same direction and have to perform the same activities. Even the score of the result of group intelligence tests is calculated by machines thus dispensing with the necessity of skilled examiners, resulting in an economy of time.

DIFFICULTIES IN THE VERBAL GROUP INTELLIGENCE TESTS

Following are the difficulties of the verbal group tests :

1. Difficulties related to Co-operation. In these tests it is difficult to judge whether the examinee is extending his full co-operatins or not.

2. Difficulties related to the Balance of the Examinee. In these tests it is difficult to determine whether the physical and emotional balance of the examinee is even or disturbed.

3. Difficulty related to the Ease of the Examinee. In the verbal group intelligence tests it is difficult to ascertain if the examinee is felling at ease and free or restrained.

4. Possibility of Cheating by the Examinee. Another difficulty in these tests is that no one can testify whether the person has written the answer himself or copied if from his neighbour.

The verbal grup intelligence tests have their own advantages due to which they are used comprehensively. The advantages are the same as the difficulties of the individual intelligence tests.

4. Non-Verbal Group Intelligence Tests. As the verbal intelligence tests are meant only for the literates, the non-verbal group intelligence tests have been developed, in which the examine makes a minimum use of language and instead performs many activities. Examplcs of the non-verbal intelligenee tests are Catell's Culture Free test, Raven's Progressive Matrices and the N.I.I.P. test. In the non-verbal group intelligence tests, the examiners have to explain to the examines even the simplest directions which are also demonstrated as far as possible. This is done to make the least possible use of language. In performance tests in the group intelligence tests, the examine draws some simple figures, or performs some simple activities. In Alexander's opinion "A complete performance battery will be a better measure than a complete verbal battery."

Characteristics of the Non-Verbal Group Intelligence Tests

The truth is that even if non-verbal group intelligence tests are not more important than verbal tests, they are certainly not less important. Some of their characteristics are as follows :

1. Comparison of Various Human Groups. The first obstacle in the comparison of human groups of various languages and cultures is the difference in their language. This obstacle can be overcome by the non-verbal group intelligence tests and a comparison between different human groups is rendered possible.

2. The Testing of Illiterate Soldiers. The verbal group intelligence tests are manifestly inapplicable to illiterate workers for the testing of their intelligence. Consequently, the abilities of illiterate workers are assessed by employing the non-verbal group intelligence tests and the possibilities of learning are known.

3. Intelligence Testing in Children. The linguistic ability is very low in the case of children and consequently the verbal group intelligence tests cannot be given to them.

MEASUREMENT OF PERSONALITY

Psychologists employ a number of methods of measure personality, *e.g.,* sitaution test, psycho-analytic test and projective method, etc. Besides these, the case history method, interview and questionnaire and rating methods have their own importance. Briefly, the methods of measuring personality are :

1. Case History Method
2. Interview Method
3. Questionnaire Method
4. Performance Method
5. Rating Method
6. Situation Test
7. Psycho-Analytic Test
8. Projection Techniques.

Among the above metioned methods, the projection techniques are the most popular. A brief description of the other methods, before we make a detailed description of this specific one, would be quite in keeping with the context.

1. Case History Method. In the case history method, as the name obviously indicates, the facts concerning the life of the subject are collected. This case history supplies all the facts related to man's environment and heredity. This method can be employed to study both normal and abnormal personality but it needs experienced testers.

2. Interview Method. The interview method is the most common of all the methods for the study of personality. It is the method widely used in the selection of people for government, semi-government and private services. In this, the subject and the tester sit facing each other and the former answers questions asked by the latter. Besides the answers which the subject offers, his personality is indicated by his expression. This method, like the case history method, needs very experienced testers who ask questions which may probe the correct thing and enable the subject to express himself without any apprehension. Thus the interview method depends as much on the tester as it does on the subject.

3. Questionnaire Method. Questionnaires have been used extensively in the investigation of personality. The name suggests that it is a list of selected questions the answers to which throw light upon different traits of personality. 'Yes' and 'No' are written in front of these questions. The subject either strikes out the wrong answer or indicates the correct one. Questionnaires are used to gain knowledge of traits like self-confidence, sociability, introversion or extroversion, tendency to dominate or be dominated, etc.

There are some difficulties in the questionnaire method. It has the following limitations :

(a) Often the subjects conceal the facts and give wrong answers.

(b) Sometimes the framing of the questions is such that the tester takes them to mean one thing and the subject another.

(c) Usually the subjects write the answer without an adequate amount of thinking thus leaving possibility of mistakes.

In spite of these difficulties, the questionnaire method has proved to be of tremendous value. Allport and Minnesota, etc., have formed questionnaires which help in the study of some subtle traits of personality. It affords a lot of assistance to comparative study because of the various answers of the subjects to the same questions. The conclusions based on these questionnaires are comparative as well as numerical. They also facilitate wide study because a number of people can be studied simultaneously.

Fig. 10.3 : Minnesota Multiphasic Personality Inventory

4. Performance Method. The performance method was developed by May and Hartshorne. In this method the subject is given a variety of specific jobs to be performed and the particular trait of his personality is examined. For example, in order to test the honesty of children some weights with little difference between them, were presented to them. The exact weight of each was written under it and the children were told to palce them in the correct order. The honest children experienced great difficulty while the dishonest read the weights under them and palced them in order promptly. A very simple method of judging the honesty of the students in the class could be something like this. Some piece should be dictated and the copies collected and examined. The mistakes of each should be secretly noted without any markings on the copy, following which the copies should be returned with the direction that the mistakes are to be noted and marks allocated. The dictation should be written on the black board. The honest will mark their mistakes while the dishonest will quietly correct them. The honesty of the students can be judged by comparing these with the mistakes previously noted.

5. Rating Method. Another method of measuring personality is the rating method, in which the procedure is of two types : one, the subject is asked to answer questions related to traits of personality. The answers which the subject offers or selects exhibit his personality. Another way of applying the rating method is to place the subject in real situations and then study his behaviour and reactions. For example, in order to judge personality traits a person is given a variety of jobs to perform.

The rating method is very simple. But it needs more skilful testers. Roughly speaking, it presents the following difficulties :

(a) Much skill and capability are essential in the tester.

(b) The possibility of prejudice is very great.

(c) It is very difficult to enumerate or evaluate the subtle traits. Mistakes are often made in this.

In spite of the above mentioned difficulties, both social and industrial psychologists make much use of this method. As has been pointed out previously too, it can be made useful to a large extent if the tester is very skilful.

6. Situation Test. As usual, the name suggests the nature of the method. In it, the subject is placed in some specific situations and the traits of his personality are ascertained. Actually, it resembles the performance method, the difference lying in the fact that in this case the person is palced in a situation while in the performance method he is given some work to do.

7. Psycho-analytic Method. In the psycho-analytic method of measurement of personality two types of tests are more popular — Free Association and Dream Analysis. Both these tests show the traits of the personality, in its unconscious aspect. In dream analysis, the subject describes his dream and without using reasoning, associates freely the dream objects and activities. Because of the absence of reasoning the truth of the unconscious mind is expressed by this association, by which the psycho-analyst discovers many characteristics of personality. The psycho-analytic method is mostly used in discovering the personality traits and mental ailments of abnormal people. Its main condition lies in the need for a skilled and experienced psycho-analyst. Often, the psycho-analyst has to analyse his own mind in order to remove the possibility of any prejudice.

8. Projective Techniques. The most popular of all the methods for the investigation of personality is the projective method. Its name suggests the fact that it is founded upon the element of projection. The Taj Mahal, to take an example is a marble building many people go to see. Different people find in it different things, in keeping with the peculiarities of their personalities. An emotional person sees it in the form of a formal symbol of emotions while, to the person who gives importance to political and economic questions, it may be a symbol of exploitation. This is an example of a material object but it does make clear the fact that a human being does not see an object as it is but also projects the traits of his own personality upon it. Many peculiarities of the personality are investigated by an analysis of this projection and a comparison of it with the projections affected by others.

Two tests in the projective techniques are more widely used :

1. Rorschach Ink-blot Test.

2. Murray's Thematic Apperception Test, known in brief as T.A.T. They are extensively used in the investigation of personality. These will, therefore, be described briefly here.

1. Rorschach Ink-blot Test. This test was developed by the Swiss scientist Hermann Rorschach. He used 10 original ink-blot cards which are still in use today. There is no picture made in these blots. Five of these are black, two black and red and the other three multicoloured. To investigate personality, they are exhibited before the subject one after the other and he is asked to describe everything he sees in the blot. These are shown for a definite interval of time. Then they are shown to the subject for a second time and he is asked to point out the location, of whatever he has seen, on the blot. In order to establish the meaning of the subject's reaction to the blots, the psychologist analyses the location, determining factors and the object. The analysis of the location serves to indicate whether the subject reacted to some particular spot on the blot or towards the blot as a whole. As a general rule, it s believed that the person who reacts more completely is more principled. The analysis of the determining factors is an attempt to find out whether the reaction of the subject is towards the shape of the blot or to the colour or motion in the blot. As to the object, the analysis shows whether the subject sees in it the figure of a man or an animal or anything else.

Besides the above analysis, facts like the time taken by the subject to react to the whole blot, the number of activities which he did and whether he did them normally or not, are also noted and observed. All these things tend to help in the analysis and investigation of the unconscious peculiarities of the subject.

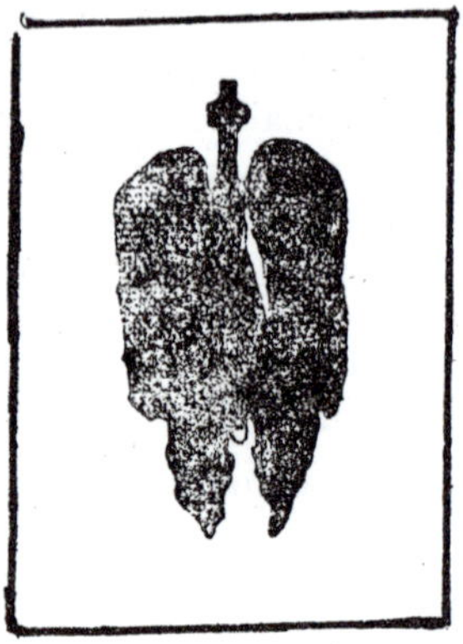

Fig. 10.4 : Rorschach's Ink Blot.

The difficulty in the ink-blot test is that the description of the subject's reaction becomes quite subjective, which conceals to some extent the correct personality traits of the subject. But efforts are being made to make this test more objective.

2. Murray's Thematic Apperception Test. The founder of this test, Murray, investigated the personality traits with the help of some pictures. These pictures are still considered to be standard. Observing these pictures, the subject, by projection, identifies himself with the characters in the picture. The pictures are presented one by one to the subject who has to compose a story on each of them within some fixed time period, say five minutes. He does not get time to think. Therefore the story expresses his natural desires, emotions, sentiments, etc. On the basis of these stories, the psychologist analyses the personality of the subject and uncovers its traits.

As in the Rorschach ink-blot test, there is some difficulty in Murray's thematic apperception test, since the personality investigation done by it is not numerical but qualitative with possibility of mistakes. But there is no doubt that an experienced and skilful psychologist can use this method to uncover many hidden traits of the personality of the subject. This test helps in the discovery of many abnormalities of personality as well.

MEASUREMENT OF SPECIAL ABILITIES

Such problems as the profession an individual may adopt, or the course of study a student may profitably pursue are ones that need guidance and for this guidance it is essential that in addition to measuring the individual's level of intelligence, his special abilites are investigated. Hence, efforts have been made to devise tests to discover special mental abilities, and they are being extensively used.

Before going on to the testing of special mental abilities, it is necessary to know the age in which these tests can be suitably administered. This question arises for the simple reason that in childhood, these special abilities are not distinctly present and psychologists are not unanimous in their opinions regarding the age in which these abilities become distinct and separate. According to some, man's special mental abilities can be separately distinguished at the age of 11, while in the opinion of Cyril Burt, it is at 13 that these abilities become distinct. Generally, it is the former opinion that is accepted. Accordingly, all educational guidance is rendered at the age of 11 or thereabouts.

Number of Special Mental Abilities

Having determined the age in which the special mental abilities become distinct, it is now essential that their number also be determined. In fact, it is very difficult to determine the exact number of special abilities, and there is no unanimity of opinion on this question. In 1938 Thurston and his associates fixed the number of special fundamental abilities at seven, calling them Primary Mental Abilities — verbal abilities or V, numerical ability or N, reasoning or R, memory or M, word fluency or W, and spatial ability or S, and perceptual speed or P. The Chicago primary mental abilities test has been based on these mental abilities. Another test battery formed on the same principle is used in the American Psychological Corporation. It contains the following seven tests :

1. Verbal reasoning,
2. Numerical ability,
3. Abstract reasoning,
4. Space relation,
5. Mechanical reasoning,
6. Clerical speed and accuracy,
7. Language uses.

Now, we can go on to a slightly detailed account of some special abilities tests.

Thurston's S.R.A. Tests of Primary Mental Abilities

To repeat, Thurston has discovered the presence of seven fundamental mental abilities through his study. This conception of primary mental abilities wrought a great change in the field of guidance and counselling. Following this discovery, in the field of guidance even more importance began to be attached to these abilities, than to intelligence, since mental abilities of different individuals with similar levels of intelligence were found to differ in the extreme. On the other hand, people with the same mental abilities were found to have different levels of intelligence. In fact, the choice of a course of study to be taken up by a student or the choice of a profession by a person requires a test of special abilities more than it requires intelligence tests since success in these fields depends more upon innate as well as acquired ability than upon intelligence. Hence in England and America, many tests of mental abilities were evolved, and they were combined to form test batteries. Then, these test batteries were used extensively in the field of education of professions.

Thurston constructed three batteries of tests for special abilities for various children in the following three age divisions and used different test items in each of them :

(a) *For Children between 5 and 7* : In the test battery for this division, he included tests of verbal reasoning, spatial ability, speed of perceptual knowledge and tests of motor ability.

(b) *For Children between 7 and 11* : Test battery for this classification includes tests of verbal ability, numerical ability, speed of logic and perceptual knowledge.

(c) *For Children between 11 and 17* : Test battery for this division includes tests of verbal ability, numerical ability, word fluency, spatial ability and power of abstract reasoning.

TESTS FOR INDIVIDUAL ABILITIES

Test batteries devised by Thurston reveal the main mental abilities of children of different ages, but in addition to this there are individual tests for separate mental abilities. It would be in keeping with the context ot describe them also.

1. Spatial Ability Tests. This reveals the person's spatial or form ability. One example of this is the N.I.I.P. form relation test devised by the National Institute of Industrial Psychology, London. It has been described earlier. The Psychological Bureau of Uttar Pradesh has been making use of it for quite some time; besides the Bureau has also formulated its own test for measuring spatial ability. Another example of such a test is the Minnesota Paper Form Board which includes 64 test items in which one has to combine various incomplete geometrical forms to complete the figures. In the Minnesota Spatial Relation Test, there are four tests of the form board. Both these tests have proved to be of immense value.

2. Mechanical Ability Tests. Through these tests, the person's ability of handling mechanical devices is measured. For this, some laboratories use paper and pencil while others use mechanical tools and objects. One example of this is the Minnesota Mechanical Assembly test. In this there are three boxes that contain the various parts of some common mechanical device. In the test, these parts have to be put together to form the complete object. Other tests of mechanical ability that are famous are the Bennett Test of Mechanical Comprehension, and MacQuarrie test for mechanical ability.

3. Motor Dexterity Tests. In these tests, the motor ability of the hands and figures us measured. Examples of such tests are Bennett Hand Tool Dexterity Test, Purdue Peg Board, Steadiness Tester and O'Conor Tweezer Dexterity Test. Only the first two will be described here.

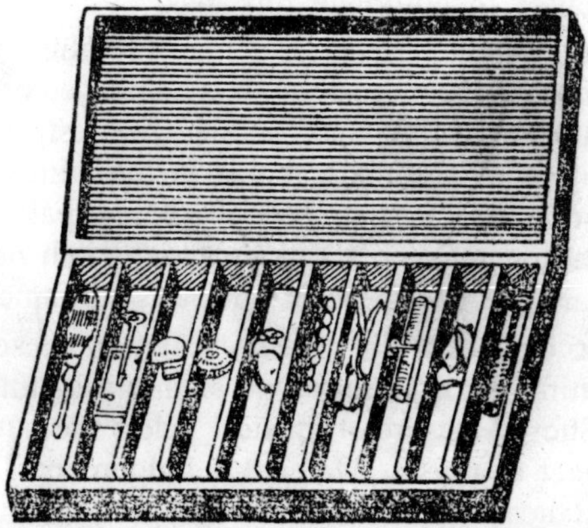

Fig. 10.5 : Minnesota Mechanical Assembly Box.

(a) *Steadiness Tester* : This device examines the steadiness of the hand and the fingers. In this, there is a box, on one side of which there are numerous holes arranged systematically so that they proceed from the widest to the smallest. The subject takes an instrument called the stylus into his hand and inserts it completely and draws it out of these holes successively. If in doing so the stylus touches any of the walls of the hole, a bell rings. The test consists in the ability to prevent the stylus touching the wall while inserting it into the hole and drawing it out. The hole in which the bell rings is tried thrice by the subject. This test helps to discover the individual's dexterity with his hand and fingers, and the extent to which he can handle minute instruments.

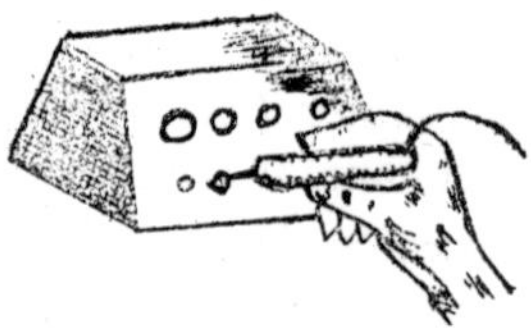

Fig. 10.6 : Steadiness Tester.

(b) *O'Conor's Tweezer Dexterity Test* : In this test, there are 100 small holes on a board, in rows of ten each. there are 100 pins placed by the side. The subject has to use a tweezer to place each of these pins in this board, one in each hole. He scores according to the short time that he takes to complete this task.

4. Clerical Tests. These tests measure the individual's ability concerning writing and composition. It is composed of tests in arithmetic, word groups, distinct reading and good writing, tests in direct knowledge, etc. One example of the clerical test is the Minnesota Clerical test which has two parts. In one part there are pairs of numbers, the correct pair having to be marked in which both numbers are given. In the other part one has to point out pairs of names that are similar.

5. Artistic or Aesthetic Ability Test. In these, the individual's ability concerning art is tested. One example of this is the McAdory Art Test. Sea Shore Measure of Musical Talent measures the individual's ability in respect of music. Meier Art Judgement Test is another test of artistic and aesthetic ability. In this test there are 100 pairs of pictures. In every pair there is one original and the other copy, and the student has to select the original and its copy in respect of every pair. Success in this depends upon his aesthetic ability and acuity since the original has more beauty than the copy.

MEASUREMENT OF ATTITUDES

Difficulties in Measuring Attitudes

Attitudes contain many elements which it is very difficult to measure. To take but one, the emotions and feelings involved in attitudes cannot be measured and hence attitudes can be measured only indirectly or by approximately guessing about them. Attitudes are internal systems. In this form, they do not possibly admit to any measurement, but the individual's external behaviour is generated by inner tendencies. Hence, attitudes can be measured from external behaviour. For the measurement of attitudes it is necessary that the immediate circumstances be controlled. The greater the amount or extent of control upon these immediate circumstances the greater will be their success and their reliability. Hence control of the conditions is necessary in the measurement of attitudes. But there are certain conditions which defy any attempts at controlling them. For example, it would be difficult to generate communal attitudes in the laboratory, or artificially anywhere else. In a situation of this kind the experimenter should keep in mind all the details of the actual circumstances in conducting the experiment upon the attitude. It is therefore evident that the degree of reality which can be obtained in the measurement of external behaviour cannot be expected in the measurement of attitudes, which in addition, do not offer the same degree of reliability. Yet it is too precipitate to conclude from this that no reliability at all can be expected in the measurement of attitudes. The accuracy of the measurement of attitude can be tested by its capacity of prediction. The extent to which any measurement can forecast and predict the future conduct of any individual, it is accurate to that extent.

Limit to Measurement of Attitudes : The following conclusions are to be drawn from the preceding discussion on the measurement of attitudes :

1. Attitudes can be measured only indirectly.

2. The greatest possible degree and extent of control should be levied upon the immediate circumstances in the measurement of attitudes.

3. In studying attitudes the uncontrolled circumstances should be carefully studied.

4. The measurement of attitudes cannot be as reliable or accurate as the measurement of external behaviour.

5. The accuracy of the measurement of attitude can be judged from the accuracy of prediction of the individual's subsequent behaviour.

Methods of Measuring Attitudes

Hence, the social psychologist has evolved various methods for the measurement of attitudes. The major ones are :

(a) Opinion Scales

(b) Rating Scales

(c) Indirect Scales.

(a) *Opinion Scales* : Opinion scales are methods of measuring attitudes through the medium of opinions. That accounts for the name. Our attitudes towards some specific person or subject can be known by analysing our opinions concerning them. Hence, psychologists evolve scales for discovering the opinions of individuals concerning different objects, problems and persons. These standards differ in respect of the method of their construction and kind. But the aim of every standard is to locate and determine the position of an individual upon a measure extending from one limit of acceptance to the other limit of refusal. We have had occasion to point out before that it is not possible to measure attitude directly by means of any available standard. The opinion scales reveal the reactions of the individual towards some particular things, and from the reactions his attitude can be deduced. Obviously, the scale should be so devised as to throw the maximum possible light upon the attitudes of the individual. For this there should be, in the scale, a selection of statements which can efficiently give expression to the concurrence or otherwise of the attitude of the person.

Characteristics of an Adequate Scale

A scale which has any claims to adequacy in serving the purpose for which it is intended must possess the following characteristics :

1. Reliability. The most prominent characteristic of the scale is its reliability. Reliability means that the scores obtained under two distinct but similar circumstances should not be too different. The more this quality is present in a scale, the greater will be its reliability.

2. Exactness. Besides being reliable, the scale should also be accurate and exact. For this the scale should possess elements which can indicate the actual mental tendency of the person.

3. Objectivity. The construction of the scale should be objective and relative to the subject matter. The choice of its various questions should not reflect and should not be influenced by the mental tendencies of the determinants.

4. Psychological Quality. The scale can be a success only when the questions contained in it and the answers which are forthcoming to them have a psychological relation with the attitudes of the individual. The choice and selection of questions of this nature depends upon the capability of the person constructing the scale.

5. Distinction in Different Items. In order to be exact, the questions, items, statements etc., should be mutually distinct. If this is not so the answers will also not be clear. This can lead to mistakes in the result.

Various Scales, Many forms of opinion scales are prevalent in social psychology, but the main among them are the following :

1. Thurston Scale Construction Method

2. Likert Scale Construction Method
3. Guttman Scale Construction Method.

In addition to these above methods, the Bogardus Scale, Rank Order Scale and Paired Comparison Scale are also important, but they are not described here because of the lack of space.

1. Thurston Scale

Thurstone and his colleagues constructed scales for the measurement of opinions and beliefs of human groups concerning such varied questions as war, the church, Negroes, capital punishment, birth control, etc., in 1929 and 1931.

Construction Method : The Thurstone Scale Construction Method was constituted of the following items :

1. Collection of numerous simple opinions related to the question or object presented.

2. To determine the value of the scale for these opinions by some definite determinant. This evaluation leads to the elimination of controversial statements, leaving only statements concerning which all specialists are unanimous. Opinions extend between a negative and a positive limit.

3. To determine the median point for every statement according to the opinions of the specialist judges.

4. Finally, it is necessary to see whether the questions contained in the scale are in a definite order or not. The order of statements should be such that they proceed from maximum to mimimum acceptance. For this, in the beginning of the scale those questions are arranged concerning which all specialists are agreed while in the end questions concerning which all specialists are disagreed are arranged.

Precautions : The following precautions are observed in the construction of the Thurston Scale Construction Method :

1. Every statement of the scale should be distinctly worded.

2. The number of determining specialists should be large enough to indicate clearly the position which should be given to the opinion professed by the subject. For this the number of judges is usually above a hundred.

3. The scale should be comprised only of those statements concerning which the judges are unanimous. For this, every specialist places all statements of maximum and minimum acceptability in eleven classes. If a particualr statement is placed in the same class by each of the specialists, it should be difinitely chosen. But if the statement is placed in a different class by each of the specialists, it should be rejected because it is controversial.

Examples : One example of the Thurstone Scale Construction Method is the scale constructed by Droba. It has 22 statements and was constructed in 1930. This printed scale is given to the individual in order to find his attitude score. The statements which the individaul finds correct, he marks them right. The median of the scale score of these statements shows the attitude of the person.

Some of the statements of Droba's scale are the following :

1. No country can gain prestige without national respect, and war is the only means by which national respect can be defended.
2. If war is declared we also should enlist.
3. It is right to start a war only if the weaker nation is protected.
4. War and peace are necessary for progress.
5. The most that we can expect is that war be partially destroyed.
6. Lack of respect for life on the part of people engaged in war results in a wave of crime.
7. Every nation should immediately disarm itself.

2. Likert Scale

In 1932, Likert constructed a scale which differed from the one by Thurston. This scale aimed at discovering the attitudes of various human groups concerning imperialism, internationalism and Negroes.

Construction Method : The following are the items in the Likert Scale Construction Method :

1. To construct many statements related to the object or problem the attitudes towards which are to be studied.
2. To show these statements to the subject and to get them classified into the following groups :

(Strongly approve)	(Undecided)	(Disapprove)	(Strongly disapprove)	(Approve)
5	4	3	2	1

3. To award points to the above classifications in the following manner.
4. To find the correlation between the total score of the subject and the scores of the statements individually.
5. To exclude those statements which bear a negligible correlation to the total score.

3. Guttman Scale

In 1941, Guttman constructed a scale to measure and study the level of morale in American soldiers. Guttman's scale possesses the following main elements :

1. To determine whether any statement can be shown upon the scale or not.

2. To prepare scalogram to test the consistency of any statement.

3. To vary the questions concerning the same problem in such a manner as to determine that the opinion of the subject is consistent.

Fastigner bitterly criticised Guttman's scale in 1947.

(b) Rating Scales. As was stated at the outset, the second method of measuring attitude, after the opinion scales, is that of rating scales. The special feature of the rating scale is that the attitudes are evaluated not on the basis of the opinions of the subjects but on the basis of the opinions and judgments of the experimenter himself.

Means of Collecting Data : In the rating scale the experimenter collects data by means of the following :

1. Non-verbal behaviour, such as accepting or rejecting customs.
2. Verbal behaviour, such as expressing concurrence or objection.
3. Secondary expressive cues such as facial expression, etc.
4. Clinical type interview.
5. Personal documents, such as autobiography, letters, diary, etc.
6. Projective techniques — such as ink-blot test.
7. Immediate experience, such as the emotions, thoughts, perception, imagination of the individual, etc.

From the above sources the experimenter gets enough data concerning the attitude. The speechless behaviour of the individual also provides a lot of information though of course precautions should be taken in interpreting it. Compared to speechless behaivour, the easier method of understanding attitude is that of conversation. In addition to conversation, various facial expressions and the fluctuations in the volume of sound are also good indicators of attitude. "It is a commonplace belief that what a man says may be less revealing than how he says it," say Krech and Crutchfield, with a happier choice of phrase. In this way the manner of expressing an opinion may be more informative than the verbal expression itself. In a clinical interview the subject can be made to respond to questions from which he would normally hesitate, but does so now under the belief that the answers are necessary for his treatment. Diary, essays, letters, poetry, story and other kinds of individual writings manifest the attitude of the individual. Among them, diary is of the greatest importance since it is the most personal. An autobiogrpahy also reveals the attitudes of the author. Projective techniques have also proved very useful in revealing attitudes. Two among them are : (a) Rorschach's Ink-blot Test and (b) Murray's Thematic Apperception Test or T.A.T. In

Rorschach's Ink-blot Test the subject is given ten original cards with ink-blots on them and he is asked to describe what he sees on them. In Murray's Thematic Apperception Test the individual is presented ten original picture cards one after another and is asked to write a story on each of them in a short but definite period of time. In the projective techniques the subject reveals his attitudes ignorant of the fact that he is doing so. Besides these, the immediate experiences such as feelings, emotions, thoughts, perceptions, etc., of the individual also help in revealing his attitude to the experimenter.

Types of Rating Scales

Roughly, rating scales are of two kinds — relative and absolute. One example of the relative method is the Rank Order Scale, while one example of the absolute type is the Percentage of Population. It should be opportune to describe both of these scales briefly.

Rank Order Scale. In this scale the experimenter gives to the individual's attitude, a postion in the scale extending from the highest quality to the lowest quality. In examining the individual in the circumstances of the human group his position, relatively to the positions of others, is kept in view. In this way, in the Rank Order method, the individual is given a relative position in the population. In this method a definite population is put to the test and then the opinions of one individual are examined. Now the examiner places the opinions of the individual on the scale, which shows the percentage of the population concurring with his opinions as well as the percentage differing from him. This also reveals the percentage of his opinions in which he leads the population and the percentage in which he is behind the population.

(c) Indirect Scales. The third method for the measurement of attitudes is that of indirect scales. All the methods so far mentioned for the measurement of attitude suffer from the defect that the subject generally realizes that he is being examined and he therefore tries to conceal his real attitudes. Hence, psychologists have favoured the indirect scales for the measurement of attitudes, in which it cannot be guessed that tendencies are being examined. In 1938 Asch, Hertzman, and other scientists attempted to study attitudes by means of the indirect scales. With the help of signs they studied changes in opinions in industrial groups. Now-a-days, many social psychologists are making efforts to study attitudes by indirect methods.

MEASURING INTERESTS

Knowledge of interests is important for the task of guidance. The task that an individual can perform with success and efficiency depends upon his interests, besides his intelligence and general abilities. In suggesting any particular course of study or subject, that an individual student shoud pursue, one must keep in mind his intelligence, his ability and also his interests. In this respect, whether the guidance be educational or vocational, it is essential for the guide to be aware of the interests of the individual whom he has undertaken to advise. Normally, most novices to the intricacies of psychology think that the only way of knowing a person's interests is to enquire them of him. People are normally seen asking each other as to their respective interests and inclinations or the task that suits them best. But science cannot rest satisfied with such inane and cursory enquiry. It requires that every element, with which it is required to deal, should be as objectively determined as possible. Hence, psychology has invented many tests whereby it discovers and measures interests.

Lists of Interests

The simplest and most prevalent test of interests is asking the individual himself. The subject is equipped with a long list of interests and he is required to pick out the vocations that interest him, the psychologist thereby coming to know what interests the subject, or, at least, what the subjet thinks is of interest to him. Of the many such lists that are in use, Margaret E. Hoppock's check list of occupations is of particular importance and deserves mention.

Limitations of Interest Inventories

The above described inventories of interests do, to a certain extent, help in guiding an individual regarding his occupation, but these lists have some limitations that are natural to them, and which must be kept in mind in making use of them. Roughly speaking, they are subject to the following limitations :

1. Difficulty in Collecting Description of Vocation. As has been pointed out, vocational inventories or lists provide description of vocations. But it is manifestly difficult to collect a complete description of any vocation, that is a description of all activities undertaken in it, the natural abilities required for those functions and the interests required, and other equally nebulous details. Let alone any psychologist, probably even the people engaged in these professions themselves could not provide a detailed account of them.

2. Redoubtable Responses. The subject to be guided is not examined as to the various occupations, interest areas and functions, but his reactions are enquired of him. Evidently, such material as is yielded by him is not sufficiently scientific since the individual's responses are questionable, being always open to doubt. In addition to this problem, there is no way of ascertaining the accuracy and validity of the answers provided.

3. Variability of Interests. Interest inventories provide information concerning interests, but interest is no permanent part or trait of the individual's nature. Interests keep on varying, to maintain the individual's interest in them. But the variability of the individual's interests creates a problem since it is not reasonable to determine from his interests of the check list the profession into which he should put himself. It is quite possible that his abilities may fit him for a particular profession in which he shows no interest at present but he may develop affection for it when he actually gets into it. It may grow on him, as they say. Of vocations, it is usually observed that one which did not interest the individal in the beginning later on interested him if he had perserved with it for some time. On the contrary, there are other vascillating individuals who profess the deepest interest in some profession so long as they have nothing to do with it, but once they have been in it, they change their minds and decide not to like it. Hence, these vocational lists or inventories are no fool-proof or even provisionally reliable methods of determining a person's interest in a particular profession.

4. No Relation of Invariable Concomitance between Interest and Success. To forecast success on the basis of interests shown in the vocational preference lists is not scientific. That an individual is definitely interested in a particular profession is no guarantee that he will also succeed in it.

5. Classification of Occupations is not Scientific. Another major fault in these inventories of occupations is that the classification by which the professions have been divided is not scientific. Truly speaking, no two occupations included in them are the same. Every profession has its own psecific functions, its responsibilities and its specific qualities that lead to sucess, and such independent occuaptions number in hundreds if not thousands. To prepare a list of all these occupations, and then to include a detailed description of each, is a difficult task.

It is improper to conclude from the above description of the shortcomings of vocational preference lists that they are completely worthless. In fact, interest itself is a subject in which the decisions reached cannot be expected to contain a high degree of objectivity. As a makeshift method, these interest inventories are very important, but when putting them to use, it is essential that the above shortcomings be kept well in mind.

1. The supervisors judge them in terms of their own self-images, appraise low level role performance by comapring it with their own high level role performance.

2. The supervisors adopt different criteria of assessment in different cases.

3. The supervisors do not give them opportunity to explain the causes of their failures or unsatisfactory performance.

4. The supervisors keep their assessment confidential so that it may not be challenged.

5. The supervisors evaluate them on the basis of certain incidents or happenings which may not be a regular feature of their behaviour or work situation.

6. The supervisors rely too much on past records and remarks by their predecessors.

McGREGOR'S THEORY OF SELF ASSESSMENT

McGregor's theory of self assessment is based on three important postulates : self-direction, self-control and self-appraisal. According to him the average human being learns under proper conditions not only to accept but to seek responsibility. The capacity to exercise a relatively high degree of imagination, ingenuity and creativity in the solutions of organisational problems is widely, not narrowly, distributed in the population. People should be given a degree of freedom to direct their own activities to achieve the goals which are set in consultation with them. This would satisfy egoistic and self-fulfilment needs. It will make them less dependent on their superiors and assume more responsibility. The philosophy of self-assessment is based on theory of human behaviour. It is successful when it ensures that the subordiantes rate themselves in an objective manner without fear of being victimised.

Proforma of Self Assessment

Self-assessment proforma should be designed in such a manner that the employee may have opportunity to tell about his performance on the job both in qualitative and quantitative terms, his interest and aptitude, his relations with the superiors, colleagues and subordinates, etc. If the assessment is done in a free atmosphere, he will not hesitate in pointing out his weak points as well as his expectations from the bosses to guide him in improving his performance and potentialities.

Result of Self Assessment by Subordinates

(i) Aceptance of the organisation goals and working activity for the same.

(ii) Co-operation with supervisors in implementing plans and policies.

(iii) Maintainence of discipline, giving due respect to superiors and working in harmony with collegues.

(iv) Improvement of productive efficiency and reducing waste and

(v) Improvement of employee morale.

QUESTIONS FOR EXERCISE

1. Define employment interview. What are its objectives? Discuss the importance of interview in employee selection.
2. Describe the limitations of interview as a technique of selection.
3. "In the process of recruitment and selection, interview the only tool is not sufficient to find the suitability of the candidates. It is to be supplemented by other techniques of selection." Elaborate this statement.
4. "Interview is not a valid tool for selection." Explain.
5. Explain various steps and principles in a good interview.
6. Discuss briefly the various methods of interviewing for employment.
7. What do you mean by psychological testing? Explain its importance in selection, etc.
8. "The need for evaluating the potentialities of men is as great in business and industry as in any field of human activities." Discuss and evaluate the part played by psychological tests in solving the problems in industry.
9. What are the characteristics of a good test? Attempt classification of Psychological tests.
10. Describe the principles of psychological testing. How would you develop a testing programme?
11. Describe the limitations of testing. What are the characteristics of a good test?
12. Explain various types of intelligences tests.
13. Explain various methods of measurement of personality.
14. Write short note on McGregor's theory of self assessment.

11

Job Changes : Promotion, Demotion, Transfer, Separation, Lay Off and Turnover

According to D.S. Beach, promotion, transfer and separation provide work force flexibility and mobility in an organisation.[1] In his career, an employee, supervisor or manager has to change his job so often. This may be due to promotion, transfer, lay off or demotion. Generally whenever promoted, the employee has to change his job for a higher job carrying better emoluments.

PROMOTION

Definition

1. *Scott and Clothier* : "A promotion is the transfer of an employee to a job that pays more money or that enjoys some preferred status."[2]

2. *Pigors and Myres* : "A promotion is the advancement of an employee to a better job-beter in terms of greater responsibilities, more prestige or status, greater skill and especially, increased rate of pay or salary."

3. *Edwin B. Flippo* : "A promotion involves a change from one job to another that is beter in terms of status and responsibility."

Basic Elements in Promotion

Thus, promotion includes are the following :

1. Transfer of an employee to some higher job having more prestige, better status, more benefits and privileges;

2. Re-assignment of an employee to a position having increased responsibilities;

3. Higher job grade.

---

1. Beach, D.S., *Personnel : The Management of People at Work,* Macmillan, New York, 1975 pp. 343-344.

2. Scott, W., Clothier, R.C. and Spriegal, W., *Personnel Management, Principles, Practices and Points of View,* Tata McGraw-Hill, New Delhi, 1977, p. 178.

Thus, promotion places employee in a position which carries greater prestige and status, increased responsibilities as well higher earnings. When the salary of an employee is increased without corresponding change in job grade, it is upgrading and not promotion. If there is an increase in responsibility without an increase in pay it is called 'Dry Promotion'.

Significance of Promotion

1. It Handles the New Job. Insiders shall have no problem in handling the new job because they are intimately connected with the organisation structure, production prcess, products and different problems.

2. It produces Higher Morale. A sound policy of promotion will keep the morale of the employee high because they know that they will be offered senior positions as and when there are vacancies. It, in this way, motivates the employees.

3. It ensures more Efficiency. It will ensure sincere efforts on the part of employees. They will try to increase their efficiency in order to get the chance for higher position.

4. It trains at Less cost. The csot to train the insider on the senior post will be much lesser.

5. It solves personnel problems. If the organisation has a sound promotion policy, several personnel problems are solved. It creates the sense of loyalty and confindence in the organisatin resulting in faithful service, meritorious performance, outstanding ability on job, good attendance, accident avoidance, higher production and lower turnover.

Principles of Promotion

1. Written. The promotion policy should be in writing. It must be understood by all employees to avoid any suspicion regarding line or promotion in the minds of employees.

2. Specify Vacancies. The promotion policy should lay down what percentage of vacancies in higher posts are to be filled up by promotion. It is better to incorporate a statement of management intention that higher paid and better jobs will be filled by promotion from within if possible rather than by hiring from outside.

3. Mention of Basis. The promotion should mention the basis of promotion. A sound policy be based on both the considerations, *i.e.,* seniority and merit should emphasise the merit giving due weightage to seniority. Seniority should be the basis of promotion of two persons who are equal in merit.

4. Based on Job Analysis. Job analysis decides the position of the jobs and their relationship to other positions. This should be done to provide clear recognition of the natural movement from one job to another. Positions may be adjusted and arranged, so that one position prepares workers for another. Natural course of advancement may be provided throughout the organisation, or within each division or department. Employees should be fully aware of the plan so that they may prepare themselves for higher positions.

5. Closely Allied to Training. Promotion programmes should be closely allied to training programme. This enables the employees to improve themselves for promotions.

6. Based on Scientific Procedure. A scientific procedure for evaluating employee performance should be followed. To justify the promotion or supersession this should be recorded period. The assessment of employee and his confidential report should be objective so that every employee has a faith in the promotion policy and thus induced for better performance of work to get promotion.

7. Based on Recommendation by Immediate Boss. The supervisor or the immediate boss should recommend the promotion. This is subject to approval by the immediate superior in the line organisation. Final decision in this respect may be taken by the top executive in the line with the advice and assistance of the personnel department in a staff capacity. This ensures that the policy will be consistently administered.

8. Contains Provision for Challenge. The promotion policy should contain provision for the challenge of a particular promotion by the employee or union within the limits of the promotion policy to ensure fairness in management decision.

9. Gives Advance Notification. A vacancy or a would be vacancy should be notified to employees in advance so that interested employees may apply within a specified period.

10. Made on Probation. At first the promotion should be made on probation. If he works satisfactory during probation period, he should be made permanent.

11. Not forced. Not all people within an organisation want promotion. Some feel that they will leave a congenial work group or they will not be able to handle the responsibilities of higher job or they may have certain other reasons. Promotion should not be forced on such reluctant employees and they should be allowed to continue their present assignment.

ROLE OF PERSONNEL DEPARTMENT IN PROMOTION

1. To give Advice. Promotion is line responsibility. The immediate boss proposes promotions which is subject to approval by his immediate superior in the line organisation. The final decision is taken by the top executive with the advice and assistance of the personnel department. It serves as a check on the fairness of promotion. It ensures that the policy is consistently administered.

2. To decide Promotion Policy. In a staff capacity personnel department can assist the line authority in designing and developing a sound promotion policy to ensrue better industrial relation in the organisation. It offers the personnel administrator or excellent opportunity to develop understanding and acceptance of management policy.

3. To provide Records. The personnel department provides the line executive necessary records available with the department which may form the basis of promotion policy.

4. To provide Tools. Job analysis, job description, job specification and performance appraisal are some of the tools which decide the lines of promotion and the ability of the person. The quantity and quality of performance should be measured periodically and should form a part of the personnel record.

5. To effect Communication. All relevant changes in the organisation that affect the workers are communicated by personnel department to them even if the results for them are negative. Every employee expects to be informed about stages of promotion, how they can prepare themselves for advancement and what will be expected of them on the higher reated jobs.

6. To solve Disputes. If the management decision on promotion is disputed by the aggrieved employees or union representiatives, the personnel manager should hold idsucsisons with them whithin the limits of promotion policy. He should convey the feelings of the representatives or the aggrieved employees to the line executive who would review the decision in consultation with the personnel manager. The conference between the representatives, personnel manager and the executive may be faithful if errors are admitted and adjustment made. If the decision on promotion appears to be fully justified after investigations reasons can be more thoroughly explained, records produced and the consequences of a deaparture from sound policy pointed out.

7. To prepare Workforce. One of the functions of the personnel department is to prepare and develop efficient workforce in the company. New avenues for their development are recommended by the personnel department. Persons are encouraged to train themselves on the job shouldering the responsibilities of higher posts. This may be done by offering the opportunities to officiate on the higher positions. However, the persons who are not interested in promotion should be not forced to hold higher positions.

To conclude the personnel department has an important role to play in promotions by assisting live executive in designing the promotion policy; communicating the promotion policy and the changes in the organisation holding talks with representatives of the employees in connection with the disputed cases; and developing promotion avenues in the organisation.

Bases of Promotion

While designing the promotion policy, there is always the problem of criterion for promotion before the management. The two formal bases of promotion are (1) Seniority, and (2) Merit.

1. Seniority. Seniority means length of recognized service in an organisation. The senior most person in the lower grade shall be promoted as and when there is an opening in the higher position. Seniority is decided on the absis of length of recognized service in the organisation and every employee knows his palce in the promotion list. By this criterion there will be no change of favouritism or dispute regarding promotion. Where seniority is the base for promotion, merit is not considered. Promotions in almost all types of organisations, particularly in organisation where trade unions are strong are based on seniority. Trade unions emphasises seniority rather than merit as the basis of promotion.

2. Merit. Merit means ability to work. The most able person in the lower grade, who is junior most in the company, shall be promoted as merit is the basis of promotion. This criteria encourages all employees to improve their efficiency. Management personnel generally prefer merit as the basis of promotion determined by job performance and by analysis of employee potential for development through written or oral examinations or personal interviews or their records of performance.

Arguments in Support of Basic Seniority

(i) *Simple* : It is very simple and easily understandable. It restricts favourism to any employee over the other.

(ii) *Popular* : Seniority has wide acceptability among workers. This system of awarding rights and privileges is very old and widespread, therefore, it promotes peach in the organisation.

(iii) *Secure* : Security is also a plus point in the use of seniority. An employee can predict when and how he will be promoted. It increases employees morale.

(iv) *Reduces labour turnover* : The basis of promotion helps in reducing the labour turnover because jan employee will not easily give up his seniority in the organisation. Sseniority is a valuable asset and nobody likes to lose it even when he is aware of somewhat better opportunities elsewhere by quitting the firm.

(v) *Single criterion* : As changes in the rights and privileges such as transfer, lay-off, demotion etc. are closely linked with seniority in the organisation, it should not be a difficult criterion for promotion.

(vi) *Gives value to experience* : It is also meaningful that experience contributes to ability. The longer an employee works at one job, the more qualified he becomes for promotion.

Arguments in Support of Merit Basis

(i) *Right person* : Only right man should be placed on a job to accomplish to overall objectives of the orgnisation. An able man can be the right man for the job. Length of service need not necessarily produce ability.

(ii) *Merit has competitive drive* : Merit has a competitive drive amongst the personnel to increase efficiency for advancement. This merit provides a base for promotion.

(iii) *Attracts able person* : The organisation may attract the able person on the job if merit is adopted as the base of promotion because they know that they will be promoted to the higher opening as soon as they attain the required ability for the same.

(iv) *Gives value to ability* : If the oldest were always the ablest, ther is no need for measuring the performance of both people and the firm. Hence, merit should be the criterion.

(v) *Support in case of challenged* : Made on the basis of merit, a promotion decision if challenged, can be supported by factual data such as written and performance tests, production records, merit rating, education and training accomplishment etc.

By analysing the above two points of view, we can conclude that a sound promotion policy should be based on both the considerations i.e., seniority and ability. It should primarily insist on the merit of the employee giving due weightage to seniority.

Objectives of Promotion

1. To put the worker in a position where he will be of greater value to the company and where he may derive increased personal satisfaction and income from his work.

2. To remove a worker from his job as an alternative to avoid the embarrassment of firing or demoting him.

3. To recognise an individual's performance and reward him for his work so that he may have an incentive to forge ahead. Employees will have little motivation if better jobs are reserved for outsiders.

4. To increase an employee's organisational effectiveness.

8. To build up morale, loyalty, and a sense of belonging on the part of the employees when it is brought home to them that they would be promoted if they deserve it.

6. To promote job satisfaction among the employees and give them an opportunity for unborken, continuous service.

7. To provide a process of "selective socialisation". Employees whose personalities and skills enable them to fit into an organisation's human relations prgoramme tend to stay on; while those whose personalities with those of the organisation tend to leave.

8. To attract suitable and competent workers for the organisation.

9. To create among employees a feeling of contentment with their present conditions and encourage them to succeed in the company.

Watkins, Dodd and others mention the following purposes of promotion :[3]

1. To furnish an effective incentive for initiative, enterprise and ambition;
2. To conserve proved skill, training and ability;
3. To reduce discontent and unrest;
4. To attract suitable and competent workers and
5. To suggest logical training for advancement.

As Yoder and others observe, "promotion provides incentive to initiative, enterprise, and ambition; minimises discontent and urest; attracts capable individuals; necessitates logical triaining of advancement and forms an effective reward for loyalty and co-operation, long service, etc."[4]

Types of Promotion

1. Multiple chain promotions. These provide for a systematic linking of each position to several others. These identify multi-promotional opportunities through clearly defined avenues of approach to and exit from each position in the organisation.

2. Up or out promotion. In it a person must either earn a promotion or seek employment elsewhere. Many universities and other organisations follow this practice. Such promotions often lead to termination of services.

---

3. Watkins, G., and others, *The Management of Personnel Relations,* 1950, pp. 447-449.
4. Yoder, D., Heneman, H.G., Turnbull, J.G. and Stone, C.H., *Handbook of Personnel Management and Labour Relations,* McGraw Hill Book Co., New York, 1958, p. 95.

3. Dry promotions. These are those which are given in lieu of increases in compensation, *i.e.,* when all compensation is adjusted upward to keep pace with the cost of living we have dry promotions.

All promotions should be on a trial basis (from 6 months to one year) for if the promoted person is not found capable of handling his job, he may be reverted to his former post and former pay scale.

Promotion poses a constant challenge to executives at all levels. It impels them to chalk out a well-thought-out programme by which the best and the most cpable individuals may find an opportunity to go up to the top. The procedure for promotion, starts right at the bottom from the shop floor and ends with the managing director of a company.

Promotion Programme and Procedure

"Organisations that have failed to reward excellence in service, or that have relied too heavily on personal relationships or length of service, suffer in terms of both efficiency and morale."

The management must provide realistic opporunities to encoruage promising employees to take the risks involved in moving upward. It must never discourage valuable employees from seeking advancement by making service in an unpopular job a prereqisite for promotion. It must provide alternatives for employees who do outstanding work but who are unwilling to take on new and additional responsibilities.

Each organisation should strike a balance between the internal and external sources of personnel promotion on the one hand and between merit and ability as against length of service on the other. "The organisation that fails to develop a satisfactory procedure is bound to pay a severe penalty in terms of administrative costs, misallocation of perosonnel, low morale, and ineffectual performance, among both non-managerial employees and their supervisors."

According to Chatterjee, following are the criteria for a sound promotion policy :"[5]

(1) *Consistency* : It will be applied irrespective of the persons concerned. Consistency demands that the policy should be so correlated to career planning that there should not be a sudden spurt of promotion in the organisation conferring premature benefits on a number of persons, followed by a long period of absence of promotion.

(2) *Fair and impartial* : The maangement should be able to remove all suspicion of arbitrariness, ad-hocism, improvisation to suit particular individuals, nepotism, etc.

5. Chatterjee, N.N., *Management of Personnel in Indian Enterprises*, Allied Book Agency, Calcutta, 1980, pp. 130-131.

(3) *Planned activity.* The management should make a correct assessment of the requirements or opportunities of promotion within the organisation so that there is no phenomena of 'bunching' or no period of 'promotional drought', *i.e.,* no overestimation or underestimation.

Elements of Promotion Policy

1. Promotion Policy statement. It should consider whether vacancies are primarily to be filled up from within an organisation or by recruitment from outside. Usually, internal promotions are preferred over external recruitment and increase is given at the time of promotion, otherwise promotion is meaningless.

2. Plan of Jobs. It decises on what basis promotions are to be given: whether on performance appraisal, or on the basis of confidential records, or job and post-bid system. Usually promotions are decided on the basis of performance appraisals. "Job-post and bid system" *i.e.,* posting of job vacancies indicating job titles, duties, pay and qualifications on company notice boards, is also utilised.

3. Transfer routes. These indicate some type of formal and systematic promotion channles. Ladders giving paths of advancement, *promotional charts, opportunity charts* or *fortune sheets* clearly distinguish each job and by lines and arrows, connect various jobs: and show the lines/routes of advancement up to and away from them. *Stepping jobs* should be clearly identified and recorded on paper. *Dead-end jobs* should be labelled and the path upward well marked.

4. Advancement through the provision of some training. This may be either on the job in professional/technical institutions, or through job rotation, multiple management, under-study and conferences.

5. Policy communication. The organisation should communicate its promotion policy in the form of manual or agreement signed with the union or a set of Standing Orders. To have a no communication of policy to the employees will only create suspicions and misgivings. However a precise formulation of such a policy may not be effective for higher level personnel.

6. Detailed personnel and service records. These are kept ready on the basis of which promotions may be made.

Indices of Suitability

For judging whether candidates are suitable for promotion the following indices are available :

1. The margin of performance. It may be on his present job, whether he runs it with ease and with margin to spare or is he barely able to manage his job.

2. Flexibility or versatility. It means whether he has been successful on different types of jobs requiring different skills and diferent abilities, or does he seem to be only interested in a restricted field?

3. Intelligence. It means how does he think? How has he learnt on work the has carried out?

4. Equipment. It means how compatible are his education, literacy, expression and personality with the critical needs of the job?

5. Motivation. It raises the questions what are his wants? What is important for him? What are his goals, his objectives in work and life?

Promotion System

A promotion system invovles clear-cut definitions of line of future advancement, detailed personnel records, specific promotion plans, definite allocation of responsibility for identifying promotable individuals and a centralised coordination of promotion function.

Very aptly describing promotion systems for different categories of personnel in the organisation, Beach observes: "For unskilled and semi-skilled workers, entry is made into 'labour pool' and thereafter and upgarding takes place on the basis of seniority or a combination of both seniority and ability. The skilled craftsmen are recruited as helpers or apprentices and thereafter upward mobility occurs upto positions of foremen, inspectors or production co-ordinators. Entry in clerical jobs is through appointment as clerks, typists or stenogrpahers and subsequently promotiions are made to higher positions such as that of secretaries or administrative assistants. In professional jobs, entry is made as assistant engineers, engineers, senior engineers, project engineers or even managers. Jobs in managerial positions are filled up by individuals who enter as management trainees or assistant supervisors, finally they are promoted to middle level managment positions and ultimately to top management positions."[6]

Two types of rank provide basis of promotion :

1. Rank-in-the-job. In it the content of the job including level of skill, efforts and responsibility form the basis. Emphasis is laid on job analysis, job evaluation, organisational planning etc. These determine the pay and status in the organisation.

2. Rank in the man. In it emphasis is put on proficiency of the individuals. It determines the position level in the hierarchy of career pattern.

---

6. Beach, D.S., *op. cit.*, pp. 134-135.

Promotion practice in India

In India, while in some companies, promotions are made on the basis of merit, potential and seniority, internal promotions are also granted, from the existing lower cadre on the basis of seniority and merit.

Elaborate rules exist for regulating the seniority of employees in different service cadres in public sector organisations. Promotions are made from this list. But often the rules are violated due to political pressures, and a person standing much lower in the list is given priority over the senior-most men.

In the private sector enterprises, efficiency is the main consideration, unless it is a a family enterprise where relationship with the proprietors or patronage might play a part. But even there only a limited number of posts would be filled upon the basis of relationship or by way of patronage. There is generally a well-defined promotion policy and nepotism is avoided in such firms where workers are concenred and well organised. The rule followed is : "*Promote the best man available*". The management must ensure that :

(a) Proper talents are first made available by a correct programme of recruitment;

(b) Employees are enabled to satisfy their own aspirations within the framework of the company's own objectives and projects and

(c) A programme of career planning, coupled with periodic assessment is followed in accordance with rules.

In a developing economy like India, it is not always possible to promote the older workers neither adequately trained nor willing to be exposed to new concepts, ideas and methods of work. According to N.N. Chatterjee, only in large organisation can a policy of promotions from within be practicable; but even there such promotions cannot be confined entirely to the existing personnel of the organsiation, unless management development and career planning are an essential part of the company's promotion policy.[7]

DEMOTION

Definition

'Demotion' has been defined as "the assignment of an individual to a job of lower rank and pay usually involving lower level of difficulty and responsility."[8]

7. Chatterjee, N.N., *op. cit.*, p. 362.

8. Beach, D.S., *op. cit.*, p. 362.

It refers to the lowering down of the status, salary and responsibilities of an employee. It is used as a punitive measure when there are serious breaches of duty on the part of an employe. It is often a preliminary to a dismissal.

Causes of Demotion

1. Reduction in number of jobs. When departments are combined and jobs eliminated, employees are often required to accept lower-level position until normalcy is restored. Such demotions are not a black mark against an employee.

2. Inadequacy in terms of job performance, attitude and capability. This happens when an individual finds it difficult to meet job requirement standards, following his promotion.

3. Inadequate output. When, because of a change in technology, methods and practices, and hands are unable to adjust, or when employees, because of ill-health or personal reasons, cannot do their job.

4. Disciplinary Measure. Demotion is also used as a disciplinary measure.

Demotion Policy

In regard to demotion practices, Yoder, Heneman, Turnbull and Stone have suggested a five-fold policy :[9]

1. A clear and reasonable list of rules should be framed, violations of which would subject as employee to demotion;
2. This information should be clearly communicated to employees;
3. There should be a competent investigation of any alleged violation;
4. If violations are discovered, there should be a consistent and equitable application of the penalty, preferably by the immediate supervisor;
5. There should be a provision for review. (In a unionised case, this will be automatic via the grievance procedure; in a non-unionised case, the employer will need to make other provisions for review.)

Principles of Demotion

1. Demotions should keep the employees alert and alive to their responsibilities and duties.

2. There should be no demotion for persons with a long and meritorious service. However, some of their duties and responsibilities

9. Yoder, D., Heneman, H.G., Turnbull, J.G. and Stone, C.H., *op. cit.,* p. 19.

may be taken from them and assigned to others to create a job for the person at the same pay and status but with lower job demands.

3. A demotion should never be made as a penalty for a violation of the rule of conduct, poor attendance record, or insubordination because such action will not improve the performance of the individual.

4. Demotions have a serious impact on need fulfilment. Needs for esteem and belonging are frustrted, leading to a defensive behaviour on the part of the person demoted; there is complaining, emotional turmoil, inefficiency or resignation. Hence, many managers prefer to discharge employees rather than face the problems arising from demotion.

TRANSFER

Yoder and associates have defined transfer as "a lateral shift causing movement of individuals from one position to another usually without involving any marked change in duties, responsibilities, skills needed or compensation."[10]

Nature of Transfer

A transfer is a horizontal or lateral movement of an employee from one job, section, department, shift, plant or position to another at the same or another place where his salary, status and responsibility are the same.

Objectives of Transfers

1. To satisfy organisational needs. These may arise out of a change in the quantity of production, fluctuations in work requirements, and changes in the organisational structure; the introduction of new lines of production, the dropping of existing product lines, the reallocation of, or reduction in the workforce due to a shortage or a surplus in same section so that lay-offs may be avoided; filling in of the vacancies which may occur because of separations or because of the need for suitable adjustments in business operations. Such transfers are known *as production transfers, flexibility transfers, or organisational transfers* generally controlled centrally through and by the personnel department. Their purpose is to stabilise employment in an organisation.

2. To meet an employee's own request. When an employee feels uncomfortable on the job because of his dislike of his boss, or his fellow workers, or because better opportunities for his future advancement do not exist there, or because of family circumstances which may compel him to change the place of his residence, he seeks transfer generally known as *personal transfers* which enable employees to feel at home in the work of their choice.

10. *Ibid.*, p. 20.

3. To properly utilise the services of an employee. When an employee is not performing satisfactorily and adequately and when the management feels that he may be more useful or suitable elsewhere, such transfers are called *remedial transfers.* They act as a follow-up measure of the selection-and-placement procedure. They help employees to adjust themselves to suitable jobs.

4. To increase the versatility of the employee. This is done by shifting him from one job to another so that he may have ample opportunities for gaining a varied and broader experience of work. Such transfers are known as *versatility transfers* which make it possible for an employee to enjoy the facility of job enrichment, which provides the management a more effective and experienced employee for a higher job.

5. To adjust the workforce of one plant with that of another. This is done particularly when a plant is closed down for reasons beyond the control of the employer. Known as *plant transfers* such transfers are generally effected on humanitarian grounds to ensure that persons who have been long in service of an organisation are not thrown out of employment.

6. To replace a new employee. Replacement is done by an employee who has been in the organisation for a sufficiently long time. Such transfers are known as *replacement transfers.* Their purpose is to give some relief to an old employee from the heavy pressure of work.

7. To help employees work according to their convenience. For example, an employee is transferred from night shift to morning shift or from the first to the second shift particularly in the case of women workers who may like to look after their children and do the necessary domestic work in the morning hours. Such transfers are known as *shift transfers.*

8. To penalise the employee. In Government organisations, this practice is widespread, and is also preferred by the employee to the grim alternative of disciplinary action. A difficult trade union activist or intriger or sealawyer may be transferred to a remote branch or office where he cannot continue his activities.

9. To maintain a tenure system. Such transfers occur in senior administrative services of the Government and also in industries, or where there is a system of annual intake of management trainees. The employee holds a certain job for a fixed tenure but he is made to move from job to job to enable him to acquire a variety of experience and skills and to ensure that he does not get involved in politicking.

Classification of Transfer

Scott and others have classified transfers as follows :[11]

1. **According to the convenience of the company**

(i) *Temporary transfers*. These arise from temporary absenteeism; shifts in the work load; vocation;

(ii) *Permanent transfers*. These arise out of shifts in the workload; vacancies which need the special skill or ability of the transferred employee.

2. **According to the convenience of the employee**

(i) *Temporary transfers* : These arise from the ill-health of, or an accident to, an employee; for family reasons or for taking care of some private affair;

(ii) *Permanent transfers* : These arise out of ill-health or accident; out of outside interest — for example, of the purpose of attending a professional school or similar activities; out of family consideration; out of a desire to learn a particular skill.

Transfer Policy

The responsibility for effecting transfers is usually entrusted to an executive with power to prescribe the conditions under which requests for transfers are to be approved.

A successful transfer policy should have a proper job description and analysis. Frequent and large-scale transfers should be avoided by laying down adequate selection and palcement procedures for the purpose.

Following are the characteristics of a good transfer policy :

1. Specifically clarifying the types of transfers and the conditions under which these will be made.
2. Locating the authority in some officer who may initiate and implement transfers.
3. Indicating whether transfers can be made only within a sub-unit or also between departments, divisions/plants.
4. Indicating basis for trnasfer — *i.e.,* whether it will be based on seniority or on skill and competence or any other factor.
5. Deciding the rate of pay to be given to the transferee.
6. Intimating the fact of transfer to the person concerned well in advance;
7. In writing and duly communicated to all concerned.
8. Not frequent and not for the sake of transfer only.

---

11. Scott, W., Clothier, R.C. and Spiegel, W., *op. cit.,* p. 1.

In making transfers, the employee is paid the actual cost of moving the household to the place of transfer.

Procedure for Transfer

1. Intra-departmental transfers. These are transfers within the same section of the same department decided by the foreman or plant manager. These are effected without the issue of any transfer order to the employee, through oral instructions. However, the personnel manager must be informed of such transfers.

2. Inter-departmental transfers. There are transfers from one department to another decided by mutual consultations among the departmental heads/plant managers when such transfers are of a permanent nature or of long duration. Here, written orders, signed by the personnel manager are issued to the employee. Transfers from one palce or unit to another place or unit, involving a considerable change in working conditions and cost to the company, have to be made in writing, after giving due notice to the employees. But; generally such transfers are discouraged.

SEPARATION

Meaning and Causes

"Separation" means cessatiion of service of agreement with the organisation. The employee may be separated from the pay roll of a company as a result of following :

1. Resignation;
2. Discharge;
3. Dismissal;
4. Suspension;
5. Retrenchment;

1. Resignation. Resignations may be put in *voluntarily* by the employees on grounds of health, physical disability, better opportunities elsewhere, or maladjustment with company policy and officers, or for reasons of marriage (frequent in case of young girls). Resignations be *compulsory* when an employee is asked to put in his resignation if he wants to avoid termination of his services on the ground of gross negligence of duty on his part, or some serious charge against him.

2. Discharge. It involves permanent separation of an employee from the pay-roll for violation of company rules or for inadequate performance. It becomes necessary under the following conditions :

(i) When the volume of business does not justify the continuing employment of the persons involved.

(ii) When a person fails to work according to the requirements of the job either because of incapacity or because he has deliberately slowed down on work, or because there is no suitable place where he can be transferred.

(iii) When an individual forfeits his rght to a job because of his violation of a basic policy often involving the safety of others, the morale and discipline of a group.

Causes of Discharge

(i) *Frequent Causes* : Inefficiency, dishonesty, drunkenness, carelessness or indifference, violation of rules.

(ii) *Infrequent Causes* : Accidents, insubordination, personal conduct, uncleanliness, infraction of rules, destructve negligence, wastefulness, and physical unfitness.

(iii) *Other Causes* : Carelessness, lack of co-operation, laziness, tardiness in startiing work, frequent absences without leave, dishonesty, lack of specific skill, preventing promotion, adverse attitude towards the organisation.

Discharge Procedure

Following evidence needs be produced to demonstrate that a discharge is justified and does not arise out of unfair discrimination or personal prejudice of the supervisor :

(i) Permanent records of all merit ratings made by the supervisors;

(ii) Permanent records of ratings of the defendant's traits maintained by persons other than the foreman;

(iii) A memorandum bearing on the efforts made by the foreman to help the defendant to overcome his weakness;

(iv) A copy of any warnng that had been sent him;

(v) The letter of discharge, especially if the letter states the cause of the discharge.

Elements of Discharge Programme

According to C.B. Mamoria the following elements should be present in a discharge programme :[12]

(i) The reasons for discharge should be clearly stated.

(ii) The individual concerned should be adequately informed about the reasons for his discharge.

(iii) The supervisor, in-charge of initiating discharge action, should

---

12. Mamoria, C.B., *Dynamics of Industrial Relations in India*, Himalaya Publishing House, Bombay, 1983, pp. 410-413.

be fully conversant with rules and regulations of the organisation.

(iv) The facts regarding the violations of the rules and regulations should be carefully analysed.

(v) Line officials should handle the discharge affairs.

(vi) There should be a well thought-out procedure for setting the discharge case.

(vii) Adequate provision should exist for review of the discharged employee's case.

(viii) A discharged employee needs a reasonable notice or an equivalent of pay in lieu of notice. It carries with it certain penalties, such as difficulty of re-employment, loss of benefits and, in certain cases, the loss of a part of the provident fund, etc.

3. Dismissal. It is the termination of the services of an employee by way of punishment for some misconduct, or for unauthorised and prolonged absence from duty. Before dismissal an employee is given an opportunity to explain his conduct and to show cause why he should not be dismissed. There should be no violation of the principle of natural justice, which ensures that punishment is not out of all proportion to the offence.

4. Suspension. It is a serious punishment generally awarded only after a proper enquiry has been conducted. For reasons of discipline, a workman may be suspended without prejudice during the course of any enquiry. During suspension, the employee receives a subsistence allowance.

5. Retrenchment. The Industrial Disputes Act, 1947, defines retrenchment as the "termination by the employer of the services of workmen for any reason". It is permanent termination of the services of an employee for economic reasons in a going concern.

Termination of services as a punishment given by way of disciplinary action, or retirement either voluntarily or on reaching the age of superannuation, or continued ill-health, or on the closure and winding up of a business, does not constitute retrenchment. Retrenchment means continuing operations where a part of the workforce is found to be superfluous.

Conditions of Retrenchment

(i) The worker he has been given 3 months' notice in writing, indicating the reasons for retrenchment, and the period of notice has expired; or he has been paid wages in lieu of such notice for the period of the notice;

(ii) The worker has been paid, at the time of retrenchment, compensation which is equivalent to 15 days' average pay for every completed year of continuous service or any part thereof in excess of 6 months;

(iii) Notice has been served on the appropriate government authority and the permission of such authority has been obtained.

An employee is entitled to both retrenchment compensation and gratuity. Compensation is intended to give a worker some relief and to soften the hardship which retrenchment inevitably causes.

Principles of Retrenchment

The principle in the procedure of retrenchment is "*last come, first go*" that is the last person employed in each category must be the first person to be retrenched. The employer prepares a list of all the workers arranged according to the seniority of service of the employees in that category. This list is displayed on the Notice Board at least 7 days before the actual date of retrenchment. When vacancies arise after retrenchment, the employer gives an opportunity to the retrenched workers to offer themselves for re-employment; and they are given preference. Such vacancies are generally notified at least 10 days before they are filled up.

LAY-OFF

It refers to an indefinite separation of the employee from the pay-roll due to factors beyond the control of the employer. The employee is expected to be called back in the foreseeable future. It involves a temporary or permanent removal from the pay-roll of persons with surplus skills. The purpose of a lay-off is to reduce the financial burden on an organisation when human resources cannot be utilised profitably. Thus, a lay-off means the failure, refusal or inability of an employer to provide employment to a workman whose name is borne on the muster roll of his establishment. It is resorted to as a result of some such bonafide reasons as factors which are beyond the control of the employers.

Definition of Lay Off

According to Section 2 (KKK) of the Industrial Disputes Act, a lay-off has been defined as "the failure, refusal or inability of an employer, on account of shortage of coal, power or raw materials, on the accumulations of stocks or breakdown of machinery for any reason, to give employment to a workman whose name is borne on the muster roll of his individual establishment and who has not been retrenched."

Causes of Lay Off

(i) Breakdown of machinery;

(ii) Seasonal fluctuations in markets and loss of sales;

(iii) Accumulation of stocks or financial slump;

(iv) Shortage of raw material, coal and power;

(v) Production delays and

(vi) Other technological reasons.

The Labour Contract

Hourly-paid employees are first affected by lay-offs, followed by white-collar and salaried employees. In a unionised organisation, the labour contract governs the order of lay-off and the method of recall. It defnes what a lay-off is, fixes the maximum period during which a laid-off employee has to be recalled, and mentions the other rights which he has.

Prnciples of Lay-Off

Workmen must not be laid off capriciously, nor as a part of a manoeuvre to lower labour costs. "Whom to let go and whom to retain" is decided by the top management. But the general principle to be followed is to lay-off the junior most, temporary and probationary employees first — last in, first out (LIFO); and when they are recalled, the principle is LOFI (last out, first in).

Lay off Policy

A lay-off polcy has to be very cautious, otherwise it will lead to a high labour turnover, affect effective teamwork, destroy morale and increase the cost of unemployment insurance. The best plicy is *to reduce the work days of all the employees or transfer the excess workforce of one departmnet to a department where it is needed.* Sometimes other criteria may be used, such as ability, job performance, age, length of service, number of dependants, financial obligations, etc. *Usually, job performance and ability are given the greatest weight, followed next by length of service.*

Compensation

A laid-off worker is paid 50 per cent of his basic wages and dearness allowance for every working day on which he reports for work. If there is a previous agreement between the worker and management to this effect, lay-off compensation need not be paid for more than 45 days during any period of 12 months. When a workman is laid-off for more than 45 days, and when the lay-off after the expiry of the frst 45 days is a continuous period of one week or more, the workman may be paid at the above rate for all the days of every such subsequent period of one week or more, unless there is any agreement to the contrary between him and the employer. Where a workman has been paid lay-off compensation beyond 45 days and is retrenched, the employer may deduct the amount so paid, from the retrenchment compensation payable to him.

In order to receive his lay-off compensation, the workman must present himself on each working day at the appointed time. Sometimes he may be required to report a second time during the same day. At the time of this second report, he is paid as if he had been employed for the full day provided that he has not been given employment at either time of report.

Elements of Lay off

(i) *Failure of the Employer* : There must a failure or refusal or inability of the employer to continue to employee workers in his employment.

(ii) *On the Muster roll* : The employees laid off must be on the muster roll of the organisation on the date of lay-off.

(iii) *Proper Reasons* : The reasons for lay-off must be shortage of coal, power or other similar reasons.

(iv) *Temporary* : Such inabilty to give employment to the workers must be temporary.

(v) *Only Suspended relationship* : The relationship of employee does not come to an end, but is merely suspended for a short period.

Conditions of the Lay Off

Under the Industral Disputes Act 1947 the purpose of lay-off is to reduce the financial burden, but the employer has a statutory obligation to give compensation to the workers who completed one year of continuous service with the organisation and whose names are borne in the muster roll on the date of lay-off whether intermittently or continuously, which shall be equal to 50% of their basic wages and dearness allowances that would have been payable had they not been so laid off. Lay-off is burdensome to the employees also because they get only 50 per cent of their wages.

Lay-off thus involves a greater cost to the employer. On the one hand he loses all benefits of the expenses incurred on selection, placement or training of the employees. On the other hand he has to pay compensation to the workers are an obligation under Act. So the employer should take every possible step to avoid the causes of lay-off. All possible adjustment of palcement of workers such as demoton, transfers etc. should be made.

Characteristics of a Sound Lay-Off Policy

(i) *Agreement on the provision* : There should on the provisions regarding lay-off, between trade union and management. The policy of lay-off should be designed in the light of such agreement.

(ii) *Prior Measures* : It should be made clear in the policy what measures should be taken by the employer before he is forced to take such decision.

(iii) *Emphasis on seniority* : Length of service should be reckoned at the time of decision to lay-off, worker at the bottom of seniority list should be laid off first and at the top, in the last but at the time of re-employment, senior-most persons should be re-employed first and junior-most in the last.

(iv) *Proper Notice* : A proper notice of lay-off should be given to employees in advance to keep the agitations off.

(v) *Placement with other firms* : The company may take an effort to place laid-off employees with other firms in the community.

(vi) *Provision of Severance pay* : In temporary lay-off, severance pay may be provided by some concerns of repute.

During a lay-off period, a workman ceases to be eligible for lay-off compensation if —

(i) He refuses to accept alternative employment at a place within 5 miles of the establishment from which he has been laid-off (*badli* and *casual* workmen are not eligble for lay-off compensation);

(ii) If he does not present himself for work at the appointed time during normal working hours at least once a day; or

(iii) If the lay-off is due to a strike or slowing down of production on the part of workmen in another part of the establishment.

LABOUR TUNROVER

Meaning

Labour turnover has been defined as "the rate of change in the working staff of a concern during a definite period."[13] It signifies the shifting of the workforce into and out of an organisation. It is a measure of the extent to which old employees leave and new employees enter into service in a given period. It is a measurement of inarticulate labour unrest. While trikes are regarded as articulate expressions of discontent amongst workers; labour turnover is expressed not by striking work but by quitting the job. It is the cause and effect of

13. *Indian Labour Statistics*, 1962, p. 16.

instability of employment, apart from being a measure of the morale and efficiency or otherwise of workers.

Calculation of Turnover

It is generally expressed in a number of different formulas which involve such forms as *accessions* (*i.e.*, addtions to the pay-rool); *separations* (quits, discharges, retirements, deaths, etc.); *replacements* (*i.e.*, one accession plus separation); and *average work force* (*i.e.*, number at the beginning of a period plus the number at the end divided by 2).

Example

If in particular industry, the average workforce per month is 1000, and there are 20 accessions and 25 separations during that period :

(i) The *accession* rate is : $\frac{20}{1000} \times 100 = 2$ per cent

(ii) The *separation* rate is : $\frac{25}{1000} \times 100 = 2.5$ per cent

(iii) The *replacement* rate is : $\frac{20}{1000} \times 100 = 2$ per cent.

Impact of Turnover

The heavy rate of turnover implies a reduction in skill and efficiency on the part of the worker and reduced output for the industry. However, some amount of labour turnover is inevitable and even natural, particularly when it stems from the retirement of old employees and the accession of new blood. In some cases, it arises because of resignations and dismissals. This is harmful to the efficiency of the worker and impairs the quality of production. "From the workers' side, they are not only deprived of various advantages of continued employment, *viz.,* opportunities of graded pay, bonus, provident fund and leave, but they have even to purchase their re-engagement; and their is bound to be less solidarity among workers who move from mill to mill".[14]

Costs of Turnover

1. Hiring costs, involving time and facilities for recruitment, interviewn, and examining a replacement;
2. Training costs, involving the time of the supervisor, the personnel department and the trainee;

14. Mukerjee, R.K., *The Indian Working Class,* Hind Kitabs, Bombay, 1951, p. 42.

3. The pay of the learner is in excess of what is produced;
4. Accident rates of new employees are often higher;
5. The loss of production in the interval between the separation of the old employee and the repalcement by the new;
6. The production equipment is not fully utilized during the hiring interval and the training period;
7. Scrap and waste rates rise when new employees are involved and
8. Overtime pay may result from an excessive number of separations causing trouble in meeting contract delivery dates.

Magnitude of Labour Turnover

The Rege Committee collected some data on labour trunover in respect of some industries during the Second World War and observed : "The cotton textile industry in Bombay has a somewhat higher monthly turn-over rate than in Madurai, Nagpur, Calcutta and Akola, for the probable reason that the number of mills in Bombay is far greater than anywhere else and it is possible for the workers to move from mill to mill....In the engineering group, the rates are fairly high in Calcutta. The highest rates for any industry are those for the glass indusry, wherein labour has proved extremely mobile owing to the scarcity of trained hands and the anxiety of employers to obtain such men at any cost from anywhere. In the mining section, iron ore has a higher range of turnover rates than gold, mainly because the former requires much less skilled labour than the latter, and also because labour supply from tribal sources in the iron ore areas is much more plentiful than in gold mining areas....In plantations, no data are available due to the peculiar system of recruitment in them...In their industries like printing presses, woollen textiles, cement, potteries, rice mills, etc., the rates do not, on the whole, appear to be exccessive except in particular localities."[15]

Causes of Labour Turnover

1. *Resignations.* Resignations may be due to such causes as dissatisfaction with working conditions, insufficent wages, bad health, sickness, old age, family circumstances and exodus to the village for agricultural operations. When workers return from their villages after a long time, they do not find their old jobs and have to seek employment elsewhere.

2. *Dismissals* : These may occur due to participation in strikes or union actvities, misconduct, insubordination and inefficiency. But dismissal is a lesser cause of labour turnover.

15. *Report of the Labour Investigation Committee,* New Delhi, 1946, p. 104.

3. *The badli system.* It contributes to a high turnover because, with a view to providing work for *badli* workers, many workers are forced to leave. Dr. Mukerjee has observed : "The excessive turnover among the *badlis* in the different establishments in India is largely due to the fact that jobbers are pecuniarily interested in extending their circle of patronage so that *badli* workers obtain a few days' employment in a month in a factory."[16]

In this connection, the Bombay Textile Labour Enquiry Committee on bserved : "Improvement in the methods of recruitment is one of the principal remedies for excessive labour turnover. But more radical and effective methods....such as the establishment of exchanges, the restriction of the powers of jobbers and the organisation of a personnel department are required. Improvement in working conditions, the adoption of an enlightened policy of management in respect of wages, transfers and promotions, leave and holidays, the provision of facilities for education and training, the promotion of welfare work, the introduction of unemployment and sickness insurance, gratuity and pension schemes, will all contribute to make the labour force more stable than it is at present. Not the least important factors contributing to the stability will be the attitude of the employers' and workers' organisations and the provision of an effective machinery of the ventilation and redressal of the grievances of the workers."[17]

QUESTIONS FOR EXERCISE

1. Describe the meaning, significance and principles of promotion.
2. What is the role of personnel department in relation to promotion.
3. What are the bases of promotion? What arguments have been given in their favour?
4. Seniority is the best policy. Discuss.
5. Write short note on Demotion.
6. What is the nature and objective of transfer? Explain good transfer policy.
7. Explain the meaning, causes and elements of discharge.
8. Write short note on Lay off.
9. What is labour turnover. Discuss its impact, costs and causes.

---

16. Mukherjee, R.K., *op. cit.*, p. 40.

17. Report, *Ibid.*, p. 63.

12

Employee Training

TRAINING AND DEVELOPMENT

'Training', 'education' and 'development' are three terms frequently used together. In all 'training' there is some 'education' and in all 'education' there is some 'training'. And the two processes cannot be separated from 'development'.

Training is a process of learning a sequence of programmed behaviour through application of knowledge which gives people an awareness of the rules and procedures to guide their behaviour. *Development* is a related process which covers not only those activities which improve job performance but also those which bring about growth of the personality and helps individuals in the progress towards maturity and actualisation of their potential capacities so that they become good employees and better men and women. Training a person for a bigger and higher job is development which may include not only imparting specific skills and knowledge but also inculating certain personality and mental attitudes. Pointing out the distinction between training and development, said steinmetz : "*Training* is short-term process utilising a systematic and organised procedure by which non-managerial personnel learn technical knowledge and skills for a definite purpose....*Development* is a long-term educational process utilising a systematic and organised procedure by which managerial personnel learn conceptual and theoretical knowlege for general purpose."[1]

While "Training" refers only to instruction in technical and mechanical operations, "development" refers to philosophical and theoretical educational concepts. In the words of Campbell, "training courses are typically designed for a short-term, stated set purpose, such as the operation of some piece(s) of machinery, while development involves a broader education for long-term purposes."[2]

1. Steinmetz, Lawrence, L., Age : Unrecognised Engima of Executive Development, *Management of Personnel,* Quarterly, Vol. VIII, 1969.
2. Campbell, J.P., Personnel Training and Development, *Annual Review of Psychology*, Vol. 22, No. 1, 1971.

Training and development differ in four ways :

(a) "What" is learned;

(b) "Who" is learning;

(c) "Why" such learning takes place and

(d) "When" learning occurs.

Following chart shows the difference between training and development.

CHART 12.1

Learning Dimensions	Training	Development
Who?	Non-managerial personnel	Managerial personnel
What?	Technical and mechanical operations	Theoretical, conceptual ideas
Why?	Specific job-related purpose	General Knowledge
When?	Short-term	Long-term

DEFINITION OF TRAINING

1. *Dale S. Beach* : "Training is the organised procedure by which people learn knowledge and/or skill for a definite purpose."

2. *Edwin B. Flippo* : "Training is the act of increasing the knowledge and skill of an employee for doing a particular job."

3. *Michael J. Jucius* : "The term training is used here to indicate the process by which the aptitudes, skills and abilities of employees to perform specific jobs are increased."

4. *L.L. Steinmetz* : "Training is a short-term process utilising a systematic and organised procedure by which non-managerial personnel learn technical knowledge and skills for a definite purpose."

5. *J.P. Campbell* : "Training refers only to instruction in technical and mechanical operations. Specifically stated, training is the organised procedure by which people learn knowledge and skills for a definite purpose. The objective of training is to achieve a change in the behaviour of those trained. In the industrial situation, this means that the trainee shall acquire new techniques, skills, problem-solving abilities and develop work attitude. It is expected that the employees apply their newly acquired knowledge on the job in such a way as to help them in the achievement of organisational goals."

IMPORTANCE OF TRAINING

A vital and necessary activity in all organisations training plays a large part in determining the effectiveness and efficiency of the establishment. Following is the need or importance of training to a business firm or industry:

1. Increase in productivity. Increase in productivity is possible only when there is an increase in quantity of output. Training programmes, by increasing skills, aptitude and abilities of workers result in increased productivity.

2. Improvement in performance. Training applies not only to new employees but to experienced people as well. It can help employees increase their level of performance on their present job assignments.

3. High morale. Possession of needed skills helps to meet such basic human needs as security and ego satisfaction. Elaborate personnel and human relations programme can make a contribution towards morale, but does not work if there is no solid core of meaningful work done with knowledge, skill and pride.

4. Reduced supervision. A trained employee is one who can supervise himself. Both the employee and the supervisor want less supervision, but greater independence is not possible unless the employee is adequately trained.

5. Reduced dissatisfactions, complaints, absenteeism and turnover. Through this the employees can experience the direct satisfactions associated with a sense of achievement and knowledge that they are developing their inherent capabilities at work.

6. Less accidents and wastage. An important advantage of training is that accidents, which spoiled work and damage machinery and equipment can be kept to minimum by well trained employees.

7. Fulfilment of manpower needs. When technical skills are required by a company it often finds it most practical to select and train from within the organisation rather then seek the skilled personnel from the outside labour market.

8. Benefits to employees. As employees acquire new knowledge and job skills they increase their market value and earning power. The possession of useful skills increases their value to their employer and thereby increase their job security. Training may also qualify them for promotion to more jobs. This, of course, increase their pay and status.

9. Increase in organizational stability and flexibility. Stability, the ability of an organization to sustain its effectiveness despite the loss of key personnel, can be developed only through creation of a reservoir of trained replacements. Flexibility, the ability to adjust to short-run variations in the volume of work, requires personnel with multiple skills to enable their transfer to jobs where the demand is highest. There is no greater organizational asset than the trained motivated personnel.

10. Prevention of obsolence. Training and development programmes foster the initiative and creativity among employees and help to prevent manpower obsolence which may be due to age, temperament, lack of motivation or the inability of a person to adapt himself to technological changes.

11. Reduction in learning time. A well-knit training programme reduce learning time to reach the level of acceptable performance.

Thus, training is a must for all concerns. The management has no choice between 'training' or 'no training'. The only choice is to select a suitable method of training.

OBJECTIVES OF TRAINING

1. To increase Productivity. According to L.C. Scott, instruction can help employees increase their level of performance on their present assignment. Increased human performance often directly leads to increased operational productivity and increased company profits.[3] To quote Baum and other "increased Performance and productivity, because of training, are most evident on the part of new employees who are not yet fully aware of the most efficient and effective ways of performing their jobs."[4]

2. To improve Quality. According to Boocock, "Better informed workers are less likely to make operational mistakes. Quality increases may be in relationship to a company product or service, or in reference to the intangible organisational employment atmosphere."[5]

3. To help a Company Fulfil Its Future Personnel Needs. As Fine points out, "Organisations that have a good internal educational programme will have to make less drastic manpower changes and adjustments in the event of sudden personnel alternations. When the need arises, organisational vacancies can more easily be staffed from internal sources if a company initiates and maintains an adequate instructional programme for both its non-supervisory and managerial employees."[6]

3. Scott, L.C., "The Economic Effectiveness of On-the-job Training," *Industrial and Labour Relations Review*, Vol. 23, No. 2, 1970.

4. Baum, Bernard H., Sorensen, Peter F., and Place, W.S., "The Effect of Managerial Training on Organization Control : An Experimental Study," *Organisation Behaviour and Human Performance* 5(1), 1, 1970, pp. 170-182.

5. Boocock, Sarane S., "Technology and Educational Structure," *Educational Technology*, 9(1), 1969, pp. 19-21.

6. Fine, Sydney S., "The Use of Dictionary Occupational Titles as a source of Estimates of Educational and Training Requirements," *Journal of Human Relations*, 3(3), 1968, pp. 363-372.

4. To Improve Organisational Climate. In the words of Greer "An endless chain of positive reactions results from a well-planned training programme. Production and product quality may improve : financial incentives may then be increased, internal promotions become stressed, less supervisory pressures ensure and base pay rate increases result. Increased morale may be due to many factors, but one of the most important of these is the current state of an organisation's educational endeavour."[7]

5. To Improve Health and Safety. As Florsheim said, "Proper training can help prevent industrial accidents. A safer work environment leads to more stable mental attitudes on the part of employees. Managerial mental state would also improve if supervisors know that they can better themselves through company-designed development programmes."[8]

6. Obsolescence Prevention. In the words of Arnoff, "Training and development programmes foster the initiative and creativity of employees and help to prevent manpower obsolescence, which may be due to age, temperament or motivation, or the inability of a person to adapt himself to technological changes."[9]

7. Personal Growth. According to Bowley, "Employees on a personal basis gain individually from their exposure to educational experiences."[10] Again, in the words of Wiener and Attwood, "Management development programmes seem to give participants a wider awareness, an enlarged skill, and enlightened altruistic philosophy, and make enhanced personal growth possible."[11]

O Jeff Harris, Jr. observes: "Training of any kind should have as its objective the redirection or improvement of behaviour so that the performance of the trainee bcomes more useful and productive for himself and for the organisational of which he is a part. Training normally concentrates on the improvement of either *operative skills* (the basic skills related to the successful completion of a task),

---

7. Greer, Thomas V., "Some Behavioural Aspects of Training," S.A.M. , *Advancement Management Journal,* 32(7), 1970.
8. Florsheim, Henry, "Employee Training Vital for Reduction of Costs : Problems to Get Worse," *Supervision*, 32 (7), 1970.
9. Aronoff, J., and Litwin, "Achievement Motivation, Training and Executive Advancement," *Journal of Applied Behavioural Science*, 7(1), pp. 215-229.
10. Bowley, Roger L., Schriver, William R., "Non-Wage Benefits of Vocational Training, Employability and Mobility," *Industrial and Labour Relations Review*, 23(4), 1970, pp. 500-509.
11. Wiener, E.L., and Attwood, D.A., "Training for Vigilance, Combined Cueing and Knowledge of Results," *Journal of Applied Psychology*, 52(8), 1968, pp. 474-479.

interpersonal skills (how to relate satisfactorily to others), *decision-making skills* (how to arrive at the most satisfactory causes of action), or a combination of these."[12]

CAUSES OF NEED OF TRAINING

1. An increased use of technology in production;
2. Labour turnover arising from normal separations due to death or physical incapacity, for accidents, disease, superannuation, voluntary retirement, promotion within the organisation and change of occupation or job;
3. Need for adidtional hands to cope with an increased production of goods and services;
4. Employment of inexperienced, new or *badli* labour requires detailed instruction for an effective performance of a job;
5. Old employees need refresher training to enable them to keep abrest of the changing methods, techniques and use of sophisticated tools and equipment;
6. Need of enabling employees to do the work in a more effective way, to reduce learning time, reduce supervision time, reduce waste and spoilage of raw material and produce quality goods, and develop their potential.
7. Need for reducing grievances and minimising accident rates;
8. Need for maintaining the validity of an organsiation as a whole and raising the morale of its employees.

A programme of training becomes essential for the purpose of meeting the specific problems of a particular organisation arising out of the introduction of new lines of production, changes in design, the demands of competition and economy, the quality of materials processed, individual adjustments, promotions, career development, job and personnel changes and changes in the volume of business. Collectively, these purpose directly relate to and comprise the ultimate purpose of organistional training programmes to enhance overall organisational effectiveness.

MEN RESPONSIBILE FOR TRAINING

1. *The top management* : That which frames the training policy;
2. *The personnel department* : That which plans, establishes and evaluates instructional programmes;

---

12. Harris, O. Jeff. *Managing People At Work : Concepts and Cases in Interpersonal Behaviour,* John Wiley & Sons, Inc., New York, 1976, p. 422.

3. *Supervisors* : Those who implement and apply developmental procedure; and
4. *Employees* : Those who provide feedback, revision and suggestions for corporate educational endeavours.

LEVELS OF TRAINING

According to Prof. John Mee, the work of traning should be done at two levels,[13] *viz.,*

1. The Training Department. It should assume the primary responsibility for the instruction of trainers in methods of teaching; for normal orientation; for the training of supervisors in human relations; for the development to executives, for co-operative education in schools and colleges; and for the general education of employees.

2. Line Supervisors and Employees. They should carry the bulk of the teaching load in the following areas: On-the-job instruction of employees; instruction in the technical and professional aspects of a business; daily development of superiors and executives through counselling; departmental communication and staff meetings as part of an over-all training programme. It is needless to say that the top line executive has the responsibility for :

(i) Authorising basic training policies;
(ii) Reviewing and approving the broad outlines of trianing plans and programmes and
(iii) Approving training budgets.

HOW TO CREATE A DESIRE FOR TRAINING?

According to Chin, the employees can be persuaded to be interested in training programmes in one of the following three ways :[14]

1. They will respond to programmes involving changed behaviour if they believe that the resulting modification in the behaviour is in their own interest, that they will receive personal benefits as a result of their new behaviour.
2. Trainees will change their behaviour if they *became aware* of better ways of peroforming (more productive or otherwise more satisfactory ways) and *gain experience* in the new pattern of behaviour so that it becomes their normal manner of operation.

---

13. Mee, John (ed.), *Personnel Handbook*, The Ronald Press Company, New York, 1955.
14. Chin, Robert and Kenneth D. Benn, "General Strategies for Effecting Changes in Human System," in Bennis, Warren G., Kenneth D. Benne, and Robert Chin, *The Planning of Change,* Holt, Rinehart and Wintson, New York, 1969, pp. 32-59.

3. A trainee may change his behaviour in compliance with the forced demands of his superiors.

PRINCIPLES OR CONCEPTS OF TRAINING

1. **Training as Solution to Problems.** According to Bass and Vaughan, trainees in work organisations tend to be most responsive to training programmes when they feel the need to learn, *i.e., the trainee will be more eager to learn training if training promises answers to problems or needs he has as employee.* The individual who perceives training as the solution to problems wll be more willing to enter into a training programme than will the individual who is satisfied with his present performance abilities.[15]
2. **More Effective Learning.** According to Skinner, learning is more effective where there is reinforcement in the form of rewards and punishments.[16] *Individuals do things that give pleasure and avoid things that give pain.* If satisfier is received after an action the action will be repeated. If no satisfaction is received, the action will not be repeated.
3. **Role of Awards.** According to Bugelski, in the long run, awards tend to be more effective for changing behaviour and increasing one's learning than punishments.[17]
4. **Rewards Performance.** According to Fryer, rewards for the application of learned behaviour are most useful when they quickly follow the desired performance.[18]
5. **More Reward More Reinforcement.** According to Clark Hull, the larger the reward for good performance following the implementation of learned behaviour, the greater will be the reinforcement of the new behaviour.[19]
6. **Disruptive Effect of Negative Reinforcement.** Negative reinforcement, through application of penalties and heavy criticism following inadequate performance, may have a

15. Bass, Bernard M. and Vaughn, James A., *Training in Industry : The Management of Learning,* Wordsworth Publishing Company, California, Belmont, 1966, p. 56.
16. Skinner, Burrhust, F., *Behaviour of Organism,* D. Appleton Century Company, New York, 1938, pp. 228-231.
17. Bugelski, Richard B., *The Psychology of Learning,* Holt & Co., New York, 1956, pp. 250-255.
18. Fryer, Douglas H., Fiemberg, Mortimer R. and Zalkind, Sheldon, *Developing People in Industry,* Harper and Brothers, New York, 1956, p. 95.
19. Hull, Clark, *Principles of Behaviour,* Appleton-Century-Crofts, New York, 1963, pp. 131-133.

disruptive effect upon the learning experience of the trainee than positive reinforcement.

7. **Training Though Desirable Behaviour.** According to Bess and Vaughan training requesting the trainee to make changes in his values, attitudes, and social beliefs, usually achieves better results if he is encouraged to participate, discuss and discover new, desirable behaviour norms.[20]

8. **Feedback on Progress.** The trainee should be provided with 'feedback' on the progres he is making in utilising the training he has received. As Miller has stated, "If a person with the required abilities is to improve his performance, he must (i) know what aspect of his performance is not upto par; (ii) know precisely what corrective actions he must take to improve his performance."[21] *The feedback should be fast and frequent,* particularly for the lower level jobs which are often routine and quickly completed.

9. **The Development of New Behaviour Norms and Skills.** It is facilitated through practice and repetition. Skills that are practised often are better learned and less easily forgotten.

10. **Meaningful Training Material.** The training material should be made as meaningful as possible. If the trainee undestands the general principles underlying what is being taught, he will probably understand it better than if he were just asked to memorize a series of isolated steps.

Principles of the National Industries Conference Board, U.S.A.[22]

1. The purpose of the training is to help meet company objectives by providing opportunities for employees at all organisational levels to acquire the requisite knowledge, skills and attitudes.
2. The first step in training is to determine needs and objectives.
3. The objectives and scope of a training plan should be defined before its development is begun in order to provide a basis for common agreement and co-operative action.
4. The techniques and processes of a training programme should be related directly to the needs and objectives of an organisation.

---

20. Bass, and Vaughan, *op. cit.,* p. 54.
21. Miller, L. *The Use of Knowledge Results in Improving Performance of Hourly Operators,* Behavioural Research Service, New York, quoted by Bass and Vaughan, *op. cit.,* p. 25.
22. *The National Conference Board Management Record,* New York, Vol. 12, No. 12, December, 1950, p. 447.

5. Training is properly the responsibility of any one in the management who wants to attain a particular objective.
6. The purpose behind the training of personnel is to assist line management in the determination of training needs and in the development, administration, conduct and follow-up of training plans.
7. To be effective, training must use the tested principles of learning.
8. Training should be conducted in the actual job environment to the maximum possible extent.

METHODS OR TECHNIQUES OF TRAINING

1. On-the-job methods. On-the-job means while working on a job. Numerous training methods may be used while the man is engaged in the process of productive work. These on-the-job training methods are suitable for all levels of personnel. Following are the various methods of on-the-job training :

1. On specific job: (i) Experience; (ii) Coaching; (iii) Understudy; 2. Position rotation; 3. Special projects; 4. Selective reading; 5. Apprenticeship; 6. Vestibule school; 7. Multiple management.

2. Off-the-job training methods. In these off-the-job training methods, the trainees have to leave their work, place and devote their entire time to the development objective. Development of trainees is primary in these methods and work of production during training is secondary. Following are off-the-job training techniques :

1. Special courses and lectures; 2. Conferences; 3. Case studies; 4. Brainstorming; 5. Laboratory method — A. Simulation (i) Role-playing; (ii) Gaming; B. Sensitivity Training; On-the-job Training Methods.

On-the-job Methods

1. On specific job. Training for a specific job is the most common and formal on-the-job training programme. Current practice in job training has been strongly influenced by the war time training within industry (T.W.L.). This was first designed to improve the job performance through job instruction training. It also included training for supervisors to improve job performance. Following are the methods of training on specific job :

(i) *Experience* : Experience is the oldest method of on-the-job training. Learning by experience cannot and should not be eliminated as a method of development, though as a sole approach, it is wasteful, time consuming and inefficient. It has proved to be very efficient in some cases though it should be followed by other training methods to make it more meaningful.

(ii) *Coaching* : On-the-job coaching by the superior is an important and potentially effective approach. It is superior, properly trained and oriented. It involves direct personnel instruction and guidance, usually with extensive demonstration and continuous critical evaluation and correction. It has the advantage of increased motivation for the trainee and the minimisation of the problem of learning transfer from theory to practice. In this method the danger lies in the possible neglect to coaching by superior.

(iii) *Understudy* : It is considered a somewhat different approach from those described above. In it a person is specifically designated as the heir apparent. It makes the trainee an assistant to the current job holder. The trainee learns by experience, observation and imitation. If decisions are discussed with him he can become informed on the policies and theories involved. The training is conducted in practical and realistic situation. However, it tends to perpetuate mistakes and deficiencies of existing managerial practices. Moreover, the understudies are frequently neglected by those they assist.

2. Position rotation. It is the broadening of the background of trainee in the organisation. If a trainee is rotated periodically from one job to another job, he acquires a general background. The main advantages of position rotation are : providing a general background to the trainee, training in actual situation, stimulating competition among the rotating trainees and stimulating a more co-operative attitude by exposing a man to other fellow's problems and view-points. A disadvantage of this method is that productive work suffers because of the obvious disruption caused by such changes. As Specialisation proceeds rotation becomes less useful as few people have the breadth of technical knowledge and skills to move from one functional area to another.

3. Special projects. These assignments grow ordinarily out of an individual analysis of weakness. The trainee may be asked to perform special Assignment, in which he learns the work procedure. Sometimes a task force is created which consists of a number of trainees representing different functions in the organisation. Trainees not only acquire knowledge about the assigned activities, but also learn how to work with others.

4. Selective reading. Through this method the individual in the organisation can gather and advance their knowledge and background. Selective reading may include professional journals and books. Some business organisations maintain libraries for their executives. Some executives become members of professional associations. They exchange their ideas with others. This is a good method for assimilating knowledge. However, some executives point out that it is very difficult to find time to do reading other than that absolutely required in the performance of their jobs.

5. Apprenticeship. This method may be traced back to medieval times when those intended on learning trade skill used to bind themselves to a master craftsman to learn by doing the work under his guidance. During earlier periods, apprenticeship was not restricted to artisans. It was used in training for the professions including medicine, law and teaching etc. Today's industrial organisations require large number of skilled craftsmen who may be trained by this system. Apprenticeship training is either provided by the organisation or it is also imparted by government agencies. Most concerns have apprenticeship laws with supervised plans for such training. Such arrangements usually provide a mixed programme of class-room and job experience.

6. Vestibule schools. Large organisations frequently provide vestibule schools, a preliminary to actual shop experience. As far as possible, shop conditions are duplicated. But here major objective is instruction, not output. Vestibule schools are widely used in training for clerical and office jobs as well as for factory production jobs. Vestibule training is usually shorter and less complex than that adaptable to the apprenticeship system. It is relatively expensive, but these costs are justified if the volume of training is large, or if uniform, high standard results are important.

7. Multiple management. This method emphasises the use of committees to increase the flow of ideas from less experienced managers and to train them for positions of greater responsibility. Such a programme was developed by the McCormik & Company of Baltimore, U.S A. This company claimed that the plan has increased employee efficiency, reduced labour turnover and absenteeism, and enabled the company to pay higher wages than those prevailing in the area and industry. A junior board was authorised to discuss any problem that the senior board may discuss, and its members were encouraged to put their mind to work on the business as a whole, rather than to concentrate to their specialized areas.

Off-the-Job Training Methods

1. Special Course and Lectures. Special courses and lectures are presented by business organisations in numerous ways as a part of their development programmes.

(i) *Own Regular Instructor* : There are courses which the organisations themselves establish to be taught by members of the organisations. Some organisations have regular instructors assigned to their training and development departments such as Tata and Hindustan Lever in private sector; Life Insurance Corporation, State Bank of India and other nationalised commercial banks, Reserve Bank, Hindustan Steel, Fertilizer Corporation and many others in public sector.

(ii) *Instructions by Instructors from Institutes* : Courses and lectures in organisations to work with university or institutes in establishing a course or series to be taught by instructors by these institutes.

(iii) *Sending Personnel to Programmes* : Courses for the organisations to send personnel to programmes established by the universities, institutes and other bodies. These courses are organised for a short period ranging from 2-3 days to a few weeks. The first such programme was the Slogan Fellowship Programme, established in 1931 at the Massachusetts Institute of Technology, U.S.A. In India, such courses are organised frequently by the Institutes of Management, Administrative Staff College of India, National Productivity Council, NITIE, All India Management Association and some other organisations and universities.

2. Conferences. Holding Conference is a favourite training method. Many organisations have developed guided-discussion type of conferences in their training programmes in order to escape the limitations of lectures. In Conference the participants pool their ideas and experience in attempting to arrive at improved methods of dealing with the problems which are common subject of discussion. Conference may include buzz sessions that divide the conference into small groups of four or five for intensive discussion. These small groups then report back their conclusions or questions to the whole conference. Conference method allows the trainees to look at the problem from a broader angle. However, unless the discussion is directed to the felt needs of the participants, they may feel that whole exercise is useless.

3. Case Studies. It is one of the most common form of training. A case is a written account of a trained reporter or analyst seeking to describe an actual situation. Some cases are merely illustrative, others are detailed and comprehensive demanding extensive and intensive analytical ability. Cases are widely used in a variety of programmes. This method increases the trainees power of observation. It helps him to ask better questions and to look for broader range of problems. A well chosen case may promote objective discussion. However, the lack of emotional involvement may make it difficult to effect any basic change in the behaviour and attitude of trainees.

4. Brainstorming. Brainstorming which stimulates trainees to creative thinking was developed by Alex Osborn inhibiting forces by providing for a maximum of group participation and a minimum of criticism. In Brainstorming a problem is posed and ideas are invited. Quantity rather than quality is the primary objective. Ideas are encouraged while criticism of any idea is discouraged. Often chain reactions develop from idea to idea. Later, these ideas are critically examined. There is no trainer in brainstorming. The introduction of known experts into it reduces the originality and practicability of the group contribution. Brainstorming favours divergence. This explains why Brainstorming is so little used in developing countries where no solutions carry the highest premium. Its immediate use is limited to new ideas only. It does not lead to change in behaviour.

5. Laboratory Training. Adding to conventional training, laboratory training provides situations in which trainees themselves experience some of the conditions they are talking about through their own interaction. Thus, they more or less experiment on themselves. More concerned about changing individual behaviour and attitude. Laboratory training is more successful in changing job performance rather than conventional training methods. Following are two methods of laboratory training : simulation and sensitivity training.

(A) *Simulation* : Its performance is an increasingly popular technique of management development. In it, instead of taking participants into the field, the field can be simulated in the training session itself. Simulation is the presentation of real situation of organisations in the training session. It covers situations of varying complexities and roles for the participants. It creates a whole field organisation. It relates participants through key roles in it. It exposes them to simulated specific situations of a kind they encounter in real life. There are two common simulation methods of training : role-playing and business game.

(i) *Role-playing* : It is a laboratory method which may be used rather easily as a supplement to conventional training methods. Its purpose is to increase the trainee's methods. Its purpose is to increase the trainee's skill in dealing with other people. One of its greatest use is in connection with human relations training. It is also used in sales training as well. It is spontaneous acting of a realistic situation involving two or more persons under class-room situations. Dialogue spontaneously grows out of the situation. It is developed by the trainees assigned to it. Other trainees in the group serve as observers or critics. Since people act roles every day, they are somewhat experienced in this art. With a certain amount of imagination they project themselves into roles other than their own. As a manager is regularly acting roles in his relationship with others, it is essential for him to have role awareness and to do role thinking so that they may size up each relationship and develop the most effective interaction position. By role-playing a trainee can broaden his experiences by trying different approaches, while in actual situation, he often has only one chance.

(ii) *Gaming* : It simulates the problems of running a company or even a particular department. It is used for a variety of training objectives, from investment strategy, collective bargaining techniques, to the morale of clerical personnel. It is used at all the levels, from the executives to the production supervisors. It is a laboratory method in which role-playing exists. But it focuses attention on administrative problems, while role-playing tends to emphasise feeling tone between people in interaction. It involves several terms, each of which is given a firm to operate for a number of periods. Usually the period is short one, one year or so. In each period each team makes decisions on various matters such as fixation of price, level of production, inventory level, and so forth. Since each team competes with others, each firm's decisions are fed into a computer which is programmed to behave somewhat like a real market. The computer provides the results. The team which has accumulated largest profit is the winner. Strength and weakness of decisions are analysed in the light of such result.

(B) *Sensitivity Training*. It is the most controversial laboratory training method. Some of its advocates exhibit an almost religious zeal in their enhancement with the training group experience. Some of its critics match this fervour in their attacks on the technique. As a result of criticism and experience it is somewhat revised. It was first used by National Training Laboratories at Bethel, U.S.A. The training groups called themselves 'T Group'. Since then its use has been extended to other organisations, universities and institutes.

DIFFERENT TRAINING FOR DIFFERENT LEVELS

The basic objective of training programme for a particular level differs from that of other level. Rank and file employees need specific job training while management group needs broad-based training. Thus, a particular training programme would be suitable only to a particular group of people. Again, within a particular group, an individual may need a particular training while others may need some other programme. Thus, the training programme would be determined by the level of an individual in the organisation and his own personality characteristics. The level is more emphasised to assessing the suitability of training programmes.

Levels of Employees

The entire personnel of an organisation may broadly be classified into the following three levels :

1. Rank and File Level. Most extensive of all training programmes are those designed to meet the needs of rank and file employees. They require training either at the time of entry or to keep pace with the technological development at subsequent time. Such training is mostly of technological nature. Pre-employment training may involve preparation, not for a single job, but for the many types of related jobs that may be given to workers subsequently. Retraining or refresher courses may be given as a means of avoiding personnel obsolence.

2. Supervisory Level. The practice of management begins where a trainee is assigned to supervisory position. The new incumbent practises with full responsibility for results over a range of time what he has learned about supervision. He thus refines his peculiar techniques of inter-personnel relationships. His career depends upon his developed skills. Outstanding men become candidates for promotion to middle-management positions. Candidates for frontline supervisory positions and incumbent supervisors need the same kind of training opportunities. They need to know how to develop and carry out approved programmes within a budget to obtain and use service and staff help, and to meet the requirements of their superior managers.

3. Management Level. Management level differs from supervisory groups in the training need. People at this level do not have any direct contact with working force. Their outlook is broad-based. Management group may further be divided into following two levels — middle management and top management.

(i) *Middle Management* : The men to enter the middle management group are generally supervisors who have had several years of on-the-job practice. These are most in need of knowledge of management theory. On the practical side, they know much about management informally. Now, when they are about to manage managers and not technicians, they can no longer rely on their technical proficiency to get things done. To manage managers, they need a comprehensive understanding of the functions of managers because these are the means they must utilise to accomplish their job.

(ii) *Top Management* : Men to be trained at top management level are normally functional managers who are candidates for general management positions. They have stepped up the promotion ladder within their division. They require training in the management of functions which are strange to them. They are required to have a substantial grounding in the fundamentals and techniques of management.

As the knowledge and technical aspects of managing are rapidly changing, it is one of the objectives of top management training to review management theory and principles and the updating of knowledge and technical development in managing.

TRAINING PROGRAMMES FOR VARIOUS LEVELS

Following specific training programmes may be recommended for people at various levels :

I. For rank and file employees. 1. Job training, 2. Apprenticeship, 3. Pre-employment training, 4. Retraining.

II. For supervisory levels. 1. Supervisory skills training, 2. Coaching, 3. Special courses and classes, 4. Conferences, 5. Job rotation, 6. Brainstorming, 7. Case studies, 8. Special projects and task forces, 9. Simulation role-playing, 10. Sensitivity training.

III. For management level. 1. Coaching, 2. Special courses and classes, 3. Conferences, 4. Job rotation, 5. Brainstorming, 6. Committee assignments, 7. Selective reading, 8. Understudy, 9. Case studies,10. Multiple management, 11. Simulation role-playing, gaming, 12. Sensitivity training.

IV. For All Levels. 1. Job experience 2. Induction and orientation.

STAGES OF ORGANISATION OF TRAINING PROGRAMME IN A LARGE CONCERN

1. Assessing training needs in the enterprise. This is done on the basis of identifying organisational and production problems, analysing jobs and men, anticipating future problems, using check-lists for nature and extent of training. This assessment will help in determining as to how many persons are to be trained and what kind of training is necessary for them.

2. Contents of training. This depends upon the major types of employees who are to be trained. Five distinctive groups of employees may be noted : rank and file, supervisory staff, middle management and top management. Rank and file employees have no administrative or supervisory duties. Supervisory staff is composed of specialised technical and professional persons attached to the operating line to provide counsel and aid. Various types of training should be outlined on the basis of these distinctions. Organisational analysis, operational analysis and workers analysis techniques help in determining the contents and scope of training.

3. Selection of training method. Training method should be ascertained with the advice of personnel manager and high officials about the system which will suit the training.

4. Preparation of training. This involves two stages :

(i) *Preparation of the trainer* : A trainer must be ready before the start of the training. He should ascertain as to what is to be taught and by which method. The success of a training programme depends to a large extent on the interest and capabilities of the instructors.

(ii) *Preparation of trainees* : A trainee is the person to whom training is to be imparted. Trainee must be mentally prepared to learn. Training must recognize individual difference in abilities, interest, learning speed and other significant personnel characteristics.

5. Rule for conducting the training. The following rules should be observed while imparting training :

(i) *Proper time-table* : The instructor must prepare time-table of the training and only one sub-job should taught in one instance.

(ii) *Orderly jobs* : All jobs should be orderly. This order should be made to understand and time for each sub-job should be distributed.

(iii) *Personal care of trainee* : Every trainee should be personally cared.

(iv) *Clear work* : Work should be made clearfully and legibly. Important points should be stressed. For this all orders should be clear.

(v) *Timing* : Work should be clearly and slowly told, *i.e.*, one action or sub-action told at a time.

(vi) *Employment on job* : Trainee should be employed on work. He should be asked questions while working and mistakes should be removed.

(vii) *Left alone for working* : After some time, when the trainee works he should be left alone for working.

6. Examination of the trainee's job. Trainee's job should be examined while working. It he makes mistakes, he should be told. After that he should be asked to repeat the whole work again. He should repeat the work till he gets competence in it.

7. Follow-up. The trainee should be allowed to work after the whole training. Later on, his work should be checked. He should be provided necessarily guidance and help in case of any difficulty. Regularity and vigilance are the key to a successful training programme.

RELATIVE EFFECTIVENESS OF DIFFERENT TRAINING METHODS

CHART 12.2

Questions	Types of Programmes						
	Lecture	Conference	Case Study	Role Playing	Simulta-tion	Sensi-tvity Train-ing	Programmed Ins-truction
1. Does this technique develop its training objectives on the basis of organisational operations, and man analysis? *i.e.*, is the technique oriented to the specific needs of trainees?	Possibly	Possibly	Possibly	Normally Yes	Possibly	May. Say No	Possibly
2. Does this traning technique help the trainee to see the benefits he mayachieve by completing the training this technque concentrates upon?	Not Particu-larly	Some-what	Yes	Yes	Yes	Yes	Somewhat
3. Does thing training technique attempt to relate itself to sary the previous experi-ences of the trainee?	Not Neces-sarily	Possibly	Not Neces-sarily	Not Neces-sarily	Not Neces-	Yes	Not Neces-sarily
4. Does this technique progress through small, carefully planned, steps to completion?	Not Neces-sarily	Possibly	Possibly	Not Neces-sarily	Not Neces-sarily	Not Neces-sarily	Yes
5. Does this technique attempt to influence the organisational conditions in which the trainee lives and works?	Not Particu-larly	Not particu-larly	Not particu-larly	Not particu-larly	Not particu-larly	Possi-bly	No
6. Does this technique utilise a variety of the senses as it works?	Possibly	Possibly	Not Neces-sarily	Yes	Possibly	Yes	No

7. Does this technique make allowances for individual rates of learning?	No	Yes	Some-what	Some-what	Yes	Some-what	Yes
8. Does this technique get the personal involvement of the trainee in the process?	Not	Yes	Yes	Yes	Yes	Yes	Yes
9. Does the technique provide for rewards as new behaviour results?	Not Neces-sarily	Possibly	Possibly	Possibly	Possibly	Possibly	Yes
10. Does the technique provide for regular constructive feed-back to the trainee?	No	Possibly	Possibly	Yes	Possibly	Yes	Yes
11. Does this technique provide assistance to the worker when he encouters obstacles?	No	Yes	Not Neces-sarily	Not Neces-sarily	Possibly	Possi-bly	Possibly

STEPS IN TRAINING PROGRAMMES

1. Identifying the training needs.
2. Getting ready for the job.
3. Preparation of the learner.
4. Presentation of operations and knowledge.
5. Performance try-out.
6. Follow-up and Evaluation of the programme.

1. Identifying Training Needs. As a training programme is established only to assist in the solution of specific operational problems, the most important step is to make a thorough analysis of the entire organisation, its operations and manpower resources to find out "the trouble spots" where training may be needed. However, training is not a cure-all.

Three Types of Analysis

According to McGhee, identication of traning needs must contain three types of analyses — organisational analysis, operations analysis, and man analysis.[23]

23. McGhee, William, and Thayer, Paul W., *Training in Business and Industry*, John Willy & Sons, New York, 1961, pp. 25-26.

(i) Organisational analysis. It centres primarily upon the determination of the organisation's goals, its resources, and the allocation of the resources as they relate to the organisational goals. The analysis of the organisational goals establishes the framework in which training needs can be defined more clearly.

(ii) Operations analysis. It focuses on the task or job regardless of the employee doing the job.[24] It includes the determination of the specific worker behaviour required, if the job is to be performed effectively.

(iii) Man analysis. It reviews the knowledge, attitudes and skills of the incumbent in each position and determines what knowledge, attitudes or skills he must acquire and what alterations in his behaviour he must make if he is to contribute satisfactorily to the attainment of organisational objectives.[25]

Five Tasks

According to William Berliner and William McLarney discovering training needs involves five tasks.[26]

1. Task Description Analysis

(i) List the duties and responsibilities or tasks of the job under consideration, using the Job Description as a guide.

(ii) List the standards of work performance on the job.

2. Determining Training Needs

(iii) Compare actual performance against the standards.

(iv) Determine what parts of the job are giving the employee trouble — where is he falling down in his performance?

(v) Determine what kind of training is needed to overcome the specific difficulty or difficulties.

The above numbers (i) and (ii) comprise basic *task description step* in identifying training needs. Numbers, (iii), (iv) and (v) involve determining job related training needs. Problems and performance discripencies are noted and training goals set.

(1) Task Description Analysis. It aims at determining what constitutes the job, the methods used on the job, and the human skills required to perform the job adequately. It lays out the requirements of task in terms of actual duties to be performed. The job specification lists the human skills and knowledge required.

24. *Ibid.*, p. 26.

25. *Ibid.*, p. 27.

26. Berliner, W., and McLarney, W., *Management Practice and Training,* Richard D. Irwin, Homewood, Illinois, 1974, pp. 438-39.

(2) Determining Training Needs. Training needs may be determined for the new as well as the present employees and for solving the specific problem in the following ways :

(i) *Identifying Specfic Problems* : These include productivity, high costs, poor material control, poor quality, excessive scrap and waste, excessive labour-management troubles, excessive grievances, excessive violation of rules of conduct, poor discipline, high employee turnover and transfers, excessive absenteeism, accidents, excessive fatigue, fumbling, discouragement, struggling with the job; standards of work performance not being met, bottlenecks in production, deadlines not being met, and delayed production.[27] These problems suggest needed training.

(ii) *Anticipating Impending and Future Problems* : These bear on the expansion of business, the introduction of new products, new services, new designs, new plant, new technology and of organisational changes concerned with manpower inventory for present and future needs.

(iii) *Management Requests* : The supervisors and managers may make specific request for setting training programmes. However, requests may not coincide with each other or organisational goals.

(iv) *Interviewing and Observing the Personnel on the Job* : This may also reveal training needs.

(v) *Performance Appraisal* : An analysis of the past performance records of the trainee and comparing his actual performance with the target performance may provide clues to specific interpersonal skills that may need development.

(vi) *Questionnaires* : These may be used for eliciting opinions of the employees on topics like communication, satisfaction, job characteristics, their attitude towards working conditions, pay, promotion policies etc. These will reveal much information about where an employe's skills and knowledge are deficient.

(vii) *Checklist* : Checklist is a useful supplement to interviews and observations. It provide more reliable information and the data are quantifiable. It facilitates evaluating the training programme's effectiveness.

(viii) *Morale and Attitude Surveys* : An occasional personnel audit may be conducted to forecast future promotions, skill

27. *Ibid.*, p. 438.

requirements, and merit rating, to initiate informal discussions and an examination of records and statistics regarding personnel, production, cost, rejects and wastages. All the generally reveal the potential problems to be tackled through training programmes.

(ix) *Tests* : According to McGhee tests of the interpersonal skills through handling of posed cases and incidents, may also reveal training needs.[28]

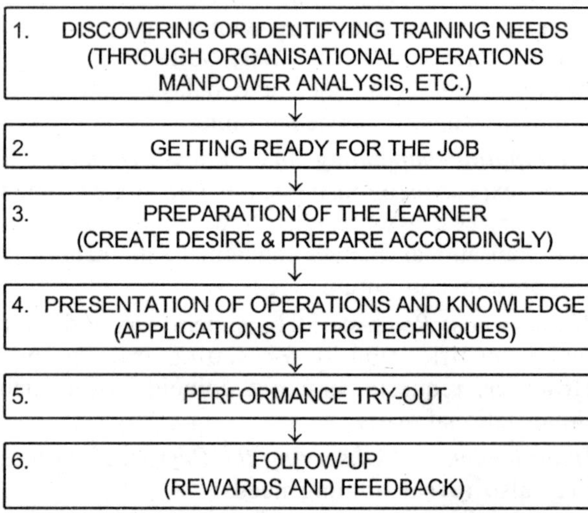

Fig. 12.1 : Sequence of Training Programme.

According to Wendell French, "the determination of training needs in American industry ranges from subjective beliefs about the value of training and education to a systematic identification of problems requiring solutions. The latter seems to be the wisest course in order to ensure that training contributes to the goals of an enterprise."[29] In a survey of 150 firms, by Mahler and others it was found that the training needs of an organisation were determined generally by requests from the top management.[30] The determining factors in these requests were perception, judgement intuition, the expressed needs of the first level and middle managers, or a desire to follow the practices of

28. McGhee, W. and Thyer, P.W., *op. cit.,* p. 125.

29. French, Wendell, *The Personnel Management Process, Human Resources Administration,* Honghton Mifflin Co., 1970, p. 484.

30. Mahler, Walter, R., and Willys, H. Monroe, *How Industry Determines Need for and Effectiveness of Training,* 1952, pp. 24-28.

other firms. The other methods often used were informal observations, talks with supervisors, group discussions and conferences. Methods used less often were analysis of various reports (such as cost, turnover, grievances, suggestions, etc.), formal training advisory committees, employee questionnaires and merit or performance rating.[31] In enquiry by Rudrabasavaraj, it was found that the development of training needs was based on supervisory recommendations in 73 per cent of the firms, on the analysis of job requirements in 58 per cent and on an analysis of job performance in 32 per cent. Suggestions by employees were a factor in 66 per cent of the firms.[32] Organisations have several sources of information which assist them in determining their training needs; and supervisors play a major role in this determination of needs.

In India, it was found in a survey by William Tracy that in all the 13 private sector comapnies where the survey was undertaken, the training needs were determined on the basis of supervisory recommendations, analyses of job performance and job requirements, and on the basis of employee suggestions. In the case of steel and tobacco industries, the employees themselves suggested the type of training that was needed.

The following chart based upon William Tracy gives a checklist for identifying training needs.[33]

CHART 12.3

Check List for Identifying Training and Development Requirements

1. Determine Immediate Needs

A. Evaluate current training and development programmes to determine whether training produces the desired behavioural changes.

(i) Evaluate ongoing training programmes :

(a) Review training documents for adequacy.

(b) Observe trainers and trainees in the learning environment of a classroom, a shop or a laboratory.

(c) Analyse in-course and end-of-course test results.

(d) Interview trainers and trainees.

31. Dudley, Waite, 'Using Performance Reports for Identifying Foreman Training Needs, *Journal of American Society of Training Direction,* Vol. 12, May 1958, pp. 25-27, *Personnel Procedures in Factory and Office*, p. 56.

32. Rudrabasvaraj, N.M., *Personnel Administration Practice in India*, Vainkathalal Mehta Institute of Cooperative Management Pune, 1969, pp. 321-323.

33. Tracy, William, *Designing Training and Development Systems,* American Management Association, pp. 37-40.

(ii) List and analyse shortfalls in the process or products. Determine whether they are due to:

(a) Poor organisation;

(b) Inadequate supervision;

(c) Poor communication;

(d) Improper personnel selection or policies or procedures;

(e) Unclear policies;

(f) Poor job design;

(g) Equipment or materials problems;

(h) Work methods;

(i) Inappropriate work standards;

(j) Inadequate operator or supervisor training.

B. Survey all the aspects of the operations of an enterprise to determine the areas where additional training is required :

(a) Compare job descrciptions and applicant specifications with personnel records.

(b) Analyse performance ratings.

(c) Analyse all the records of an enterprise to identify areas of possible deficiency.

(d) Identify and analyse operating problems.

(e) Use interviews, questionnaires, group conferences, tests, and work samples to determine training problems.

(f) Subject each problem to a careful analysis to determine whether it is due to:

(1) Poor organisation;

(2) Inadequate supervision;

(3) Unclear or ambiguous policies;

(4) Poor communication;

(5) Improper personnel seletion policies;

(6) Poor job designs;

(7) Equipment or material deficiencies;

(8) Improper work methods;

(9) Inappropriate work standards;

(10) Training deficits.

II. Determine Long-range Training Needs

(a) Analyse an enterprise's plans, policies, and forecasts to determine their potential impact on staffing needs.

(b) Identify and analyse future systems, equipment, techniques, and procedures to determine their impact on personnel requirements.

(c) Determine whether current training systems will support future personal requirements in terms of:

(i) Operative personal (workers);

(ii) Supervisory personnel;

(iii) Managerial personnel.

(d) Identify training system shortfalls.

III. For each training requirement, **determine whether training be provided on or off the premises,** and whether it should be normal or on-the-job. Consider :

(a) Comparative costs; and

(b) The availability of in-house personnel, equipment and facilities.

IV. **Summarise training needs.**

V. **For off-the-premises programmes,** develop objectives, prepare contract specifications, solicit and evaluate proposals, and select contractors.

VI. **For in-house programmes,** develop objectives and guidlines following the procedures laid down for the purpose.

2. Getting Ready for the Job. Now, it is to be decided who is to be trained — the newcomer or the older employee, or the supervisory staff, or all of them selected from different departments. The trainer has to be prepared for the job, for he is the key figure in the entire programme. This calls for a decision on support material for training; Training period; Training for different employees and Training methods.

3. Preparation of the Learner. It consists : (i) in putting the learner at ease (so that he does not feel nervous because of the fact he is on a new job); (ii) in stating the importance and ingredients of the job, and its relationship to work flow; (iii) in explaining why he is being taught; (iv) the creating interest and encouraging questions, finding out what the learner already knows about his job or other jobs; (v) in explaning the 'why' of the whole jobs and relating it to some job the worker already knows; (vi) in placing the learner as close to his normal working position as possible and (vii) in familiarising him with the equipment, materials, tools and trade terms.

4. Presentation of Operations and Knowledge. The trainer should clearly *tell, show, illustrate* and *question* to put over the new knowledge and operations. The learner should be told of the sequence of the entire job, and why is each step in its performance necessary. Instructions should be given clearly, completely and patiently. There should be an emphasis on key points. One point should be explained at a time. The trainer should demonstrate or make use of audio-visual aids and ask the trainee to repeat the opeations. The trainee should be encouraged to ask questions in order to indicate that he really knows and understands the job.

5. Performance Try. The trainee is asked to go through the job serveal times slowly, explaining him each step. Mistakes are corrected, and if neccessary. The trainee is asked to do the job, gradually building up skill and speed. As soon as he demonstrates that he can do the job in a right way, he is put on his own.

The effectiveness of a training programme evaluated by the following :

(i) By giving written or oral tests to trainees to ascertain how far they have learnt the techniques and principles taught to them and the scores obtained by them;

(ii) By observing trainees on the job itself and administering performance tests to them;

(iii) By finding out individuals or a groups' reaction to the training programme while it is in progress and getting them to fill up evaluation sheets;

(iv) By arranging structured interviews with the participants or sending them questionnaires by mail;

(v) By eliciting the opinion or judgement of the top management about the trainees' performance;

(vi) By comparing the results obtained after the training with those secured before the training programme in order to find out whether any material change has taken place in attitude, opinion, in the quality of output, in the reduction in scrap, breakage and the supplies used and in overhead costs.

(vii) By study of profiles and charts of career development of the partcipants and related assignment techniques.

The validity of training programmes may be ascertained through one or a combination of these devices. If there are any errors or weaknesses, they should be corrected and instruction repeated.

6. Follow-up. Undertaken to test the effectivenes of training efforts. It consists in :

(i) Putting a trainee "on his own".

(ii) Checking frequently to be sure that he has followed instructions; and

(iii) Tapering off extra supervision and close follow-up until he is qualified to work with normal supervision.

OBJECTIVES OF TRAINING POLICY

1. To indicate a company's intention to develop its personnel; to provide guidance in the framing and implementation of programmes and to provide information concerning them to all concerned;
2. To discover critical areas where training is to be given on a priority basis and
3. To provide suitable opportunities to the employee for his own betterment.

TRAINING COURSES

1. Training in General Areas. Training in general areas is given in such subjects as general and home economics, basic English, instruction in letter writing and report drafting, reading using gauges, the operation of machines, fire-fighting and safety devices on the job, shop practices and secretarial practices, elementary mathematics, sociology, industrial psychology, time study, personal hygiene, public speaking and public relations, selling and communication with people.

2. Training for women employees. They are given training in hygiene, good grooming, sales talk and handling of sales and courtesy.

3. Support Material for Training. Training material has to be prepared with great care and distributed among the trainees so that they may come well-prepared to a session and are able to understand the operations and/or demonstrations quickly and correctly. Support material consists of the following :

(i) Lectures (learning by hearing supplemented by reading assignments); conferences, seminars and staff-meetings (learning by seeing); and short courses, through coaching.

(ii) Role-playing (learning by doing) and job rotation (learning by experience).

(iii) Case or Project studies and problem-solving sessions (learning by personal investigation).

(iv) Use of pamphlets, charts, brochures, booklets, handbooks, manuals, etc.

(v) Graphs, pictures, books, slides, movie projectors, film strips, tape recorders, etc.

(vi) Posters, displays, notice and bulletin boards.

(vii) Reading rooms and libraries where specified books and journals are maintained for reference and use.

(viii) Understudy and visits to plants.

(ix) Correspondence courses under which knowledge about business law, statistics, industrial management, marketing, office procedures, retailing and many other similar subjects may be imparted.

(x) Teaching machines.

(xi) Membership of professional or trade associations, which offer new techniques and ideas to their members.

EVALUATION OF TRAINING EFFECTIVENESS

The effectiveness of training is determined by all the three partners in it : (1) The institution imparting formal training, (2) The participants and (3) The word organisation. All the three should be evaluated before and after the training. This may be done as follows :

1. Training programmes. The basic question for evaluation of the training programme is : to what extent did the programme achieve its objectives ? A training programme is started with certain objectives. Its success can be measured in this context after the programme is over.

McMurry has suggested eight tests that must be met by any successful management training programme : (1) train candidates for specific positions, (2) define necessary qualities and skills, (3) include only trainees with adequate potential, (4) carefully determine which qualities can be developed through training, (5) use tested and proved techniques and procedure, (6) assure qualified trainers, (7) assure adequate trainee motivation and (8) demonstrate results of the programme.

Evaluation at the end of the programme disclose the new knowledge, understanding and skill that the participants have gained during training. At various stages of the post-training phase the same kind of data show how stable these gains are and to what extent they have survived transfer to the work situation.

2. Training objectives. If the objectives were inadequately formulated even a good training programme has no chance to be effective. Sometimes this is due to faulty job analysis. Sometimes participants are shifted from one work to another so frequently that no one job analysis or training may be relevant to their future work. For example, I.A.S. personnel exposed to civil administration in their training programmes, fail miserably when they are given charge of business organisations. Thus, training failure happens whenever training objectives are not rooted in definite plan. Thus, changes on the job or when the change occurs as a whole, failures happen through inadequate organisational commitment and support.

3. Deliberate policy. A deliberate policy is required which may guide the establishment and revision of training objectives. If the policy is realistic, clear, regular and of frequent evaluation followed by marginal adjustments it can keep training objectives in tune with shifting needs. This assumes a close relationship between the training institution and the work organisation.

4. Training institution. Evaluation of training objectives is the responsibility of the work organisation. The training institution may contribute procedural experience and consistent and sustained interest. Collaboration between the organisation and the institution ensures rapid use of evaluation results in selection and preparation of participants in programme designs and in preparing the organisation for change.

5. Participants. With the training objectives formulated clearly in terms of changes to be effected at work, the work organisation is in a position to evaluate the effect of training on individual participants. This can be done in the context of precisely defined training objective. The objective may be changed in behavioural approach. Some behavioural approach may be immediate and direct, and the other secondary, less direct, and more obviously subject to hazards of contamination. The impact of training may be to evaluate in parts by direct measurement of the time required for the trainee to reach the accepted standard of productivity. It may also be expected to influence through less direct behaviour, work attitudes, morale and turnover. All these secondary outputs are subject in the influence of many other factors. Some of these may not become evident for some time.

TRAINING FACILITIES IN INDIA

Categories of Training Facilities

Various training facilities in India can be divided into three categories : training of lower level workers, training to supervisory and middle level personnel, and finally training facilities to the managerial personnel.

1. Worker's training. Worker's training is comparatively a new idea in India. It came into light after the world War II. Real progress in the direction was made only after Independence.

(i) *Apprentice Training Act 1961* : During 1961 was passed the Apprentice Training Act. More than 500 Industrial Training Institutes were established. 300 centres were established for Apprenticeship Training. Madras had Advanced Training Institute, Calcutta had the Central Staff Training and Research Institue, Bangalore had the Foreman Training Institute. The Directorate General of Employment and Training, Government of India established Training Centres under Craftsman

Training Scheme. The National Apprenticeship Training Scheme was extended to other industrial houses also.

Child Training Schemes were developed under Apprenticeship Scheme and now this has been extended to many new works.

(ii) *Private Sector* : As a general rule the private sector has not introduced any formal training programme to its workers. But many concerns have an induction programme for their new employees aimed at informing and educating them about the company, its products, policies and management, etc. These programmes are generally conducted by their personnel department with the help of the supervisory staff. Now, many well established private sector concerns are conducting in company programmes based on their worker's needs and job requirements.

(iii) *Public Sector* : The public sector undertakings use their internal training facilities for training their non-supervisory employees. In some cases, employees are also encouraged to avail of the external training facilities. Sometimes they sponsor their candidature and meet the costs also some public sector organisation such as banks, insurance etc. have started well-organised training programmes.

2. Supervisor's Training. (i) *General Education* : An organisation recruits its supervisors either by promotion from the ranks or by direct recruitment. The latter is the more widely followed practice in India, though promotion from the ranks is more common in western countries. Illiteracy and poor educational background very much limit the possibility of promotion to supervisory jobs from the ranks in India. The problem of supervisory training has, therefore, to be talked at the root and in order to bridge the gap between the potentiality of a worker for sueprvisory work and the post itself, the level of general education needs to be raised. Many organisations have successfully undertaken training of junior and senior hands in Mathematics, Elements of Science, etc., through regular routine classes during working hours.

(ii) *T.W.I.* : Some supervisory training is imparted through T.W.I. or Training Within Industry. T.W.I. was formally introduced in India with the help of I.L.O. experts. A number of organisations, both in public and private sectors, have had persons trained by T.W.I. Centre staff, so that they may undertake supervisory training in their respective organisations. T.W.I. programmes have had mixed results. The managements who have realised complacency by the simplicity of T.W.I. have obtained highly successful results and the programmes.

(iii) *Training Institutes* : The Central Training Institute for Instructors has an additional course meant for supervisors which covers non-technical subjects such as leadership, foundations for good relations, handling of problems, induction of new entrants, effective communication, and so on. Some institutes, particularly Small Industries Service Institute, N.I.T.E., etc., organise short-term training programme for supervisors.

3. Management Training. The management training and development has attracted the greatest attention of both practising managers and academicians in this filed. This is due to the fact that management has very much lagged behind the imperative demand of the country. The major gap in the developing countries is managerial rather than technological. While advanced technology may be imported, managerial competence has to be home-grown to suit the ethos, temper and needs for our society.

Employee Training in India

In an endeavour to build up the career of young persons in their adolescence, Directorate General of Employees and Training has evolved various training programmes. These are formulated within the national framework as far as possible and also in collaboration with foreign countries.

1. Craftsmen Training. Industrial Training Institutes (ITIs) were set up all over the country to impart skills in 42 engineering and 22 non-engineering trades to young men and women in the age group of 15-25. By July 1994, 2,721 such institutes with a total capacity of about 407 lakh were providing training to craftsmen in the country. The duration of the course is one or two years for engineering trades and one year for all non-engineering trades. Educational qualification for admission vary from 8th stnadard to 12th standard depending upon the trades. Besides these 64 trades, some state governments and union territories have introduced training in certain trades to meet requirements of local industries under the jurisdiction of state councils for vocational training.

2. Crafts Instructors Training. Advanced Training Institutes (ATIs) at Howrah, Bombay, Kanpur, Ludhiana and Hyderabad and the Central Training Institute for Instructors at Madras, train instructor trainees in the techniques of imparting industrial skills, who in turn train and make available skilled manpower for industry. These institutes with a seating capacity of 988 offer a series of one year courses which provide comprehensive training, both in skill development and principles of teaching. Refresher courses are also conducted to update and upgrade the knowledge and skill of the instructors and keep them abreast of technological development in industry. Facilities for training of instructors in some selected special trades continue to be available in printing trades at ATI, Kanpur, farm-mechanic trades at ATI, Ludhiana, mill-wright trades at ATI, Kanpur, Howrah and Ludhiana, where seats for scheduled caste and scheduled tribe candidates are reserved as per the Government of India norms.

3. Advanced Vocational Training Scheme. Advanced Vocational Training Scheme was launched in October 1977 for training of highly skilled workers and technicians in a variety of advanced and sophisticated skills not available from other vocational training programmes. Regular full time courses of two to twelve weeks duration are offered under the scheme in a variety of advanced skill areas. The scheme was introduced in six advanced training institutes located at Bombay, Calcutta, Hyderabad, Kanpur, Ludhiana, Madras and 16 selected industrial training institutes under 15 state governments. These institutes which were modernised to conduct various advanced courses under the scheme have an annual capacity to train about 10,000 industrial workers.

4. Women Vocational Training Programme. At present vocational training facilities for women are available through a network of 400 ITIs/wings exclusively for girls with seating capacity of about 32,609 besides general ITIs. Under the state sector, 100 new women ITIs/ wings are being set up, and new trades being introduced in 64 existing ITIs/wings in the Eighth Plan with the assistance of World Bank. Under Women's Vocational Training Programme, NVTI for women at NOIDA, Regional Vocational Training Institutes (RVTIs) at Bombay, Bangalore, Thiruvananthapuram, Calcutta, Hissar, Tura, Allahabad, Indore and Jaipur have seen set up with the intake capacity of 1,496 in 18 basic, advanced and instructional skills.

5. Central Instructional Media Institute. Central Instructional Media Institute (CIMI) has been set up in Madras to make available instuctional materials in the form of Media Packages (MPs) for the use of trainers and trainees in the ITIs and apprentices under the Apprenticeship Training Scheme. The Institute has developed various elements of instructional media packages (IMPs) comprising instructional materials, instructors guide wall charts, overhead text-books, transparencies on technology land workshop calculations and science.

6. Foremen Training/Supervisory Training. Training programme for supervisors/foremen from industry are organised at two Foremen Training Institutes located at Bangalore and Jamshedpur.

7. Central Staff Training and Research Institute. Central Staff Training and Research Institue, Calcutta was set up in 1968 by the Government of India in collaboration with the Government of Republic of Germany. The Institute has three wings — Training, Reserach and Development. The Training Wing provides training to the executives and administrators of vocational and industrial training in the country. The Research Wing conducts problem-oriented studies on different aspects of vocational training and Development Wing is to develop and disseminate instructional material and air/models for effective execution of industrial training.

8. Apprenticship Training Scheme. The Apprenticeship Act, 1961 makes it obligatory for employers in specified industries to engage apprentices for undergoing apprenticeship training which varies from one year to four years. The training consists of basic training followed by on-the-job or shop floor training in accordance with standards prescribed by Government in consultation with Central Apprenticeship Council. So far 218 industries have been specified and 132 trades have been designated for trade apprentices.

The Apprenticeship Act, 1961 was amended in 1973 to bring under its purview the training of graduates and technician vocational apprentices, graduates and diploma holders in engineering and technology. The Act was again amended in 1986 to include technician (vocational) apprentices for the benefit of the students passing out of 10+2 vocational education stream.

9. Vocational Training Research. A Central Staff Training and Research Institute was set up at Calcutta in 1970 for developing indigenous training techniques. The Institute conducts training programmes for officers and staff of the central and state governments as well as from industry who control, regulate and direct training programmes. It also carries out research in trades and training techniques, prepares training aids, and advises industry on industrial training methods.

10. Vocational Training Programme for Women. The Central Training Institute for Women at New Delhi has been upgraded into a National Vocational Training Institute for Women. The Institute provides instructor training, basic training and advanced training in selected trades particularly suitable for women. Two Regional Vocational Training Institutes for Women have also been set up at Bombay and Bangalore.

QUESTIONS FOR EXCERCISE

1. What do you understand by training of workers? Describe the different methods of training?
2. What is the importance of training in industry? Explain the different methods of training which are generally used in industries now-a-days.
3. Explain the importance of workers' training. How will you organise a training programme in a large industry?
4. Explain the utility of training as a tool to the management control. Evaluate the various methods of training the industrial workers.

5. What is the relationship between training programmes and employee level? Discuss.
6. How will you organise a training programme in a large industry? Explain the importance of workers training.
7. What are the principles of training? How will you evaluate training effectiveness in an organisation?
8. Describe the training facilities available in India.
9. What facilities are available for management training in India? Evaluate them and point out their limitations.